THE DROVE ROADS OF SCOTLAND

The Highland Drovers' Departure for the South

(From the painting by Sir Edwin Landseer, R.A., in the Victoria and Albert Museum—Crown Copyright)

THE DROVE ROADS
OF SCOTLAND

A. R. B. HALDANE

THOMAS NELSON AND SONS LTD
LONDON EDINBURGH PARIS MELBOURNE
TORONTO AND NEW YORK

THOMAS NELSON AND SONS LTD
Parkside Works Edinburgh 9
3 Henrietta Street London WC2
312 Flinders Street Melbourne C1
5 Parker's Buildings Burg Street Cape Town

THOMAS NELSON AND SONS (CANADA) LTD
91–93 Wellington Street West Toronto 1

THOMAS NELSON AND SONS
19 East 47th Street New York 17

SOCIÉTÉ FRANÇAISE D'EDITIONS NELSON
25 rue Henri Barbusse Paris Vᵉ

———

First published June 1952

THIS BOOK IS DEDICATED TO
MY WIFE

ACKNOWLEDGMENTS

THE list of those who have helped me in the production of this book is a long one, and I can only attempt to mention by name a few of those to whom I am principally indebted.

In the first place, I must record my very great indebtedness to the staff of the Signet Library, Edinburgh, who have helped me throughout, and particularly to Mr John Robertson, who has not only helped me in my search for sources of information, but has undertaken the long and laborious task of checking the references. Without the help of the Signet Library and its staff the time and labour involved in the collection of material would have been immensely increased. I am also indebted to the staffs of the Central Library of Edinburgh Public Libraries; the National Library of Scotland; the Historical Room at H.M. Register House, Edinburgh; the Public Record Office, London; the Map Room at the British Museum, and The Royal Scottish Geographical Society.

Dr H. W. Meikle and Professor W. Croft Dickinson have helped me greatly with suggestions and encouragement, and I wish particularly to thank them.

I am also much indebted to the following : Mr Charles McInnes, Curator of Historical Records, H.M. Register House; Mr Angus Graham, Secretary to the Royal Commission on Ancient Monuments in Scotland; Mr K. J. Bonser, Leeds, and Mr R. J. Adam, Lecturer in Mediaeval History, St Andrews University, through whose kindness I have had access to material in the Sutherland Estate Papers at Dunrobin.

I wish also to express my thanks to Mr N. G. Matthew for the great care which he has taken in the preparation of the map, to Mr Robert Adam for allowing me to use a number of his fine photographs illustrating the country through which the drovers passed, and to numerous other friends and correspondents who have helped me in my search for illustrations.

In addition to those mentioned, I have received valuable help and information from landowners, factors, farmers, crofters, shepherds and others in many parts of Scotland who have given me the benefit of their knowledge of local history and tradition.

ACKNOWLEDGMENTS

The extent of my indebtedness to other writers, contemporary and modern, is, I hope, sufficiently apparent from the notes and references.

Finally, I must record my thanks to the Carnegie Trust for the Universities of Scotland whose generosity has helped to make possible the publication of this book. and to the publishers for the great care which they have given to every detail of its production.

A. R. B. H.

EDINBURGH, 1951

CONTENTS

LIST OF PLATES

ABBREVIATIONS

In the Notes and References the following abbreviations have been used :

A.P.S. Acts of the Parliament of Scotland

R.P.C. Register of the Privy Council

O.S.A. The Statistical Account of Scotland, 1791–99

N.S.A. The New Statistical Account of Scotland, 1845

H.R. & B. Reports of the Commissioners for Highland Roads and Bridges, 1804–60

P.R.O. Public Record Office

NOTE

The Author wishes it to be clearly understood that the mention in the text or the notes or the marking on the map of routes or areas used as drove roads, rights of way or stances during the period of which he writes, cannot in itself be taken as any indication that these routes or areas retain today the character of rights of way.

Except in the quotations or in passages directly referring to quoted matter, the spelling of the place names is that given in W. & A. K. Johnston's Gazetteer of Scotland, 1937.

INTRODUCTION

DURING the autumn of 1942 I had occasion, in the course of certain work on which I was then engaged, to call to mind an old road which crosses the Ochils immediately behind my home near Auchterarder in Perthshire. For a mile or two back into the hills the road serves as an access to upland farms, but at the sheep farm of Coulshill it loses this character, and from that point to its junction with the main road through Glendevon it is now little more than a lonely grass-grown track crossing the hills. Little used as it now is, the grassy road retains the clear marks of extensive use by the traffic of former days, and it occurred to me that it would be of interest to try to trace something of its history. Local inquiries left little doubt that the road had seen much and varied traffic. Over the Ochils passed at one time coal and lime from West Fife going north to the rich farm lands of Strathearn, while slates from Glenalmond and Glenartney, together with grain, flax, wool and timber went south to the Forth basin. It may be that a part of this traffic crossed the Ochils by this Coulshill road in preference to the parallel routes through Gleneagles or by Dunning to Yetts of Muckhart; but besides all this, local tradition marked the road as one which was in use in the latter part of the eighteenth and much of the nineteenth centuries by droves of cattle and sheep bound from the Highlands to the great market at Falkirk. I knew little or nothing of the nature or extent of this traffic and my informants were in little better case, but the subject seemed to be one of interest and I determined, as opportunity offered, to get to know more of this droving traffic, the routes by which it reached the Lowlands, its ultimate destination and the methods of the men whose work it was. The material contained in the pages which follow has been gathered over the past eight years, partly from the personal recollection or inherited tradition of men and women in many parts of Scotland, but in the main from scattered references contained in a wide variety of manuscript and printed sources in Scotland and England, from which has been gradually pieced together to the best of my ability the story of the drove roads of Scotland.

The main intention at the outset was to discover the routes

I

by which the cattle of the Highlands were brought to the markets or trysts in the centre of Scotland, and to a substantial extent this intention has been adhered to ; but at an early stage it became apparent that before any intelligent appreciation of the drove routes could be gained, a wider knowledge of the history, nature and extent of the droving traffic must be acquired than could be obtained from any sources then available to me, while the growing interest of the subject, as research proceeded, suggested that a more comprehensive study would be worth attempting.

To anyone attempting to trace the origin and development of the movement of livestock the problem must immediately arise of deciding to how early a date the research is to be carried. In Scotland, as in all other largely pastoral countries, the breeding and movement of livestock was fundamental to the life of the people and can be traced back as far as historical records exist. Part of this movement was clearly of a normal and legitimate character called for by the need to move stock from one grazing area to another, or by the droving of beasts to such markets as then existed. To this extent it forms part of the history of droving which may thus claim to date back at least as far as recorded history. The Register of the Privy Council from which much of the early historical material has been drawn shows, however, that as late as the sixteenth and seventeenth centuries a large part of this movement was the result of cattle thieving. That the cattle traffic of the earlier centuries was largely of a like character seems certain, and the early history of the drove roads is to a large extent the story of the gradual transition from lawless cattle driving to lawful cattle droving. The evidence available suggests that this process of change began to be apparent about the end of the fifteenth century, gradually acquiring momentum during the two centuries which followed. The Union of the Crowns helped the trend towards the legitimate movement of livestock, but it was only after 1707 that droving in the sense of large-scale organised movement of live-stock on foot to established markets became a marked feature of Scotland's economy.

The century which followed the Union of the Parliaments witnessed several great developments which fundamentally affected the commercial life of the country and not least the trade in livestock. During these hundred years the Union with England became a reality and Scotland was finally integrated as an essential part of the commercial life of Great Britain, losing in some degree her identity and with it certain Continental markets, but gaining in return the advantages of a growing market in England and the vast markets and resources of the extending Empire. The Union with England had involved Scotland in the full consequences of British foreign policy, and the constant wars which filled much of the eighteenth and early nineteenth centuries were of direct and vital consequence to the droving trade. The eighteenth century saw the final pacification of the Highlands and the transformation of Highland communications brought about first by Wade and the builders of the military roads who immediately followed him, and later by the great work of the Commissioners for Highland Roads and Bridges. Most important of all in its effect on the livestock trade, the second half of the eighteenth century saw the start of a great revolution in farming practice comparable in scope to the industrial revolution with which indeed it was closely connected and to which it was in many ways complementary. Coinciding as it did with other changes, political and economic, the agricultural revolution at first brought a great extension to the droving industry, and only in its later stages in the second quarter of the nineteenth century brought into play factors which led in the end to the decline of the trade. It is, then, of this century and a half which followed the Union of the Parliaments, of the growth, fortunes and vicissitudes of the cattle trade during these years that the story of the drove roads of Scotland mainly tells.

The magnitude of the changes, social, political and economic, which took place during this period of 150 years presents a formidable problem in attempting to construct an intelligible picture of a trade which persisted throughout. The main wealth of the material available for the task comes from the Statistical Account of 1791–99, the New Statistical Account and the many surveys of Scottish agriculture which were undertaken in the years between ; but much comes also from the early and middle part of the eighteenth century. From all we know of them it is very evident that drovers were adaptable fellows. Handicapped by few preconceived ideas or perhaps even by any too rigid code of commercial morality, they were quick to change their methods to suit the needs of their rough-and-ready trade. So it is that the fleeting and scattered glimpses of the droving trade through-

3

out the long years of its continuance reveal a variety of custom and technique. The main outlines are clear, but any comprehensive survey of a drover's life and work must almost inevitably include detail and colour belonging to different phases in the history of the trade.

A similar difficulty presents itself in considering the routes used by the drovers. Without a doubt these changed from time to time according to the political and social conditions of the time, the market requirements, the type of beasts forming the drove, the weather or even the individual tastes, prejudices and idiosyncrasies of the drovers. It can be little, if any, exaggeration to say that there are few glens in the Highlands, even few easy routes leading to the South over moor or upland country, which have not known the tread of driven cattle on the way to the Trysts. At an early stage in the research it became apparent that to construct a map on which were marked all the routes, the use of which at one time or another as drove roads could be established by reasonable evidence, would be an unmanageable task, and that such a map, through the very multiplicity of routes, would lose much of its meaning. It was, therefore, decided to show only the main routes used by the drovers, with such subsidiary routes as appeared to be of substantial importance or interest, and no claim is made that the map is in any way exhaustive.

For the purpose of exact historical record this work has been too long delayed. Had it been undertaken even twenty years earlier, much information now lost might have been secured. The written and printed sources, scanty and widely scattered though they be, remain, but the generation of those who can recall the last days of the droving trade is almost gone, and there survives only a small and fast-dwindling band of old men who themselves took cattle to Falkirk Tryst in the last years of its existence and can speak either from their own recollection or at least from information handed down to them from the generation before. How often in the course of inquiries in all parts of the Highlands has a request for information been met with an expression of regret that it had not been made during the lifetime of those not long since dead. If this has often provoked tantalising speculation as to what might have been, it has no less brought realisation of the importance of securing what can still be secured before that too becomes obliterated by the passage of time ; but perhaps the delay in attempting this research has been not without some advantage, for it may be that had the work been started earlier, at a time when droving was still a part of everyday life or even a very recent memory, the picture might have lost something from over-abundance of detail and from the absence of that perspective which distance lends.

The work has for me been full of interest and growing fascination. Once the initial difficulty of grasping the few scattered threads leading to the true sources of information had been overcome, these threads quickly led to others, and the number and variety of sources finally used have been incomparably greater than seemed at first possible. Throughout I have had the very great advantage of having access to the resources of the Signet Library, Edinburgh, and the ready help of those who care for and know so well that fine collection ; of the National Library of Scotland ; of H.M. Register House, Edinburgh ; of Edinburgh Public Libraries and, through the Central Library for Students, of local collections in Scotland, England and Wales. Apart from the printed and manuscript sources the search has led to many parts of Highland Scotland ; to Wester Ross-shire where on an autumn day a crofter working in his harvest field on the eve of his hundredth year told of his early life as a drover in voluble Gaelic interpreted by his daughter ; to Skye ; to the Lorn and Knapdale districts of Argyll ; to the banks of the Upper Don and to many parts of Perthshire and the Southern Uplands. I can only hope that any who read these pages may perhaps derive a small part of the pleasure which the collection of the information has given to me, and that the picture I have tried to paint may help to preserve for the future a reflection, however faint and imperfect, of what was once a vivid and vital part of the life of Scotland.

1

THE EARLY DROVERS

THE beginning of the story of Scotland's cattle lies far back in her remote past. In all parts of the world, before man came to possess knowledge, skill or implements to enable him to till the ground, hunting and the grazing of livestock provided him with his only means of livelihood, and in the possession of that stock lay almost his only source of wealth. As the years went on, bringing with them increasing knowledge, the richer lowland areas came gradually into cultivation for crops, but in the mountains and upland valleys, sheep and cattle remained the mainstay of the people.

So it has been with Scotland. The early records bear witness to the number of sheep and cattle in the country and the importance of stock grazing. In the early Charters few superficial areas of land are given, the extent being in general measured by the number of cattle and sheep which it would support, while rents, taxes and fines were regularly paid in livestock. The monks and religious houses, particularly in the south of Scotland and the valley of the Tweed, soon became among the best and most prosperous farmers. Indeed it seems probable that at the time of the Reformation the monks, and especially those of the Cistercian Order, had raised the standard of farming in the lands under their control to a level which was not surpassed till well on in the eighteenth century. In this the monks of Melrose Abbey were prominent, and at the end of the twelfth century they were deriving much of their revenue from the pasturing of stock. In 1180 Melrose was given the right to build a ' vaccaria ' for 100 cows in Threipwood.[1] Newbattle Abbey had from the Lord of Lynton and Romanno the right of pasturage for 1,000 sheep and 60 cattle—a ' mirabilis concessio,' [2] while the records of the period are full of other references showing the value and extent of stock-raising particularly in the Lowlands. These rights of grazing were often in conflict with the interests

---

[1] *A.P.S.*, I, 387
[2] *Chartulary of Newbattle Abbey*, xxxv, 97 (Bannatyne Club 89). Cosmo Innes, *Sketches of Early Scottish History*, 133

of the huntsman and game preserver. A grant by Robert Avenel of lands in Upper Eskdale to the monks of Melrose reserved deer, boar and other game.[1] In an early Grant of Pasturage in the Lammermuirs it was provided that moveable folds should accompany the flocks of the Abbey to provide shelter, but avoiding the establishment of permanent settlements in the forests, and statutory penalties incurred by the owners of cattle found trespassing in the forests recur frequently in the early Acts of the Scots Parliament.

On Matthew Paris's map of thirteenth-century Scotland he has shown the far North and West of the country as ' marshy and impassable, fit for cattle and shepherds,' [2] and a century later John Fordoun found ' the upland districts and along the Highlands ' to be ' full of pasturage grass for cattle and comely with verdure in the glens along the water courses.' [3] Of the total number of cattle in the country in these early times, no accurate estimate can be made, but the Exchequer Rolls for 1378 show the number of hides exported as being nearly 45,000.[4] Major, writing of Scotland in the early sixteenth century, reported that many men possessed as many as 10,000 sheep and 1,000 cattle,[5] and when, in 1544, Henry the Eighth sent the Earl of Hertford and later in the same year, Sir Ralph Eure to lay waste the Border country, the tale of the losses suffered by Scotland shows that the beasts driven back to England included 10,386 cattle and over 12,000 sheep.[6] Estienne Perlin, describing Scotland in the middle of the century, speaks of the abundance of cattle in the country,[7] and towards the end of the century Bishop Leslie described how ' in the mountanis of Aargyl and Rosse lykewyse and sindrie utheris places ar fed ky, nocht tame, as in utheris partes, bot lyke wylde hartes, wandiring out of ordour and quhilkes, throuch a certane wyldnes of nature, flie the cumpanie or syght of men.' [8] Well might they fly the company of men, for the story of these days and of the two centuries to follow is the story of an unkindly age with cattle the pawns in a rough and

---

[1] *Liber Sancte Marie de Melros* (Bannatyne Club), I, 178
[2] Hume Brown, *Early Travellers*
[3] Hume Brown, *Scotland before 1700 ; from Contemporary Documents*, 11
[4] *Exchequer Rolls*, II, xc
[5] Hume Brown, *Scotland before 1700 ; from Contemporary Documents*, 48
[6] Brewer, *Historic Note Book*, 105, and Ridpath, *The Border History of England and Scotland*, 1776, 548–50
[7] Hume Brown, *Early Travellers*, 74
[8] Hume Brown, *Scotland before 1700 ; from Contemporary Documents*, 132

cruel game. The early records are full of instances of the cruel treatment of stolen cattle. The Acts of the Lords of Council covering the years 1496–1501 contain a complaint about the chasing and poinding of cattle ' garring thame cast calfis ' and ' spoliation of certane oxin and puttin furth of thair ene,' [1] while in 1668 Sinclair of Dunbeath and others are charged with stealing cattle from the lands of Lord Reay and ' incarcerating and imprisoning them in great dungeons and pitts and keeping them their in great miserie be the space of many dayes.' [2]

In an unsettled age and a lawless country where cattle were the main form of transportable wealth, it was inevitable that much of the early traffic in livestock should be the result of raiding between glen and glen and between Highlands and Lowlands. From the middle of the sixteenth century the Privy Council was responsible for the general maintenance of peace and order. The Records of the Council contain details of the cases heard before it, and during the next hundred years complaints of thefts of cattle follow close one on another with a regularity almost wearisome in its monotony. From all parts comes the same story ; from Caithness and Ross, from Glen Isla and Strathardle, from west Perthshire and Lochlomondside, and above all from the East, West and Middle Marches of the Borders. It almost seems that cattle raiding was in the sixteenth and early seventeenth centuries the chief occupation of the people of Scotland. From the highest to the lowest few could resist their neighbour's beasts. Scott of Harden drives the cattle of Drumelzier and Dreva in Upper Tweeddale,[3] Douglas of Drumlanrig those of Branerig [4] ; Stuart of Ardvorlich steals from his neighbours in West Perthshire [5] ; Forbes of Towie in Strathdon from Glen Farquhar in Kincardineshire,[6] while the Angus glens were the happy hunting ground of the men of Lochaber and Badenoch. From Reay in Sutherland comes news of losses, from Morayshire, from Locheil's country and from the Argyllshire hills. In an attempt to check the traffic in stolen beasts bonds were taken from landowners who controlled the numerous ferries on lochs and rivers, and these included the boat

[1] *Acts of the Lords of Council in Civil Causes 1496–1501*, II, Introd., cxiii
[2] *R.P.C.*, 3rd series, II, 566–7   [3] *R.P.C.*, 1st series, IV, 709
[4] *R.P.C.*, 1st series, V, 273   [5] *R.P.C.*, 1st series, V, 28
[6] *R.P.C.*, 1st series, VI, 363

at Aberfeldy, the coble at Fonab, the ferry boat at Pitnacree, the 'curroch of Innergarrie' and even the 'littill coble of Tulloche.' [1] It would be hard indeed to find one corner of the Scottish Highlands, the Southern Uplands or the Border country the inhabitants of which, now as victims more often as perpetrators of cattle thefts, do not figure in these records. Many of the raids were on a small scale involving the theft of the few 'nolts' and the scanty household goods of humble folk, and sometimes the complaint is against the wanton malice of 'houghing and hounding' cattle too weak or thin to drive away. Most were under 'cloud and silence of nycht,' but not all. In a complaint against Alastair Stuart of Ardvorlich and others for the theft of 160 cattle from neighbouring lands in 1592, the defendants are charged with having come onto the complainers' lands 'with twa bagpypis blawand befoir thame.' [2] Some were on a larger scale, involving a major operation of real war. In 1602, men of Glen Garry raided the grazings in Glen Isla, Glen Shee and Strathardle, driving off 2,700 cattle pursued by the owners who overtook and partially defeated them near the Cairnwell Pass.[3] In the following year, a raid by the Clan Macgregor on Colquhoun of Luss ended in a fight in Glenfruin with the loss of 80 men and the theft of 600 cattle, an expedition which led to the proscription of the Clan Macgregor.[4]

Against this flowing tide of lawlessness the Crown and the Privy Council, as the central body responsible for the maintenance of law and order throughout the land, could do little. Chieftains and large landowners were held responsible for their tenants, or answerable for those to whom they had given protection or for whom they had acted as resetters of the stolen beasts; but seldom did they appear to answer the charge, and time after time all the Privy Council could do was to find the charge proven and pronounce sentence of outlawry against the guilty party, safe and untroubled in the fastnesses of Lochaber, Argyll or the Border hills.

By an Act of the Scots Parliament in the reign of William the Lion in 1175 it had been made unlawful for anyone to buy cattle without 'lauchful borch of hamehald.' [5] This was a form of 'guarantee' or 'caution' required by the buyer of cattle from

[1] *R.P.C.*, 3rd series, VIII, 532, 575   [2] *R.P.C.*, 1st series, V, 28
[3] *R.P.C.*, 1st series, VI, 501   [4] *R.P.C.*, 1st series, VI, 534, 535
[5] *A.P.S.*, I, 373

the seller that the beasts had not been stolen, heavy penalties being due from the latter or from him who guaranteed the seller's good faith if the beasts should later turn out to be stolen property. As late as 1634 the Baron Court held at Killin found it necessary to provide that no dealer in cattle should buy from strangers or even from neighbours dwelling 'between the ford of Lyon and Tyndrum' without sufficient 'caution,' of 'burgh and hamer.' [1] In 1606 the Privy Council, acting in its legislative capacity, sought to compel 'dryvers of sheape and nolt' to buy only from those answerable to the King's Laws under pain of confiscation of their 'whole drifte.' [2] Twelve years later, in an attempt to stop cattle thefts in the Middle Marches, the Privy Council ordered that no carcase be brought to market unless with the skin attached,[3] a precaution which was still in force in the Island of Islay as late as 1725. The Islay regulations required that before cattle or sheep were slaughtered they must be shown to two witnesses who knew the brand-marks of the person in whose possession they were, to prove that they were his own property or that evidence must be brought to show how he acquired them. The hides of slaughtered cattle were to be kept till the carcase had been eaten, to prove the ownership.[4] By such measures did King and Council seek to bring law and order into the cattle dealing of Scotland, but the frequent recurrence of such orders shows with what small success they met in checking or changing what had grown to be a tradition and custom ingrained and deeply rooted in the character of the people.[5] It shows a country stocked with cattle and a people trained up in a warlike school to a hardiness, a way of life and a knowledge of their native hills which was to be passed down from father to son and at last to droving descendants of cattle-reiving ancestors.

In such conditions it might well be imagined that any legitimate trade in cattle was almost an impossibility, but as early as

---

[1] Cosmo Innes. *Sketches of Early Scottish History*, 381–2. *Black Book of Taymouth* (Bannatyne Club), 389   [2] *R.P.C.*, 1st series, VII, 744
[3] *R.P.C.*, 1st series, XI, 289   [4] *Stent Book of Islay*, 280
[5] In many parts of the country the King's Writ did not run and many decrees were dead letters as soon as they were passed. An Act of the Scottish Parliament of 1503 refers to 'greit abusioun of Justice in the northt partis and west partis of the realme sic as the northt Ilis and south Ilis for lak and falt of Justice Airis Justicis and Shereffis and thairthrou the pepill ar almaist gane wild.' (*A.P.S.* II, 249), while in 1527 letters of apprising issued in the King's name against 'Alexander McLeod of Dunveggan' refers to Alexander as dwelling 'in ye Hieland where nane of ye officeris of ye law dar pas for fear of yair lyvis' (*Scot. Hist. Rev.* ii, 356).

the days of Alexander II travellers on the King's Highway had a common law right to spend one night on common land through which the road passed and there pasture their beasts ' saving corn and meadow,' [1] while frequent reference to ' viridis via ' in early Charters would seem to be an indication of routes which were at least of the nature of drove roads. To claim this as early evidence of droving in the sense in which the word came to be used in later years may be to claim too much, but that droving existed at least as early as 1359 is shown by a letter of safe conduct of that year granted to Andrew Moray and Alan Erskyn, two Scottish drovers, with three horsemen and their servants, for travelling through England or the King's foreign dominions for a year with horses, oxen, cows and other goods and merchandise,[2] and ten years later the Scots Parliament allowed cattle to be sold to Englishmen, fixing the customs dues on beasts leaving the country.[3]

During the three centuries which followed, the Scots cattle trade, in common with trade in other items on the short list of Scotland's exports, was to be the victim of an uncertain commercial policy. That policy—if policy it can be called—blended of ignorance, opportunism and self-interest, was dictated by a combination of factors, complex and often inconsistent one with another. The relative freedom of export and import trade which Scotland had formerly enjoyed came to an end with the start of the Wars of Independence, and from now on till the close of the seventeenth century antagonism and jealousy towards England

[1] *Chartulary of Newbattle Abbey* (Bannatyne Club), XXXVII, 158

[2] Rymer, *Foedera*, III. Record Comm. Edn., 1825, III, part 1, 415
The opening of the struggle with England marked the beginning of a long period during which commercial relations between the two countries were strained and constantly broken. From the date of the meeting of Edward I with the Scots barons at Norham in 1291 till 1348, only three safe conducts were given to English merchants to trade with Scotland, and during those years there is no record of a safe conduct granted to a Scots merchant to trade with England. (Davidson and Gray, *The Scottish Staple at Veere*, 97 ; Tytler, *History of Scotland*, 2nd Edn., II, 262–3)
In contrast to this, after 1357 very many safe-conducts were granted to Scots merchants trading with England, their number reflecting the desperate efforts made by Scotland to meet the crushing ransom required by Edward II for the release of David II who had been taken prisoner at the Battle of Neville's Cross eleven years earlier. (*Rotuli Scotiae, passim*)

[3] *A.P.S.*, I, 508, 547
In an English Writ dated 1384 mention is made of ' Johannes Kereslegh, Drovere et civis, London ' (Early Chancery Proceedings 61/387,' *Bulletin of the Institute of Historical Research*, III, 68 and *cf.* I, 97). Quoted by Professor C. Skeel in *Cattle Trade between England and Wales from the 15th to the 19th centuries* (Royal Historical Society Transactions, 4th series, IX, 1926, pp. 137/8).

fought with the hard fact that here lay a natural market. High prices at home, constant wars and recurring threats of famine, called periodically for retention in Scotland of the livestock and victuals which were a large part of her exportable products as urgently as the precarious state of her national economy called for export trade. The powerful Convention of Burghs looked on questions of commercial policy solely from the point of view of those privileged trading classes whose interests they so jealously guarded. Free-traders only if the trade passed through their hands, national interests meant little to them, and the development, except by them, of commerce or industry met with their bitter opposition. While the tanning industry wanted hides from home-killed beasts, the Crown, whose revenue came largely from export dues, preferred to encourage the export of hides on the live animals. In such conditions the policy of the Crown, the Acts of the Scots Parliament and the Orders of the Privy Council during the fifteenth, sixteenth and early seventeenth centuries present a maze through which the cattle trade threads a hard, devious and precarious way.

The trade to England which had been, at least by implication, recognised by the Act of 1369 appears to have been carried on partly on a credit or possibly a barter basis, for in 1451 the Scots Parliament prohibited any trade to England except in cash,[1] and during the famine of 1480, while all restrictions on foreign merchants trading with Scotland were lifted, south-bound cattle traffic across the border was entirely forbidden. Five years later the export of hides was prohibited, the object being to increase the livestock population of the country[2]; but men who could brave the perils of droving through fifteenth-century Scotland were not to be deterred by Acts of Parliament, more especially when King and Council possessed little of the will or the power to enforce the law. So the traffic continued without effective check, and the year 1542 saw a complaint to the Scots Parliament, this time that the profit on cattle sold out of the country was not paid to the Customs Officers.[3] A few years later a further complaint that owing to the negligence of the Wardens of the Marches the export of Scottish products has caused great dearth in Scotland, leads to an Order of the Council that no sheep or cattle are to be exported nor are English beasts to be

[1] *A.P.S.*, II, 40   [2] Davidson and Gray *op. cit.*, 62. *A.P.S.*, II, 174
[3] *A.P.S.*, II, 424

pastured in Scotland.[1]　In the next year the cattle traffic to England is again prohibited, and also the export of barrelled beef, particularly to Flanders,[2] owing to the scarcity of food in the country, a scarcity which for the next half-century is reflected in repeated measures to check both export trade and meat consumption in Scotland.　An Order of the Privy Council in 1561 ordained that as meat deteriorates at Lentryne and bad weather has caused scarcity, no one except those who are sick may eat meat before 29th March.[3]　Five years later the Council again forbids anyone to eat meat during Lent in that or future years,[4] while in 1592 the King, ' understanding the greit wrang done to the comoun weill be certane privat personis for thair awin comoditie transporting in england yeirlie, woll, scheip, and nolt, abone the nowmer of ane hundreth thowsand punds quhairby sic derth is rasit . . .' prohibited the export of sheep and cattle to England under pain of forfeiture [5] ; but once again the trade goes on, recognised, or at least tolerated, and an Act of the King in Council in 1598 aimed against those who ' daylie transportis grit nowmeris of nolt and scheip furth of this realme ' without licence or ' undir cullour of prevey licenceis unlawfullie and surreptitiouslie stollin and purchest ' from the King, annuls all export licences.[6]　In such a tangled skein it is hard indeed to find one firm, continuous thread, but, confused as the records are, they do show beyond any doubt the existence at least as early as the sixteenth century of a cattle trade to England spasmodic and interrupted but clearly recognisable as a forerunner of the great droving traffic of the days to come.

　While the drovers of the sixteenth century thus strove in the face of so many dangers and discouragements to take their beasts

---

[1] *R.P.C.*, 1st series, I, 114, 115
　Complaints of beasts pastured across the Border were not confined to the Scots. In their *View and Survey of Waste Lands along the East and Middle Marches of England* in 1542, Sir Robert Bowes and Sir Ralph Elleker observed ' also upon the said Elterburne [near the head of Bowmont Water] we did perceive and see two brode waies or rakes commonly used occupied and warne with cattall broughte out of Scotland to be contynually and daily pastured and fedde wythin the ground of England. . . .' (p. 177) : ' also hygher upon the said burne [Elter] appeared twoo comonly used waies or rakes of great bredth where the cattalles of Scotland had bene accustomed to have been dryven into the grounde of England to their contynuall pastures. Also the townes of Scotland boundinge upon England have eared plowed and sowen muche of all the grounde that was wounte to be their pastures and pasture all their shepe and cattall in great nombres within the Realme of England.' (Hodgson *History of Northumberland*, Part III, vol. 2, 219)　　　　[2] *R.P.C.*, 1st series, I, 127
　[3] *R.P.C.*, 1st series, I, 200　　　　　　　　[4] *R.P.C.*, 1st series, I, 611
　[5] *A.P.S.*, III, 577　　　　　　　　　　　　　[6] *R.P.C.*, 1st series, V, 476, 477

13

to England, the first signs were appearing within Scotland itself of an internal cross-country cattle trade breaking the trail for the droving traffic of later times. By the early years of the sixteenth century Skye had already started sending beasts to the mainland, and before the century ended a regular traffic was being carried on between the island and the East of Scotland, running the gauntlet through the trackless hills of a wild countryside of the losses and dangers which ' discourages all peceable and guide subjectis to direct or send ony guidis to the mercattis and fairis of the incuntrie.' [1] Argyllshire cattle, too, were being driven to the Lowlands, and by 1556 so many Highlanders were coming to the Lowlands to trade that the Privy Council found it necessary to take measures for the preservation of order at the markets. [2]

Like the drovers of later times, these early cattle dealers had no doubt little use for the beaten track or the fixed line of march, and of made roads there were few, but tolls on bridges in the late sixteenth and early seventeenth centuries show the existence of a regular cattle traffic. An Order of the Privy Council of 1594 levies a toll of 2d an ox for the repair of the bridge of Linton in East Lothian, [3] and a similar sum a few years later for the repair of Auchendinny Bridge at Glencorse [4] ' being the only direct passages between Edinburgh and the South. . . .' In 1605, 4d an ox was charged for those crossing the Water of Leith, for building a bridge at Saughtonhall, [5] and in 1607 a toll of 8d an ox was exacted for beasts passing through Dumbarton to any market, for the preservation of the town from flooding. [6]

While the course of legislation towards the Scots cattle trade throughout the greater part of the sixteenth century was determined by few considerations other than the immediate and changing needs of the moment, the last quarter of the century did in fact see the first signs of a new outlook. Scots trade policy, based hitherto purely on fiscal considerations and sectional interests, began now to show some signs of a national complexion, and an Act of 1592 forbidding the export of skins aims for the first time at the encouragement of industry and the increase of employment in Scotland. [7] The new outlook had shown itself in

---

[1] *R.P.C.*, 1st series, VI, 184
[2] *R.P.C.*, 1st series, I, 470–1. Hume Brown *Scotland in the Time of Queen Mary*, 27–8.
[3] *R.P.C.*, 1st series, V, 216   [4] *R.P.C.*, 1st series, VI, 207
[5] *R.P.C.*, 1st series, VII, 741   [6] *R.P.C.*, 1st series, VII, 431
[7] Davidson and Gray op. cit., 66 ; *A.P.S.*, III, 579, IV, 29

a practical step to improve the trade channels between Scotland and England. The Border areas which presented such a formidable barrier to trade with the South had despite the efforts of the Wardens of the Marches so far remained beyond the effective reach of the law. This was partly the result of the inability of the Crown to make them otherwise ; but partly it was an act of policy. The Scots saw something of advantage in having on their southern border a belt of wild unsettled country which, while it cost them dear in raids on the rich lands of Berwickshire, Roxburghshire and Dumfriesshire, preyed equally on Northumberland and Cumberland. Scots and English alike were content that this turbulent land should lie, a buffer state between them, looked on by each as a potential safeguard against invasion, and tolerated by either country for its value as a thorn in the flesh of the other. Hitherto what measures had been taken by Scots and English against the Border dwellers, were aimed only against those who were common enemies, against those who ' stole the beeves which made their broth from Scotland and from England both.' In the middle of the sixteenth century the state of the Border lands was as bad and as unruly as it had ever been. The policy of Henry VIII was hostile to Scotland, but the reign of Elizabeth saw a steady improvement in the political relations of the two countries possessing at last a common interest in the defence of the Reformation. Now for the first time the lawlessness of the Border country began to be regarded by the Scots as endangering peace with England, and an Order of the Privy Council of 1597 reflects the new outlook in providing for the release of prisoners and the return of cattle and other booty taken by Border raiders in a recent raid on England.[1] On the English side of the border the power of the great family of Percy had at last been broken, and Redesdale and Tynedale had come finally under the effective control of the English Crown. On the Scottish side, the hard core of Border unrest was attacked in the gradual eviction of the raiders from the strongholds which had hitherto proved inaccessible and unassailable. So the last quarter of the century saw the first successful efforts of Scots and English alike to put an end finally to what had been for centuries a disturbing influence in the relations of the two countries, now linked by a common religion and soon to have a common Crown.

If the close of the sixteenth century saw the end of the most

[1] *R.P.C.*, 1st series, V, 405

bitter period of antagonism between England and Scotland, the Union of the Crowns in 1603 had little immediate effect in drawing closer the commercial bonds between them. The old jealousies and prejudices largely remained, and the trade passing between the two countries continued to be regulated by few considerations other than the immediate and individual needs of each. For the drovers of Scotland's cattle the gradual pacification of the Borders had removed one of their main sources of anxiety, but their trade still remained at the mercy of a legislative policy marked as in the past by opportunism rather than continuity. The conflict of interests which had so hampered the drover of the sixteenth century largely continued, and the first half of the seventeenth century showed only a gradual, tacit and unofficial recognition of the trade ; but from now on the emphasis is laid less on efforts to stop the trade than on measures to secure that the fullest advantage is obtained from its existence. The Commission which under James VI had been appointed to consider terms for a treaty between the two countries had recommended the virtual adoption of free trade between them, and that the inhabitants of either Scotland or England should enjoy the privileges of free-born subjects in the other. The Scots Parliament agreed to the Commission's proposals, and in 1607 passed an Act providing that, with certain exceptions, all such wares as were the growth or handiwork of Scotland might be exported to England without paying any customs dues or other exaction.[1] Cattle, sheep, wool, hides and linen were among the items which were still to be subject to customs, and the first step to give effect to this was an attempt to canalise the traffic crossing the Border and to ensure that it passed through certain fixed points which acted as customs posts. An Order of the Privy Council in 1611 provided that no merchant or trader passing between Scotland and England should take his goods by the ' West groundis or washes,'[2] and in the following year complaints that the King is prejudiced by loss of customs dues on cattle and sheep led to an Order that all goods passing across the West Border must pay toll at ' the Kirk of Graitnay in Annandale,' those crossing the Middle Border at Jedburgh or Kelso, while those crossing the East Border must go by way of Duns, all on pain of confiscation.[3] The tolls were fixed at high levels both to limit the traffic and to ensure that the public revenues profited to the full by such as did

[1] *A.P.S.*, IV, 366   [2] *R.P.C.*, 1st series, IX, 267–8   [3] *R.P.C.*, 1st series, IX, 394

persist. In the autumn of 1612 the customs dues on cattle leaving the country were fixed at £10 Scots a head and on calves at £5, while barrelled beef paid £10 a barrel or carcase.[1] In 1644 the Customs Officers were directed to keep a record of the number of cattle, the names of the drovers and the dates when they passed, records which, if kept, have not survived.[2] An Order of 1635, aimed at the suppression of bad coinage in circulation, provides that drovers of cattle be compelled to pay customs dues in good coin,[3] and in 1661 the dues on cattle exported were fixed at 2 oz. bullion for every four cows or three oxen[4]; but the art of evading tolls was one with which the drovers had long been familiar. Across the grassy hills of the Border country they had a wide choice of routes, and much of the traffic crossed the Border unobserved and untaxed. An application in 1611 for a tack or lease of the right of collecting customs on cattle and other goods passing over the West Marches was refused on the ground that the probable yield of the customs dues was unknown,[5] and when the annual value of exports from Scotland in 1614 was estimated at £736,986 Scots this excluded 'greit quantetie of lynning claythe, lynning yairne, sheip, nolt, etc. that is transpoirrted by land dalie.'[6]

While the authorities sought to regulate and tax the cattle traffic to England, there is no lack of evidence that they fought a losing battle and that, harassed and hampered as it might be, the droving trade went on little deterred or controlled. This led during the first quarter of the seventeenth century to continued complaints of shortage of food and high prices in Scotland. In 1615, owing to the scarcity of meat, export was banned and the eating of beef during Lent was once again prohibited. The preamble of the ordinance refers to 'suche a continewing storme of froist, snaw, rayne, and wind that the most pairt of the bestiall and goodis of the cuntrey ar outher deade or become so feble and waik that thay ar not able ony lang tyme to indure.'[7] In 1627 the Justices of the Peace for the Counties of Fife and Stirling tried to prevent the export of hides from the country, the droving of cattle to England having caused a shortage of supplies for the tanning industry,[8] while two years before Commissioners had been appointed in Nithsdale, Annandale and Roxburghshire to

[1] R.P.C., 1st series, IX, lxix   [2] A.P.S., VI, Pt. 1, 242
[3] R.P.C., 2nd series, VI, 94   [4] A.P.S., VII, 252, 253
[5] R.P.C., 1st series, IX, 608
[6] Hist. Manuscripts Commission, Mar and Kellie Papers, 1904, 74
[7] R.P.C., 1st series, X, 312, 313   [8] R.P.C., 2nd series, I, 684

prevent the export of cattle.[1] A complaint to the Privy Council in 1626 described how 'the most pairt of the nolt within this Kingdom ar ather alreadie boght to be transportit or els some conditioun or bargane is maid for the same afoirhand, sua that now the poore labouraris of the ground can haif no nolt to buy, and, if some few ar to be had, the pryceis thairof ar so extraordinair and heigh as thay can not be boght to the grite hurt . . . of all . . . within this Kingdome.' [2] So serious was the rise in prices that the Justices of the Peace were ordered to make annual reports on the position in the light of which export policy could be reviewed, an Order which seems to have been only very partially obeyed.[3] The customs dues paid by cattle exporters or the fines levied on those who sought to evade them were sometimes earmarked for specific purposes. In 1628, fines exacted from drovers were allocated for the building of the King's castle at Lochmaben,[4] and when in 1646 General Leslie was granted a sum of 50,000 merks Scots in recognition of his services at the Battle of Philiphaugh, £10,000 Scots of this was to be paid from dues on exported cattle.[5] It seems probable that Leslie may have had to wait for his money, for as late as 1683 the total customs including those on cattle collected at Kelso for the half year to November, amounted only to £1,683 Scots, while those collected at Ayton for the same period totalled only £806 Scots, of which cattle dues made up only a small proportion.[6]

By the middle of the seventeenth century the cattle trade to England had, despite all its handicaps, grown to such proportions that Scotland was described as little more than a grazing field for England. The number of beasts passing through the town and paying toll at Carlisle in 1663 reached the considerable total of 18,574,[7] and in the following year the House of Commons

---

[1] *R.P.C.*, 2nd series, I, 138   [2] *R.P.C.*, 2nd series, I, 300

[3] The Justices of Kincardineshire appear to have been among those who sent in reports on prices, for in 1627 they complained that the price of cattle at 50 merks for oxen and 40 merks for cows is even higher than in the previous year. ' If remeid be nocht provydit speidalie ' they declare ' puir men laboraris salbe forcit to quyte their tillage of the ground.' From this it seems clear that the hardship lay in the price of working cattle rather than in the price of beef. (*R.P.C.*, 2nd series, II, 554 and 2nd series, I, Introduction lxxxv–lxxxvii)

[4] *R.P.C.*, 2nd series II, 473   [5] *A.P.S.*, VI, Part 1, 627

[6] *Record of Customs Dues collected at Kelso in 1683.* H.M. Register House

[7] *State Papers. Domestic.* Charles II. 1663–64, 226. ' 1663. August 1. Account of cattle brought in from Scotland to the port of Carlisle since August 1662 ; total number 18,574.' The toll dues were 8d a head. It may be noted that the number of beasts has been misquoted in various publications as 318,574.

complained of the under-selling of English cattle by Scots and Irish beasts. A Petition by Yorkshire graziers for heavier duties against Scots cattle entering England complains that ' the cattle being fed, maintained and fatted with farre less charge than can possibly be done in England they filled and quitte the markets and undersell those of English breed.' [1]

The second half of the century saw a marked change in the attitude of the authorities towards the droving industry, and an unwilling but growing realisation of the benefits of freer trade with England. An Order of 1663 aimed at the improvement of pasture and of the breed of cattle provided that exports by sea should be subject to no customs for nineteen years,[2] and in 1672, to encourage trade, the export of cattle by land or sea was made open to all.[3] The drovers too were coming to be recognised as part of the commercial life of the country and as forming a body of men engaged in an honourable trade. Orders of 1671 and 1674 aimed against those who passing as drovers ' commit severall thiftes and abuses ' provide that drovers shall carry certificates of respectability and passes giving the names of all in their company.[4]

The scarcity of money in Scotland led in 1680 to the appointment of a Commission to encourage the export of cattle and other goods,[5] and the following year brought a complaint that the growing practice among English cattle dealers of giving bills in payment lessened the value of the traffic as a balancing item in the import and export trade of the country.[6] So, in the course of two centuries, the Scottish export cattle trade had passed from active opposition, through grudging tolerance, to emerge at last into an era in which full recognition and active encouragement were given to a trade now acknowledged as an essential part of the economy of Scotland.

---

[1] *Journal of British Archaelogical Assoc.*, Vol. 87, 1932, 172–83
[2] *A.P.S.*, VII, 476   [3] *A.P.S.*, VIII, 63
[4] *R.P.C.*, 3rd series, III, 312 and IV, 280, 281. Steps to ensure the reliability of drovers seem to have been taken in England earlier than in Scotland, for by Statutes of Edward VI and Elizabeth it was enacted that a drover must be licensed annually by the Quarter Sessions of the county in which he had lived for three years and that he must be a married householder, over 30 years of age. No licence was to be granted to a servant or retainer. (5 and 6 Edw. VI, Chap. 14 Section 13. *Statutes of the Realm*, Vol. 4, part I, 150, and 5 Elizabeth Chap. 12, *Statutes of the Realm*, Vol. 4, part 1, 440)
[5] *R.P.C.*, 3rd series, VI, 431, 432   [6] *R.P.C.*, 3rd series, VII, 669

2

THE LIFE AND WORK OF A DROVER

THE development of the droving trade in Scotland and the important part which it came to play in the life of the country between the start of the sixteenth and the middle of the nineteenth centuries, was the outcome of a combination of circumstances leading logically and almost inevitably to this end. The climate and physical nature of the Highlands in comparison with the Lowland part of Scotland made them a natural grazing area, a division of function further emphasised at first by the turbulent history and later by the agricultural and industrial development of the Lowlands which, increasingly as time went on, confined cattle breeding to the hill country. Here the system of land tenure, encouraging a large tenant population all with grazing rights, led to over-stocking of the land with cattle. These were for long almost the sole form of realisable wealth, while the primitive farming methods practised throughout the Highlands up till the middle of the eighteenth century made a reduction of stock with the approach of autumn a matter of necessity. When there is added the fact that cattle supplied their own transport to market and could gather their own livelihood on the way, droving from the Highlands was the natural outcome.[1] There was, however, one more factor which, if any were needed, helped to bring the droving industry to the important place which for nearly four centuries it occupied.

The literature, the poetry and the whole history of the Scottish people show them to have been a people to whom raids and forays, often taking them over long distances and through great hardships, have for centuries possessed an almost irresistible attraction. Whether it tells of descents from Border hills on the rich pasture lands of Northumberland and the Tweed Valley, of raids from Highland glens to despoil farm lands in Lennox

---

[1] 'Live cattle' wrote Adam Smith, 'are, perhaps, the only commodity of which transportation is more expensive by sea than by land. By land they carry themselves to market. By sea, not only the cattle, but their food and their water too must be carried at no small expense and inconveniency.'—*Wealth of Nations* (Bohn's Standard Lib., 1887, I, 460)

and Strathearn, or of expeditions from Badenoch and Atholl to take toll of the Angus glens, the story of the early raiders seldom varies in its main theme, and everywhere cattle are the pawns in the game. A study of the Acts of the Scots Parliament or any attempt to reckon the time and energy devoted by the Privy Council in the sixteenth and seventeenth centuries to checking these activities, can leave no doubt that cattle raiding was one of the main pre-occupations of large numbers of the people and one of the chief sources of worry to those set in authority.

Marks of their heredity remained deeply imprinted on the descendants of these old raiders long after the arrival of more settled times in Scotland, and to this was attributed much of the adventurous and turbulent spirit which remained in vigorous life till 1745 and lingered on into the second half of the eighteenth century. A ' Memorandum concerning the Highlands ' of 1746 speaks of cattle thieving among the Highlanders as ' the principal source of all their barbarity, cruelty, cunning and revenge ' (which) ' trains them up to the use of arms, love of plunder, thirst for revenge. . . .' [1] To a Highlander of the eighteenth century, divided at the most by one generation from such a way of life and pos-sessing beyond a long lineage of cattle-reiving ancestors, it was but a short step to a more legitimate and only slightly less adven-turous form of cattle driving. ' He has felt from his early youth,' wrote Sir John Sinclair of the Highlander in his Analysis of the Statistical Account, ' all the privations to which he can be exposed in almost any circumstances of war. He has been accustomed to scanty fare, to rude and often wet clothing, to cold and damp houses, to sleep often in the open air or in the most uncomfortable beds, to cross dangerous rivers, to march a number of miles without stopping and with but little nourishment, and to be perpetually exposed to the attacks of a stormy atmosphere. A warrior, thus trained, suffers no inconvenience from what others would consider to be the greatest possible hardships, and has an evident superiority over the native of a delicious climate, bred to every indulgence of food, dress and habitation and who is un-accustomed to marching and fatigue.' [2] So heredity, aptitude and inclination, re-inforced economic necessity and produced by an easy transition the drovers of the eighteenth and nineteenth centuries.

[1] *Breadalbane Papers (Roads)*, Box 4, H.M. Register House
[2] Sinclair, *Analysis of O.S.A.*, I, 106–7

Of the men who brought the cattle from the Highlands to
the markets of the Lowlands or 'trysts' as some of these were
called, there were, as in other walks of life, many grades. There
were those, often great landowners, nobles or chieftains, who
bred the cattle on their wide estates or received them from their
tenants and sub-tenants in payment of rent or other dues. Cattle
dealing in the seventeenth and eighteenth centuries was considered a trade in no way unsuited to a gentleman, and during
this period the records of the droving industry show how deeply
concerned in it were not only the humble folk but some of the
highest in the land. Some there were who did little more than
send the beasts to market in the care of others and some, like
Rob Roy's one time associate the Duke of Montrose, merely
acted as sleeping partners or provided the capital needed for
cattle dealing enterprises.[1] Others, smaller lairds, tacksmen or
monied dealers, attended the markets themselves but entrusted
the care and transport of their droves to subordinates. Others
again, smaller men of little substance, combined the functions
of dealer and drover, buying cattle in the North and themselves
driving them to the Lowlands either on commission or, staking
their all, as a private and perilous speculation. Finally, there
were the drivers of the cattle on whom fell the day to day dangers,
hardships and responsibilities of the long journeys from Kintail
to Crieff, from Caithness to Falkirk and often from the Highlands
of Scotland to the meadows of Norfolk. Of this last class, some
were men who had small parcels of land to cultivate, and for
them the driving south of a drove in the summer or early autumn
meant welcome employment between seed time and harvest;
but many who had no ties at home stayed in the low country,
helping to shear the harvest after the droving was finished, and
some stayed on through the autumn and early winter, smearing
the sheep with the mixture of tar and butter which, in the
eighteenth century, was looked on as essential before the winter

---

[1] At the start of his career in the latter years of the seventeenth century, Rob Roy
appears to have carried on business as an honest cattle dealer. During this period,
he enjoyed the support of the Duke of Montrose who made loans to him for speculations in cattle, but latterly Rob fell on evil times owing to bad markets and finally
absconded with, it is said, £1,000 belonging either to the Duke or to other creditors.
His estate was attached for the debt and thereafter Rob lived the life of an outlaw,
supporting himself by theft and the thinly disguised blackmail of a cattle 'Protector.'
Despite his mode of life he avoided capture in the hill country west of Lochearn and
died in his bed near Balquhidder about 1738. (Sir Walter Scott, Introduction to
Rob Roy)

storms.[1] All these are in contemporary records referred to indiscriminately as ' drovers,' but though each played his essential part in the drama, it is mainly with the actual drivers of the cattle that we are here concerned in this attempt to reconstruct something of the life and work of the men who walked the drove roads of Scotland.

The characteristics and qualities required of a successful drover were many. Knowledge of the country had to be extensive and intimate, while endurance and ability to face great hardships were essential. The larger and more prosperous drovers owned ponies which they used either for riding on their long journeys to the Lowlands or for carrying supplies for use on the way, or home-made goods which were often taken for sale ; but most of the drovers did the whole journey on foot. Resource and enterprise were called for with knowledge of men and tact tempered at times with absence of too fine scruple. Knowledge of cattle was needed and good judgment wherewith to balance the varying factors on which depended the successful completion of the journey to the Lowlands. Finally, honesty and reliability were needed in a drover for the responsible work entrusted to him. The list is a formidable one, but for the most part these qualities were attributes inherent in the men from their heredity, their upbringing and their way of life. It may indeed be doubted whether the civil or military authorities in Scotland would have credited with any high degree of honesty the Highlander of the first half of the eighteenth century, but even they would not have questioned his fidelity to his chieftain, a fidelity which, when commerce took the place of war, he transferred to the interest of his employer and the welfare of the beasts entrusted to him which he drove ' with something of the pride of his ancestors when carrying off the fat oxen of the Sassenach.' [2] ' The Highlanders in particular,' wrote Sir Walter Scott in *The Two Drovers*, ' are masters of this difficult trade of driving, which seems to suit them as well as the trade of war. It affords exercise for all their habits of patient endurance and active exertion. They are required to know perfectly the drove roads which lie

---

[1] The cutting of the harvest in the central and southern districts of Scotland gave employment to large numbers from the Highlands each year. An item in the Inverness *Courier* of 26th August 1824 records that over 2,500 shearers from Skye, Mull and the Outer Isles had recently passed through the Crinan Canal bound for the Lowlands.

[2] McIan and Logan, *Highlanders at Home* (1848), 32 et seq.

over the wildest tracts of the country, and to avoid as much as possible the highways which distress the feet of the bullocks, and the turnpikes which annoy the spirit of the drover ; whereas on the broad green or grey track, which leads across the pathless moor, the herd not only move at ease and without taxation, but, if they mind their business, may pick up a mouthful of food by the way.' The need for these qualities of head, heart and body and the varying circumstances which called for them may best be shown if an attempt is made to follow in the footsteps of a drover from the glens of Ross-shire or Kintail to the markets of Central Scotland.

The dress and appearance of a drover of the early part of the eighteenth century have been described by Macky who wrote of the scene at Crieff Tryst in 1723. ' The Highland gentlemen were mighty civil, dressed in their slashed waistcoats, a trousing (which is breeches and stocking of one piece of striped stuff) with a plaid for a cloak and a blue bonnet. They have a poinard, knife and fork in one sheath hanging at one side of their belt, their pistol at the other and their snuff mull before with a great broadsword at their side. Their attendance [following] was very numerous all in belted plaids, girt, like women's petticoats down to the knee ; their thighs and half of the leg all bare. They had also each a broadsword and poinard.' [1] The New Statistical Account for the Parish of Monzie tells that people old enough to remember the Highland drovers at Crieff described them as having been ' bare-kneed and bare-headed, though many of them old men.' A century later, the drover's dress included ' a coarse plaid of a plain brown and white chequer,' [2] and towards the end of the droving period in the latter half of last century he is described as ' dressed usually in homespun tweeds which smelt of heather and peat smoke and which was so thick that those who wore them look like bears as they lounge heavily along ' ; [3] ' great stalwart, hirsute men ' they were, ' shaggy and uncultured and wild,' their clothing and physique alike suited to the hardship of their lives.

The arms carried by the drovers at Crieff Tryst in 1723 were no mere ornament. The Privy Council Records of the sixteenth and seventeenth centuries amply demonstrate their use and

[1] Macky, *Journey through Scotland*, 1723. Quoted in Bishop Forbes' *Journal*, 235.
[2] Macculloch, *Highlands and Western Isles*, 1824, I, 179
[3] R. B. Cunninghame Graham, *A Hatchment*, 1913, 212 et seq.

necessity, particularly for drovers from the north and west whose route through Lochaber, Badenoch, Rannoch and Atholl took them through the wildest part of the country. A drover from Skye in the first half of the eighteenth century, crossing the hills on the way to Glen Garry, must pass uncomfortably close to the wild country to the south of Loch Hourn where, despite the Bernera Garrison, Colin MacDonell of Barrisdale levied black-mail of about £500 per annum as 'cattle protector' of his neighbours, or stole the beasts of those who grudged this primitive insurance premium.[1] Rob Roy too in his later and less reputable days engaged in transactions of a like character, as Sir Walter Scott has described in the forceful language of Bailie Nicol Jarvie : 'Troth I wad advise ony friends o' mine to gree wi' Rob ; for watch as they like and do what they like, they are sair apt to be harried when the lang nights come on. Some o' the Grahame and Cohoon gentry stood out ; but what then—they lost their haill stock the same winter ; sae maist folk now think it best to come into Rob's terms. He's easy wi' a'body that will be easy wi' him, but if ye thraw him ye had better thraw the deevil.' Drovers were exempt from the Disarming Acts of 1716 and 1748. In 1725, General Wade issued 230 licences to 'the forresters, drovers and dealers in cattle and other merchandise belonging to the several Clans who have surrendered their arms' permitting them to carry arms. The licences were valid for two years and the weapons to be carried were gun, sword and pistol.[2] Even during the Rising of 1745 the exemption in favour of the drovers continued, and a safe-conduct granted by the Sheriff-Depute of Argyll dated 11 December 1746 permits James Macnab, drover in Craig of Glenorchy, going with two servants to buy cattle in Kintail and Skye, 'to pass to and from these countries with their arms alwise behaving themselves as Loyall subjects of His Majesty.'[3] Arms were indeed necessary for the drovers of these times, for cattle raiding was still common, and in the years immediately before and after the Rising of 1745 the task of checking the activities of raiders living in Lochaber and Badenoch was one of the main problems which faced the Hanoverian Government. General Wade reporting to George I in 1724 on the condition of the Highlands drew attention to the prevalence

---

[1] Chambers, *Domestic Annals of Scotland*, III, 616
[2] New Spalding Club, *Historical Papers, 1699–1750*, I, 160, 161
[3] *Celtic Magazine*, VIII, 586

of cattle raiding. 'The Clans in the Highlands most addicted to rapine and plunder are the Camerons in West of the Shire of Inverness, the MacKenzies and others in the Shire of Ross who were vassals to the late Earl of Seaforth, the McDonalds of Keppoch, the Broadalbin men and the Macgregors on the borders of Argileshire. They go out in parties from 10 to 30 men, traverse large tracks of mountains till they arrive at the Low Lands, where they design to commit their depredations which they choose to do in places distant from the glens which they inhabit. They drive the stolen cattle in the night time, and in the day remain in the tops of the mountains or in the woods (with which the Highlands abound) and take the first occasion to sell them at the fairs and markets that are annually held in many parts of the country.' [1] William Mackintosh of Borlum in 1742 describes the part of the country most inhabited by cattle thieves as being the west corners of Inverness, Perth and Stirlingshire and the north part of Argyll. [2]

Scott has described a drover's food as 'a few handfuls of oatmeal and two or three onions renewed from time to time and a ram's horn filled with whiskey which he used sparingly every night and morning,' [3] while R. L. Stevenson adds 'ewe milk cheese and bannock.' [4] Enough oatmeal was carried for a few days and this was replenished on the journey as opportunity offered. The oatmeal was not for the drover's use alone. Dogs were extensively used in droving, and although there is curiously little mention of them in contemporary records, their function must have been an important one on routes which crossed long stretches of open country. Those who can still remember the last years of the droving period recall that the first concern of drovers on arrival at houses or inns was food for the dogs. [5] Sometimes the drover would have his oatmeal made into porridge at

---

[1] *An Authentic Narrative of Marshal Wade's Proceedings in the Highlands of Scotland*, printed as an Appendix in Jamieson's edition of Burt's *Letters from a Gentleman in the North of Scotland* (5th ed. 1822), II, 273.

[2] Mackintosh, *A Short Scheme . . . to stop Depredations . . . so destructive to the Northern Counties of Scotland* (1742).

[3] Scott, *The Two Drovers*, Ch. I [4] Stevenson, *St Ives*, Ch. 10

[5] Some years ago the late Miss Stewart Mackenzie of Brahan, Ross-shire, informed a friend that in the course of journeys by coach in the late autumn from Brahan to the South during her childhood about the year 1840 she used frequently to see collie dogs making their way north unaccompanied. On inquiring of her parents why these dogs were alone, Miss Stewart Mackenzie was informed that these were dogs belonging to drovers who had taken cattle to England and that when the droving was finished the drovers returned by boat to Scotland. To save the trouble and

inns or cottages beside which the cattle rested for the night, but where the resting-place was in a remote part of the hills far from fuel or shelter the drover must be content with oatmeal mixed with cold water, relying for warmth on his plaid and the contents of the ram's horn. One other item may occasionally have lent variety to the drover's diet. The bleeding of cattle by farmers during a hard winter or spring was an established practice in eighteenth-century Scotland. Writing of Gairloch in 1772 Pennant says that the cattle were blooded in spring and autumn, the blood being preserved to be eaten cold, and according to local tradition the practice continued till the beginning of the nineteenth century. It seems not unlikely that drovers short of food may on rare occasions have bled cattle on the way to the Trysts. The blood, with the oatmeal and onions which they carried, would supply the main ingredients required for the 'black puddings' which were a traditional Scottish food.

Much preliminary work by the dealers and the drovers employed by them had to be done before the cattle were collected and ready for the road to the South. The agriculture of the Highlands of Scotland and the Hebrides in the eighteenth and early nineteenth centuries rested on a complex system of tacksmen, tenants and sub-tenants, broadening out in the lower strata of the social scale to the occupiers of what came to be known as the penny, halfpenny and farthing lands, among whom the country was divided and sub-divided. Each of these classes owned cattle. In many cases small tenants with a single beast or a very small parcel of beasts, sold to the chieftain or the tacksman from whom he held his land, in payment of rent, but though common this was not an invariable practice, and the drove which finally started on the long cross-country journey to the Trysts was generally made up of beasts from many grazings. The onerous 'casualties' or services which the smaller tenants owed to the tacksmen or the chieftain sometimes included, too, an obligation

---

expense of their transport the dogs were turned loose to find their own way north. It was explained that the dogs followed the route taken on the southward journey being fed at Inns or Farms where the drove had 'stanced' and that in the following year when the drovers were again on the way south, they paid for the food given to the dogs. No evidence has come to light that drovers returned from the South by boat, and it would seem that a possible alternative explanation is that the dogs belonged to drovers who had remained in the South through the autumn for the harvest when the dogs would not be needed.

to sell only to a particular drover who paid the chieftain for this privilege,[1] and in Lewis as late as the last quarter of the eighteenth century the Seaforth Factor, who leased his office ' with all its appendages,' forced the tenants, on the pretext that rents were in arrears, to sell their beasts only through him.[2] Such devices would to some extent simplify the cattle dealer's task, but the collection of the drove for market remained a formidable undertaking, and all through the summer and early autumn months the Highland glens and grazing lands were filled with busy dealers and anxious sellers.

The method by which these local sales were arranged has been so described by James Robertson in his *General View of the Agriculture of Inverness-shire*, of 1813 : ' The manner of disposing of their dry cows or young bullocks is somewhat curious. When the drovers from the South and interior of Scotland make their appearance in the Highlands, which always happens during the latter end of April or the beginning of May, they give intimation at the Churches that upon a particular day and in a central place of the district they are ready to purchase cattle from any who offer them for sale. This is a most important and anxious time to both buyers and sellers. The price of this commodity, like all others, is regulated by the demand. The farmers have only two ways of judging of the demand, first by the number of drovers that appear in the country and, secondly, by epistolary correspondence with persons in the South who have their confidence. The drovers are of two descriptions, either those who buy on commission for persons of capital who, being diffident of their own skill or averse from fatigue, choose to remain at home, or those who purchase cattle on their own account. Much address is used on both sides to feel the pulse of the market at these parochial meetings before the price for the season be mutually settled and it may happen that many such small Trysts or meetings take place in different parts of the Highlands before the price be finally determined. Their anxiety on both sides is sometimes so great that the cattle are given away upon a conditional contract ; that if the price rises within a limited time the seller will receive so much more ; but if the lean cattle fall in value the drover will get a deduction. Ready money is generally given for the cattle ; and this is the season for the Banks to

---

[1] Walker, *Economical History of the Hebrides and Highlands*, I, 78
[2] Knox, *Tour through the Highlands of Scotland and the Hebride Isles in 1786*, 191–3

circulate their paper money. These petty markets in the Highlands commence at the period above mentioned and the cattle are moved as soon as they can bear the fatigue of travelling that they may be put as early as possible on the Southern pastures. When the demand from the South continues brisk, this sort of trade is carried on with little or no interruption from May to October.' The writer of the Statistical Account for the Parish of Abernethy in Inverness-shire, complaining of these casual markets called by dealers, urged that markets should be fewer and more central, and that the estate factors should get the best information possible as to current prices and the solvency of the dealers. ' Considering what a fatiguing, hazardous business droving is,' he writes, ' men that pay should be much sought after and much encouraged.' [1]

The beasts were generally brought for delivery to some convenient spot where the purchases were gradually collected into a drove and where the real work of the drovers began. The drove might consist of 100, 200 or 300 beasts, with one drover to each 50 or 60 animals, but much larger droves were often collected by the dealers at the more important local Trysts like the Lawrence and Aikey fairs in the Garioch and Buchan districts of Aberdeenshire or the Muir of Ord Tryst in Ross-shire, and the droves belonging to the great dealers of the early nineteenth century were numbered in thousands and stretched for several miles. The profit on a drove of beasts brought from the Highlands to the Lowland markets was often little more than 2s 6d to 5s a head, and a drove of less than 200 animals, unless one of several owned by the same dealer, was thus hardly an economic undertaking. It was to eke out his small wage or his uncertain profit on the enterprise that some drovers, particularly those in a large enough way to have ponies, carried with them home-made goods for sale in the Lowlands. It is probable that this practice was most common among the drovers from the north-east, for the knitted goods and coarse cloth of Aberdeenshire and Morayshire found a ready market in the South. As late as 1876, one who remembers the last days of the droving trade in the south of Scotland recalls having seen droves passing through Liddesdale, the drovers knitting stockings as they went.

Besides the actual drivers of the cattle, a drove of 200 to 300 animals might have a ' topsman ' whose duty it was to go

---

[1] *O.S.A.*, Abernethy, XIII, 147

on ahead, usually on horseback, to arrange for grazing for the night and generally to plan the route ; but often the drovers relied on their own knowledge of the country and on their own judgment and initiative. In this lay an important part of the drover's art, for the planning and execution of a journey with stock across 150 miles of eighteenth-century Scotland called for ability of no mean order to reckon with and balance a variety of complex factors peculiar to the operation, the country and the period. It was not without reason that a writer of last century compared favourably the skill and organising ability of a drover to that of the Duke of Wellington.[1] 'To purchase 1,000 cattle from a multitude of individuals,' observes a writer of the early nineteenth century, ' and march them, in one or more great battalions, from the extremity of Scotland, into the centre of England, at the expense of only a few shillings on each, is an undertaking that requires genius, exertion and a provision for many contingent circumstances, besides the knowledge which is requisite for their disposal to such advantage, as may encourage the continuance of the trade.' [2]

Maps were, of course, during the greater part of the droving period, not available, and a drover had to rely on knowledge gained from former journeys or perhaps from other drovers. At least till 1750 the state of the country had to be taken into account, for it was not till the middle of the century that drovers traversing the hills of Lochaber, Badenoch and Rannoch could do so with confidence and security. Wet weather might make the passage of rivers dangerous or impossible, while a dry autumn might make certain hill passes less attractive for feeding cattle on the move. Tolls on roads or bridges, or customs dues payable at certain points like Crieff or Dumbarton would reduce the slender margin of profit. These factors and many more must be balanced one with another, and all in the knowledge that Crieff or Falkirk must be reached without hurry by a given date.

The tracks followed by the drovers up to the middle of the eighteenth century were for the most part ill-defined, marked principally by the passage of that very traffic for which they themselves were responsible. The duty of maintaining the roads of rural Scotland, which had been laid on the Justices of the

[1] McLeod, *Reminiscences of a Highland Parish*, 1871, 192–3
[2] Leslie, *General View of the Agriculture of Nairn and Moray, 1811*, 303–4

Peace in 1609, was largely ignored, and the system of Statute Labour introduced in 1669 for the same purpose brought little improvement. Matters improved after the Union of the Parliaments in 1707, but trade in the rural districts was carried on mainly by pack-horse throughout the greater part of the eighteenth century. In 1723, the roads of Scotland outside the main towns were little more than tracks quite unsuited for wheel traffic which was, in consequence, practically non-existent. Between 1723 and 1740, General Wade built nearly 250 miles of military roads in the Highlands. Though these, the first properly constructed roads to be made in the Highlands, were of considerable importance, they did little more than touch the fringe of the problem of Highland transport, and it was not till the military roads were taken over by the Commissioners for Highland Roads and Bridges after 1803 that the work of Highland road construction was seriously taken in hand. Telford in his first survey of Highland roads made for the Commissioners in 1803 reported that ' previous to the year 1742 the roads were merely the tracks of black cattle and horses intersected by numerous rapid streams which being frequently swollen into torrents by heavy rains rendered them dangerous or impassable.' [1] Wade, indeed, in laying out the routes of his roads appears to have followed in some places the routes of older traffic of which cattle formed the bulk, but for the most part the routes of the droves passed unrestricted over open country. Only in those parts where droving traffic passed through Lowland areas, or where the land was considerably cultivated as in parts of Angus and Dumfriesshire, were attempts made to define and restrict its route by the construction of ' raiks ' as they were called 50 to 100 feet wide with turf dykes on either side. One of the earliest examples of this was in the south-west of Scotland, where in 1619 James Murray of Cockpool reported to the Privy Council that on their instructions he had laid out a drove road from Annan to Gretna, the people through whose lands the road led being ordered, with the help of the constables, to build dykes on either side to protect their corn.[2] Again in 1697 the Privy Council as a result of disputes between drovers and local landowners, appointed a Commission to mark out a drove road between New Galloway and Dumfries.[3] In the main, however, it seems clear that during much of the droving period

[1] Telford, *A Survey and Report of the Coasts and Central Highlands of Scotland*, 1803
[2] *R.P.C.*, 3rd series, XI, 633-4   [3] Chambers, op. cit., III, 153

and over great stretches of the Highlands the droves moved as they chose through a country unmarked by tracks other than their own.

While the general lines followed by the main droving traffic in Scotland can be determined with fair accuracy from contemporary records, local recollection or tradition, the identification on the ground of the actual line of march is in many cases a matter of great difficulty. As has been seen, droving traffic was in general unrestricted, free to cross a wide area or to change its route according to the weather, the season, or the many other factors which influenced that uncertain trade. This must often have prevented the formation of a track sufficiently well defined to remain visible to this day. In some parts of the Highlands, too, the routes followed by the drovers were routes used also by pack-horse, sledge and foot traffic, often dating from a very early period, and it is in many cases now hardly possible with any certainty to distinguish the marks made by one type of traffic from those made by another. Where, however, as in parts of the Highlands, the Southern Uplands and the Cheviots are still to be seen tracks, the predominant use of which by cattle traffic alone is reasonably certain, these are characterised by a number of roughly parallel paths. Where the ground is open and level these paths may in places cover a breadth of twenty to thirty yards and often much more, a type of track which would be left by beasts moving in parallel lines or perhaps by successive droves following the same route and choosing fresh ground to avoid that cut and trampled by the passage of those before. Where the configuration of the ground has concentrated the traffic, the breadth of the track narrows with a corresponding increase in its depth and clarity. The traffic which has left these traces is often referred to as consisting of 'streams' of beasts, and indeed the characteristic marks of a drove road are very similar to those left by the passage of a stream, alternately flowing in broad shallows or narrow deeps and rapids.[1]

The use which Wade and the road-makers who followed him made of the old traditional cattle routes in laying out the new roads, and the steady development and improvement of Highland roads after Wade's time, led to increasing complaints from the

---

[1] In the recent film *The Overlanders* which describes cattle droving in Northern Australia, it is noticeable that the photographs of the droves show the animals moving in parallel strings or streams now broadening and now contracting according to the nature of the ground.

drovers. The gravel of the new roads, they said, hurt the feet of the cattle while the hard surfaces wore down their hooves.[1] To meet these difficulties, many drovers adopted the practice, particularly in autumn or in bad weather, of shoeing the beasts, at least for that part of their journey which took them over made roads. The shoeing of cattle appears to date back to very ancient times. There is some evidence that working cattle were shod in Britain as early as the days of the Romans, and while it is not clear whether shoeing continued to be practised all through the centuries following their occupation, it is known that cattle were regularly shod in England in the seventeenth century. The Welsh drovers also shod their cattle on the way to the English markets, while in parts of England, notably in Sussex, the shoeing of cattle both for working and for travelling to market appears not to have entirely died out until about the beginning of the

---

[1] It seems doubtful whether complaints by drovers about the effect of made roads on the feet of the cattle can have had much justification until well on in the second half of the eighteenth century when the system of military roads had become fairly extensive. Wade's roads in many cases followed routes not extensively used by cattle droves which, in any event, did not keep to a narrow track. The surfaces of Wade's roads appear to have been composed of gravel. It is questionable whether cattle passing over them would suffer as much damage as they caused, and it is hardly surprising to find that in an Essay by William Mackintosh of Borlum in 1742 advocating the use of Wade's roads for stopping cattle-raiding, he recommends that the soldiers to be stationed at intervals on the roads should not allow their use by cattle droves on the way to the south-country markets. ' For these fairs and markets serve only in the latter end of the year when frequent rains fall which must by the cattle's feet potch and break the solidest structure can be made : nor is there any injury done them in this since the muirs on each side of the road affords their cattle as good footing as ever former droves had before that road was made.' The relatively soft nature of the surface of Wade's roads and the effect on them of the passing of cattle may be judged by a further passage in Mackintosh's essay, which emphasises the value of the roads for showing the marks of stolen beasts driven across them. The tracks of pasturing cattle, he states, can be easily distinguished from those of stolen cattle which are being hard driven. In the case of the former, the marks of the hooves are close together, while in the latter the hoof marks are far apart, while the marks of the pasterns appear like little dimples behind the hooves. (*A Short Scheme . . . to stop depradations . . . so destructive to the Northern Counties of Scotland*, Edinburgh 1742.) The progress which had been made by the early years of the nineteenth century in the technique of road construction, is shown by an extract from Telford's Report on the eastern end of the Glen Garry Road quoted in the *5th Report of the Commissioners for Highland Roads and Bridges* in 1811. ' This being a great extent of road,' he reported, ' through a country where much rain falls and a considerable portion of it having been now for three years used by Drovers of Black Cattle and of Sheep, of carts in carrying timber sold by Glengarry and for the conveyance of material for the bridge-building, it affords a very good specimen of the durability of Highland roads made according to the specification of our contracts. I saw it after a month of very heavy and constant rain . . . yet under all these circumstances the road has sustained no serious injury . . .' In 1813, however, the Commissioners referred in their *6th Report* to continued repairs needed on the Arisaig Road as a result of timber and cattle traffic.

present century.[1] The shoeing of animals travelling long distances to market was not confined to cattle, for during the early eighteenth and nineteenth centuries when numbers of geese and turkeys were driven by road from Norfolk to the London market, the birds were 'shod' by the simple process of smearing the feet with pitch and covering the surface with sand.[2] The method of shoeing cattle was rough, for the beasts had to be thrown on their backs, often with serious damage to the horns, the head being held down and the feet tied while the shoeing was being done. The shoes used by the drovers for their cattle were thin metal plates, crescent-shaped and nailed on the outer edge of the two hooves of each foot with fine metal nails the heads of which were formed of cross pieces giving the nail the appearance of a small hammer. A beast fully shod thus required eight metal plates, but it seems that often only the outer hoof of each foot was shod, as the most wear came on this outer edge.

At what points in Scotland on the journey to the trysts shoes were first fitted cannot be exactly determined, but it seems unlikely that shoes would be fitted for the first part of the journey through the Highlands where much of the way lay over mountain tracks and moorland. Till within recent years there still lived men who could remember the shoeing of cattle at a smiddy at Trinafour on the main drove road to Crieff from the North, and at Tyndrum, and a Ross-shire drover, whose memories of the droving trade go back to 1868, recalls the shoeing of cattle from Wester Ross-shire when they reached hard well-made roads in the neighbourhood of Muir of Ord and Dingwall.

While the shoes used for the Highland droves were no doubt largely made by local smiths, an Aberdeenshire cattle breeder of last century has recorded that many were made by a smith at Crossgates in Fife, who specialised in the craft and produced such good shoes and nails for fixing them that some drovers refused to drive the cattle unless Crossgates shoes were used.[3] The shoeing of half-wild cattle fresh from Highland grazings and unused to handling must have been difficult work, but the same

---

[1] Johnson, *Byways in British Archaeology*, 1912 ; and Skeel, *Cattle Trade between England and Wales from the 15th to the 19th centuries*. Royal Hist. Society's Transactions 4th series, IX, 1926, 143–4 and 149.

[2] Defoe estimated that about 150,000 turkeys were driven to London each year from East Anglia. The journey of approximately 100 miles started in August, and took about three months.

[3] McCombie, *Cattle and Cattle Breeders*, 1867, 113

Plate 1 Cattle Shoes

(*left*) Shoes made by the family of Kennedy, smiths at Trinafour, Perthshire, about 1865 (length 2⅞ in.). (*right*) Shoe and nails made at the village of Grassington, in Wharfedale, in the second half of the 19th century (length 3⅝ in.; nails 1⅛ in.)

(*Photos by C. S. Minto of shoes in the Author's possession*)

writer has described how Robert Gall of Kennethmont in Aberdeenshire once shod as many as seventy cattle in a day, probably shoeing only the outer edge of each hoof. As the droves moved south to the harder roads of England, the shoes had to be renewed at intervals either at local smiddies where stores of shoes were made and accumulated during the winter months, or with spare shoes carried by the drovers for the purpose.[1] Donald Mackenzie, a crofter living near Broadford in Skye, states that in his youth he repeatedly took cattle from the Islands to Falkirk Tryst. These beasts were not regularly shod, but if any went lame on the journey pieces of leather were attached to the foot to protect the hooves.

Leaving the gathering-point in the northern hills the drove ' crept slowly southward day after day.' The beasts must not be hurried, especially during the first days of the march, and the usual day's journey was ten to twelve miles. At midday the drovers halted to allow the cattle to graze, and when evening came they stopped in some suitable spot where the beasts could rest, graze and drink, while the men passed the night wrapped in their plaids in such shelter as the place afforded, but always on the watch to guard the drove or to do such herding as the tired beasts needed. A party of drovers from Skye whom Bishop Forbes met at Dalwhinnie on the way to Crieff in 1723 were rather better equipped than was usual, and one of the men so described the drovers' work : ' They had four or five horses with provisions for themselves by the way, particularly blankets to wrap themselves in when sleeping in the open air, as they rest on the bleak mountains, the heathy moors, or the verdant glens, just as it happens, towards the evening. They tend their flocks

---

[1] The cattle shoes used by the Welsh drovers were known as ' ciw.' These, like the shoes of the Scots cattle, were in two parts and the method of shoeing the beasts appears to have been very similar to that employed in the North. Shoes for Welsh cattle bound for England were made in large quantities by local smiths, particularly at Bala in Merionethshire. (P. G. Hughes, *Wales and the Drovers ; the Historic Background of an Epoch*, 1943.) On the English drove roads, shoes were made at Langthorpe, near Boroughbridge, at Grassington in Wharfedale and at other points on the routes to the great cattle markets. (William Thompson, *Cattle Droving between Scotland and England. Journal of Archaeological Association*, Vol. 87, 1932.) The smiths appear to have been paid about 10d for each beast shod. In an unpublished manuscript written about 1818 Arthur Young deals at some length with the shoeing of working cattle. He reports that in Sussex cattle are shod where their work takes them frequently on hard roads. His conclusion is that except for road work or on very stony ground shoeing is not advisable because of the trouble and risk of throwing the animal in the process and the difficulty of fixing the shoes securely. (Unpublished Manuscript, *The Elements and Practice of Agriculture*, Vol. 28, 355 et seq. British Museum)

35

by night and never move till about eight in the morning and then march the cattle at leisure that they may feed a little as they go along. They rest a while at midday to take some dinner and so let the cattle feed and rest as they please. The proprietor does not travel with the cattle but has one for his deputy to command the whole and he goes to the place appointed against the day fixed for the fair. When the flock is very large as the present, they divide it, though belonging to one, into several droves that they may not hurt one another in narrow passes, particularly on bridges many of which they go along. Each drove has a particular number of men with some boys to look after the cattle.' [1]

The factor on which beyond all others depended the success of a droving venture from the Highlands to the trysts was the care of the drover to see to it that wayside grazing was provided for the beasts, with opportunity to profit by it, and that undisturbed rest, food and water were theirs at night. The stopping-places for the night were known as ' stances.' ' These stances are essential to the use of the drove roads as such. The physical powers of sheep and cattle will not suffer them to be constantly in motion, and periodical rests are indispensable for their safety on journeys continuing from day to day for weeks together. Hence the existence of stances without which the drove road would be useless. The stances may therefore be truly said to be part and parcel of the drove road just as much as any other portion of the surface trodden by cattle in the course of their transit.' [2] The choice of these stopping-places to rest and graze the cattle was dictated by the existence of pasture and water for the beasts, and by the limited day's march which the cattle could cover. While ten to twelve miles was the distance generally recognised in Scotland by the careful drover as the most the cattle could do in a day if they were to be in good condition on reaching Crieff or Falkirk, it was sometimes necessary to exceed this limit. In the Hebrides, where the route of cattle bound for the mainland entailed crossings from one island to another dependant on tides, the beasts might have to be driven farther and faster than the drovers liked. A drove starting late from Broadford in Skye might be hurried to catch the slackest of the tide at the crossing to the mainland, or bad weather at an exposed

---

[1] *Bishop Forbes' Journal*, 235–6
[2] *Macgregor and Others* v. *Breadalbane*, Court of Session Cases, 1846, 9 Dunlop's Reports, 210

part of the route might mean a forced march to cross a high pass ; but these were exceptions, and the good drover was loth to hurry his beasts or to cheat them of their midday grazing and their full night's rest.

Until the second half of the eighteenth century the drovers' stances were in most cases used without payment. As an old drover of last century said of them in giving evidence in support of the drovers' rights : ' The beasts were allowed to feed where they stopped. There was no charge made for that. They were all made welcome—a free table for man and beast.' [1] In many parts of the Highlands, indeed, until changing conditions led to a different outlook, droves were probably not unwelcome, for the passage and pasturage of large droves of cattle meant valuable manuring of the ground, and even to this day the routes of the old drove roads and the sites of the stances remain in many places appreciably greener than the surrounding hill. As the droves moved towards the lower country, however, where enclosure of land was more frequent, payment for grazing and stance rights became, as time went on, more common, especially where cottages or inns beside the stances offered, if they wished it, shelter for the drovers as well as grass for the beasts.

On arrival at a stance, which was seldom enclosed save by the sides of glen or corrie, the beasts were allowed to graze freely. The men ate their simple meal and later lay down to rest, one of their number by turns keeping watch through the night while the others slept. The beasts were usually too tired and hungry to wander far, but old men still (1948) living who in their young days took beasts to the Trysts, have told that sometimes if the moon rose late after the beasts had fed and rested they would wander and must be herded. A writer of the nineteenth century mentions the acuteness of hearing of many of the drovers which enabled them to detect the movements of an animal straying from the stance during the dark hours.[2] During the first few days of the journey, the homing instinct, strong in sheep and cattle, lingered on, and during this period there was the risk of beasts making off the way they had come. Soon the memory of the familiar pastures faded, and from then on the nights were seldom disturbed. Night marches were avoided at all costs, for,

[1] *Scottish Rights of Way Society* v. *MacPherson*, Court of Session Cases, 1887, 14 Rettie's Reports, 875 and Notes of Evidence
[2] McIan and Logan, op. cit., 37

37

like Candlish and Sym, the drovers who led St Ives over the hills of the Southern Uplands, they knew that such forced marches were 'fair ruin on the bestial.'[1] When morning came the beasts were quietly roused and collected again for the road, for cattle startled and hurried after a night's rest were liable to scatter and stampede. The degree of skill and care required of the drovers in the management of the beasts depended partly on the composition of the drove. Beasts newly come from summer grazing could be more easily spoiled by over-driving than a drove in the spring which had had no rich feeding, while a mixed drove of heifers and bullocks or one composed of beasts from several different grazings was more restless and difficult to drive than a drove of one sex or from one locality.

The movement of thousands of cattle by ten mile stages from all parts of north and west Scotland to Crieff or Falkirk by many and varying routes meant the existence of great numbers of stances throughout the Highlands. Some of these are still known by the local people and are on occasion used as stances ; some are now only fast-fading traditions, while countless others have passed far beyond the limits of memory or tradition. To attempt to enumerate them all, even if it were now possible, would lead into profitless paths of speculation and controversy. It is sufficient to know that all through the Highlands, in glens and corries or on open moorland, are grassy hollows or stretches of open grazing which once offered rest to tired beasts and wearied men.[2]

Many water hazards lay between the drovers and the Trysts. The absence of bridges over the rivers of the Highlands was one of the main obstacles to inland communication in Scotland in the seventeenth and eighteenth centuries. Wade's work indeed included the building of between thirty and forty bridges, but though he bridged the Tay, the Spean, the Tummel and the Perthshire Garry the total number was made up largely of small

---

[1] R. L. Stevenson, op. cit., Ch. 10

[2] While, for the reason given, no complete list of the stances on the main drove routes has been attempted, information based on local recollection or tradition indicates that on the drove routes from Skye to Central Perthshire stances which were regularly used included Kyle Rhea, Shiel Bridge, Clunie, Torgyle, Fort Augustus, Meallgarbh, Garvamore, Drumgask, Dalwhinnie, Dalnaspidal, Dalnacardoch and Trinafour. On one of the alternative routes stances appear to have been in use at Loch Loyne, Fedden in Glen Cia-aig, Spean Bridge, Blarmachfoldach in Glen Kiachnish, Kinlochleven, Altnafeadh, Inveroran, Bridge of Orchy, Clifton, Luib and Balquhidder.

bridges. In the latter part of the eighteenth century a number
of new bridges were built over some of the larger rivers, but when
Telford started his work as Engineer to the Commissioners for
Highland Roads and Bridges in 1803 the absence of bridges at
key points was still one of the main weaknesses in the road system
of the Highlands.[1] The Conon, the Beauly, the Spey and the
Lyon were still unbridged. The only crossing of the Don except
by ford appears to have been at the old Bridge of Balgownie
near its mouth. On the Dee there were, till 1800, only four
bridges, one of these at Aberdeen, while on the Tweed the only
bridges available for cattle before 1766 appear to have been at
Berwick and Peebles. Of the bridges which did exist, most were
naturally at the most populous parts which the drovers sought
to avoid, and over countless Highland streams and burns no
bridges of any sort existed. There were good reasons, too, why
such bridges as existed were not popular with the drovers. Many
of the early bridges were narrow wooden structures. To cattle
being driven for the first time, and unused as many of them were
to anything but their native hills, the crossing of a narrow bridge
was a terrifying experience, while the unaccustomed sound of
their feet on the timbers was liable to make them panic. Even
on the larger bridges the danger was considerable. A note in a
Dumfriesshire paper records that while a large drove was on its
way south from Dumfriesshire in the early part of last century,
it was met by the mail coach while crossing the bridge over the
Eden near Carlisle. The cattle took fright and so great was the
rush of beasts that the parapet of the bridge gave way, and both
men and cattle were thrown into the river.[2]

In these conditions the crossing of rivers by ford or by
swimming was the common lot of the beasts and part of the
familiar technique of the drovers.[3] Edward Burt has so described
the crossing of a river by a drove of cattle in the first half of the
eighteenth century : ' It was in a time of rain by a wide river
where there was a boat to ferry over the drovers. The cows were
about fifty in number and took the water like spaniels, and when

[1] Telford, *Survey and Report of the Coasts and Central Highlands of Scotland*, 1803
[2] *Dumfries and Galloway Courier*. 'Notes and Queries', 1913. Note 439
[3] In this the drovers may well have profited by the traditions and teaching of their
less reputable ancestors. Mackintosh of Borlum has described the crossing of the
Tay near Kenmore by cattle thieves. ' Each man takes hold in his one hand of
horse, bullock or cow's tail, he drove into the water and extends out his other hand
with his fusee and his pistol in his teeth, and so is drawn with his firearms dry to the
other side.' Mackintosh of Borlum, op. cit.

they were in, their drivers made a hideous cry to urge them forwards : this, they told me, they did to keep the foremost of them from turning about, for in that case, the rest would do the like and then they would be in danger, especially the weakest of them, to be swept away and drowned by the torrent.' [1] Except in time of flood the larger rivers, such as Burt described, would offer relatively little difficulty, for cattle are strong swimmers. Even so, there must have been times when the crossing of rivers such as the Dee or the Spey would be a work of great hazard, and it is hardly surprising that in the *General View of the Agriculture of Elgin* in 1794 the writer reports that drovers from the South do not attend the local sales for lack of a bridge over the Spey at Fochabers.[2] William McCombie the Aberdeenshire cattle dealer already quoted, has described how in the early years of last century, his father, in bringing a drove from Caithness to Aberdeenshire, lost seventeen beasts in the crossing of the Spey, a severe frost having come on shortly after the cattle had swum the river.[3] Difficult as the crossing of the larger rivers might be, however, the smaller ones and many a hill stream would at times present almost greater problems. Too shallow to swim and too rapid to ford, they must at times of flood have proved formidable obstacles involving detours or delays wearisome alike to tired beasts and their harassed drivers.

The period of the year during which droving from the Highlands went on lasted from May or early June, when some of the beasts had recovered from the hungry winter, till the end of October. Little or no droving took place in the winter or early spring, a season which even the old cattle raiders recognised as one during which the beasts were too weak for long journeys ; but even during the droving months, storms of wind and driving mist and rain were to be looked for on high passes or open moorland, while early snows might well come before the last beasts were delivered to the October Tryst at Falkirk. Yet, cold and wet as they must constantly have been, these hardy men the drovers, seldom sought the shelter of houses. Many, it is said, never slept under a roof between Lochaber and Lincolnshire, and those still (1948) alive can recall meeting in their youth with old drovers who, when in charge of cattle, were loth to enter a house

[1] Burt, *Letters from a Gentleman in the North of Scotland*, II, 33
[2] Donaldson, J., *General View of the Agriculture of Elgin*, 1794, 27-8
[3] McCombie, op. cit., 100

even to eat. The constant vigilance called for from the drovers no doubt made it necessary for them to rest beside their cattle, a need perhaps all the greater in the vicinity of men and habitations. A writer of the first half of last century has so described the work of the smaller type of cattle dealer in the south of Scotland : ' A mountaineer will travel from fair to fair for thirty miles round with no other food than the oaten cake which he carries with him, and what requires neither fire, table, knife nor any instrument to use. He will lay out the whole, or perhaps treble of all he is worth (to which the facility of the country banks is a great encouragement) in the purchase of 30 or 100 head of cattle, with which, when collected, he sets out for England, a country with the roads, manners and inhabitants of which he is probably unacquainted. In this journey, he scarcely ever goes into a house, sleeps but little, and then generally in the open air, and lives chiefly upon his favourite oaten bread.' [1]

While the hardiness of these men is remarkable, it may be doubted whether they were greatly the losers in shunning the inn of the period. With the great increase in road building in the Highlands during the first half of the nineteenth century some improvement took place in both the supply and the standard of Highland inn accommodation, but at no time earlier than the middle of that century did the inns of Scotland stand in good repute. ' The Band and Statutes of Icolmkill ' by which James VI sought to reduce the Western Isles to order had provided for the setting up of inns in convenient places ; but Thomas Kirke, writing in 1669, says, ' The Scots have not inns, but change-houses as they call them, poor small cottages where you must be content to take what you find,' [2] and it was the existence of too many of these primitive inns kept by lawless people that the Privy Council in 1618 blamed for much of the unrest of the Border.[3] A writer of the first half of the eighteenth century says of the inns in his youth : ' Few were to be met with in which the traveller could either eat or sleep with comfort,' [4] perhaps because the Scot of the period travelled little, and when he did, enjoyed the hospitality of friends or relations which was amply repaid

---

[1] Youatt, *Cattle, their Breeds, Management and Diseases.* Library of Useful Knowledge, 1834, 163
[2] Hume Brown, *Early Travellers,* 264   [3] *R.P.C.*, 1st series, XI, 445–6
[4] Somerville, *My Own Life and Times 1741–1814,* 356

by the relief of the tedium and monotony of the hosts' daily life. The passing of the eighteenth century saw little change in the standard of accommodation provided for the wayfarer, and at the end of the century travellers from the South coming to Scotland in increasing numbers have all the same complaint. Many of the inns of the Highlands of this period were still only wayside cottages providing little more than the rough spirit, illicitly distilled, which, with the small black cattle and the kelp of the Islands and coastal districts, were the only products with which the Highlander of the time could eke out his meagre livelihood. Kingshouse on the Moor of Rannoch was a key point on the drove roads. Here the need for an inn and the lack of incentive to keep one was early recognised by the Government, and travellers of the eighteenth and early nineteenth centuries record that the innkeeper sat rent free and had an annual Government grant. Despite this, the description of the place given by travellers during the droving period shows it to have been rough and cheerless. It is described by a traveller of 1791 as having ' not a bed fit for a decent person to sleep in nor any provisions but what are absolutely necessary for the family,' [1] and in 1802 James Donaldson, Surveyor of the Military Roads, complains that it ' has more the appearance of a hog stye than an Inn.' [2] Dorothy Wordsworth in the following year found it ' a wretched place—as dirty as a house after a sale on a rainy day,' but of the inn at Inveroran ten miles across the moor, she has left a more cheerful picture. Here, on 4 September 1803, she found the inn filled with ' seven or eight travellers probably drovers, with as many dogs, sitting in a complete circle round a large peat fire in the middle of the floor, each with a mess of porridge in a wooden vessel on his knee.' [3] As the nineteenth century wore on, and the routes of the drovers became more defined and restricted, wayside inns came to be increasingly used by them, and those inns with facilities for resting cattle started to advertise the fact in the local papers. Despite this, many drovers remained to the end true to their calling and their traditions, resting at night with their cattle, where ' wrapped in their plaids on which the frost showed white or the dew shone just as it does upon

---

[1] Newte, *Tour of England and Scotland in 1785* (1791 edn.), 120
[2] Letter to John Campbell, Esq., W.S., Edinburgh, dated 9th June 1802 : *Breadalbane Papers* (*Roads*), Box 4, H.M. Register House
[3] Dorothy Wordsworth, *Journals*, 1798–1828 (Ed. William Knight), 318, 323

a spider's web, their sticks near their hands, they slumbered peacefully.'[1]

That the connection between the Church in Scotland and the life and work of the drovers was close, is apparent from the early records of the droving trade. The local fairs which in many cases developed into the cattle trysts of the seventeenth and eighteenth centuries commemorate the names of St Lawrence, St Serf, St Faith, St Andrew, St Palladius and a score of others, and as has been seen, the help of the Church was enlisted by cattle dealers in calling together their customers ; but the Church was concerned to see to it that their help and patronage of the droving trade was not abused. In 1503 the holding of markets or fairs on Holy Days had been prohibited by statute ; but drovers were rough folk to whom it seemed that the Sabbath was made for man, and all through the seventeenth century the Register of the Privy Council and the later records of the Presbyteries and Kirk Sessions throughout the country contain constant complaints of Sunday droving and efforts to prevent it. Many of the local fairs had originally been fixed on a Monday, and as this inevitably led to the driving of cattle on the previous day, the dates were gradually changed. In 1640 the great market at Dumfries was changed from Monday to Wednesday,[2] and nearly fifty years later the date of the important fair of St Lawrence in Aberdeen-shire was changed for the same reason.[3] The Minutes of the Kirk Session of Peebles in July 1764 record the punishment of drovers passing through the town on a Sunday for neglecting to attend church.[4] Sunday droving, however, continued to be practised, and particularly in the south-west of Scotland the

[1] Cunninghame Graham, *A Hatchment*, 212
Sir Walter Scott mentions an incident described to him by one of those who took part in it as a boy. A small number of cattle which had been stolen by Highland cattle thieves had been recovered with the help of Rob Roy acting in the capacity of ' cattle protector.' The beasts were being driven homewards by a small party including the narrator, and when darkness fell they lay down for the night in an exposed place. The season was late October and the night exceedingly cold. The narrator in a desperate attempt to get warm lay down beside one of the Highlanders, and by degrees pulled over himself part of the plaid in which the latter was wrapped. In the morning, he was alarmed to see that the Highlander's neck and shoulders which had been uncovered were white with hoar frost, but the Highlander suffered little inconvenience, merely shaking himself on awakening and rubbing the hoar frost off with his plaid while he muttered that it had been a ' cauld nicht.' (Scott, *Rob Roy*, Introduction, lxxii, Border edn., Waverley Novels)
[2] *A.P.S.*, V, 297–8   [3] *R.P.C.*, 3rd series, VIII, 380
[4] Johnman, *Highways and Byways*, Transactions of Hawick Archaeological Society, 1917, 21

matter was constantly before the local Church authorities during the eighteenth century and at least as late as 1840.[1] Whether in the remoter parts of the Highlands drovers observed the Sabbath may be doubted, but Dorothy Wordsworth's description of Glendochart on a Sunday in September 1803 seems to indicate that perhaps even here men and beasts may have had their Sunday rest : ' On the side of a sunny hill a knot of men and women were gathered together at a preaching. We passed by many droves of cattle and Shetland ponies, which accident stamped a character upon places—else unremembered—not an individual character but the soul, the spirit and solitary simplicity of many a Highland region.' [2]

While the hazards and hardships of his calling must fill much of the canvas of any picture of the drover's life, there were some patches of brightness to alleviate the sombre colouring. His wayfaring life taking him far afield, did more than satisfy the love of movement and adventure handed down to him from the generations before. Gossip and talk with other travellers and drovers at inns and wayside meetings cheered his lonely journeys, and with the packsman, the pedlar and the tramp he shared the function of news carrier so dear to country people at a time when news was scarce. His was the excitement of the Tryst, of the bustle and the bargaining ; his too, the pride of recounting its every detail to eager listeners back in his Highland glen. If at times these advantages may have seemed to the drover small recompense for his life of hardship, and if he were sometimes tempted to turn his back on the drove road and to prefer his poor croft and scanty holding in Uist, Skye or Lochaber, some other thought may have come to him. Perhaps rough hard men though the drovers were, their memories brought to them as they sat by their peat fires pictures which made them forget their hardships and their sufferings : sunlight and cloud-shadow on the hills of Kintail ; gold of the birches in Glen Garry or along the Dee as they took a drove south to the October Trysts ; green of lush grass and flags set against the yellow of seaweed as the Islay cattle moved up the shores of Loch Sween ; Cruachan with an early powdering of snow ; Loch Awe and Loch Lubnaig still on a September morning, or countless other scenes of loch, river, meadow and mountain as they and their cattle passed in the autumn days on their slow journeys through the Highlands of Scotland.

[1] *Dumfries Courier*, 29 January 1840   [2] Dorothy Wordsworth, op. cit., 325

3

THE ECONOMICS OF DROVING

THE natural barriers of sea, mountain and river which faced the early drovers on their journeys from Highlands to Lowlands, formed part only of the difficulties which lay between them and the success of their hazardous enterprise. To these were added problems of finance and economics so great that it can only be a matter for wonder that trade was carried on in conditions which to a trader of later times must seem well-nigh impossible. Of the complex factors which a cattle drover had to take into account during the centuries preceding the Union of 1603, the most important were probably the political state of the country and particularly of the Border areas, the policy of the Government towards the internal trade of the country and the commercial relations of Scotland and England. By the middle of the seventeenth century, the advantages of freer trading across the Border had come to be more generally recognised, and the years which followed the Union of 1707 brought a gradual realisation that for better or for worse the fortunes of the two countries were indeed finally linked. The changing and opportunist policy which had hitherto hampered the trade of Scotland settled at last on a more fixed course, and from the early years of the eighteenth century it becomes possible to attempt to construct a clear picture of the economic and financial problems which faced the drovers and the methods by which they plied their trade.

The rapid development of droving throughout the eighteenth century was, as has been seen, the natural outcome of the state of rural Scotland at that period. In the early years of the century, road communications between Highlands and Lowlands were still almost non-existent. Markets for cattle were distant, and to reach them involved a journey over large tracts of little-known and disturbed country where, as late as 1747, it was estimated that the total annual loss suffered directly or indirectly from cattle thieving was £37,000 sterling.[1] Yet cattle constituted almost

[1] *An Inquiry into the Causes . . . of Rebellions . . . in the Highlands of Scotland*, 1747 ; Gartmore MS. printed as Appendix in Jamieson's (5th) Edition of Burt's *Letters from a Gentleman in the North of Scotland*, II, 359.

the only form of readily realisable wealth, and were in many cases the principal method of paying rents. Since dealers from the south would not face the risks of journeys to and from the Highlands, there arose this class of hardy and adventurous men —the drovers—to barter knowledge of the country and acceptance of hazard and hardship in return for a meagre daily wage, a small commission on the price realised for the beasts sold, or in the case of some, for the difference between the price paid to the Highland grazier and that realised in the markets of the Lowlands.[1]

Money was scarce in Scotland in the eighteenth century, and at the time of the Union of 1707 the total amount in circulation was reckoned to be not more than £200,000 Sterling.[2] Though the Bank of Scotland had been founded in 1695, nearly half a century was to pass before banking became an active part of the commercial life of Scotland, and even longer before banking facilities became widely available in the rural districts ; but while money was short credit was long, and the written promise to pay or bill of exchange was in active circulation. Many of these bills remained for long unpaid before they could be cashed, and meantime passed from hand to hand, fulfilling to some extent the function of the banknotes of later years. This credit

---

[1] ' It is alledged that much of the Highlands lye at a great distance from publick Fairs, mercates and places of commerce and that the access to these places is both difficult and dangerous ; by reason of all which, trading people decline to go into the country in order to traffick and deal with the people. It is on this account that the farmers, having no way to turn the produce of their farms, which is mostly cattle, into money are obliged to pay their rents in cattle which the landlord takes at his own price, in regairde that he must either grase them himself, send them to distant markets, or credite some person with them to be againe at a certaine profit disposed of by him. This introduced the business of that sort of people commonly known by the name of Drovers. These men have little or no substance, they must know the language, the different places and consequently be of that country. The farmers, then, do either sell their cattle to these drovers upon credite, at the drover's price (for ready money they seldom have) or to the landlord at his price, for payment of his rent. If this last is the case, the landlord does again dispose of them to the drover upon credite, and these drovers make what profites they can by selling them to grasiers or at markets. These drovers make payments, and keep credite for a few years and then they either in reality become bankrupts, or pretend to be so. The last is most frequently the case and then the subject of which they have cheated is privately transferred to a confident person in whose name, upon that reall stock, a trade is sometimes carried on for their behoof, till the Trustee gett into credite and prepaire *his* affairs for a bankruptcy. Thus the farmers are still kept poor ; they first sell at an under rate and then they often loose altogether. The landlords, too, must either turn traders and take their cattle to markets, or give these people credite, and by the same means suffer.' (ibid., 364-5)

[2] Hume Brown estimates it at only £60,000 in copper, £60,000 in silver and £30,000 in gold. (*History of Scotland*, III, 69)

system was one of which the cattle drovers of the eighteenth century took full advantage, and without which the financing of their operations would have been impossible. For some years before the start of the earliest Scots banks, there had been in existence mercantile houses whose business lay largely in the financing of trade. From them, a drover bound for the Highlands to buy cattle for sale at Crieff Tryst obtained a letter of credit and a slender stock of cash.[1] Armed with these, he made his appearance in the late spring or early summer among the needy tenants, tacksmen and landlords of the north and west. To men short of money and distant from markets, the temptation of a few pounds of cash and the prospect of a further payment on the sale of their beasts proved irresistible. Such scraps of information as had filtered through from the South, or the number and urgency of the drovers in the North were their only means of judging as to the fair market value of their animals. So the scales were weighted and after such bargaining as was possible in the circumstances, the cattle passed to the new owners, these ' little extorting money holders,' as Sir John Sinclair called them, ' who for affording a little supply of money when any distress occurs take the cattle at their own price.' [2] The proportion of the price paid in cash appears to have varied greatly, but probably in few cases was it more than a fraction of the value of the animals.[3] The balance was met by bills or promissory notes which the drovers gave, payable usually at the end of three months, by which time they might reasonably hope to have sold their beasts at the Trysts. Sometimes necessity drove the owners to part with their beasts for bills alone. The needs of the sellers, the optimism and ready wit of the buyers, led to great variations in the type of bargain to suit varying circumstances, but all rested on credit given and risks taken.

[1] In a case which came before the Court of Session in 1767 on the Petition of a Yorkshire cattle dealer, the ' Answers ' lodged in reply described how drovers from the South about to proceed to the remoter parts of Scotland procure in Edinburgh promissory notes for different sums payable at some distance of time, when they expect to have finished their round and picked up all the cattle they mean to purchase, the bankers in Edinburgh being re-imbursed by bills drawn on the drovers' correspondents in London. (*Old Session Papers*, Signet Library, 150, 24)

[2] Sinclair, *General View of the Agriculture of the Northern Counties*, 1795, 160

[3] In a case which came before the Court of Session in 1779 the price agreed for a sale of cattle between a Sutherlandshire farmer and a local drover was fixed at 8s to 15s a head below the normal figure because the drover undertook to pay cash when the cattle were delivered at a fixed rendezvous—an undertaking which was in fact not fulfilled. (*Old Session Papers*, Signet Library, 191, 25)

The sale effected and the drovers started on their long journey South, the bills they had signed passed quickly into circulation as part of the currency of the district. When James Boswell and Samuel Johnson visited Skye in 1772 they found that the rents due to the Lairds were paid in drovers' bills.[1] A system of finance based largely on bills of exchange seems to have been general throughout the Highlands at that time, and the Letter-book of Bailie John Steuart, an Inverness merchant of the early eighteenth century, shows such bills to have been in circulation helping to finance a wonderfully active trade not only in such home products as Easdale slate, Morayshire grain and Findhorn salmon, but in coffee beans from Rotterdam, wines from Bordeaux and olives of the Mediterranean shore.[2] Many of these Highland bills were made payable at Crieff, for during the first half of the century Crieff cattle market was probably the greatest centre of money circulation in the country, and Steuart was often represented there to try to get payment of bills held by him from the proceeds of cattle sales. After the turn of the century, the Edinburgh banks were for the same reason represented at Falkirk Tryst, which was then rapidly supplanting Crieff as the centre of the droving trade.

During the first thirty years of the eighteenth century, the financing of trade in Scotland had been done mainly by merchants and goldsmiths in Edinburgh, and by commercial houses, of which Coutts and Company, founded in 1723, was one of the most important. The years which followed the founding of the Royal Bank of Scotland in 1727, however, saw a rapid extension of the cash credit system by means of which any reputable person with two guarantors could get credit. While much of this financing was, so far as concerned the cattle trade, probably in most cases on a small scale, considerable advances were sometimes made, and a record of the British Linen Bank shows that in 1767 the cashier of the bank was sent to Falkirk with instructions to get payment on bills due by drovers and to finance John Birtwhistle, a well-known drover from Yorkshire, to the extent of £2,000 if he required it, while Robert Scott of Shelphill and James Grieve of Todshawhaugh were authorised to get advances of £500 each. The system of cash credit was popular with traders and bankers

---

[1] Boswell, *Tour to the Hebrides*, Isham Collection, 172
[2] *Steuart's Letter-book 1715/1752.* Scot. Hist. Soc,. 2nd series, Vol. 9. Introd. xxii, xxiv.

alike, for while it greatly helped the rapid growth of trade and industry from 1730 onwards, it provided the new banks with an opportunity of getting their notes into circulation. By the middle of the century branch banks had been opened in many of the larger towns, and soon small independent banks started business in many country districts, encouraged by the dangerous but convenient system then in fashion which enabled them to pay cash for their notes, or at their own option to make payment with interest at the end of six months. The dangers arising from the widespread use of this option and the multiplication of small banking companies all over the country which it facilitated soon became apparent, and an Act of 1767 prohibited the issue of notes of less than £1 and provided that all notes should be immediately convertible into cash ; but this alone was insufficient to restore stability to the country's banking system. In the face of rapidly expanding industry and rising prices, ignorance or disregard of sound banking principles produced all the conditions making for the disaster which overtook many of the smaller banks and some of the larger in 1772.

Of the abundant credit so readily available none took fuller advantage than the cattle drovers and dealers. The chance of large profits and the rising demand for cattle in the markets of England in the latter years of the eighteenth and early nineteenth centuries, induced many to go into the business with little or no capital other than their hardiness, their spirit of adventure and their boundless assurance. Though many of them would have found difficulty in raising a few hundred pounds, these men thought little of buying from the Highlands in a single autumn cattle to the value of £10,000 to £12,000, giving in return a little cash and the balance in the customary bills. The existence of the new small banks each vying with its neighbours to extend its business and its note circulation, enabled the cattle owners to discount the bills in disregard, or possibly in ignorance, of the fact that by so doing they themselves became, with the drovers, jointly responsible to the banks which cashed the bills. So long as prices at the Trysts kept up, all went well, but no trade was more vulnerable than the droving trade to the chances of fortune, and losses were frequent and heavy. Few of the drovers were men of any substance, and the Banks which had advanced money to them, or had later discounted their bills for the farmers, saw to it that when repayments were made their advances to the drovers,

which were in most cases the least secure, were the first to be can-
celled. 'A drover at starting,' writes Webster in his agricultural
survey of Galloway in 1794, 'agrees with a banker for money or
credit which the latter knows how to make safe and profitable.
With some money and this credit he attacks the country and
grants his own acceptance at such date as may be agreed upon,
not exceeding three months for what he purchases. These
acceptances being discounted by the farmer, the banker gets the
country as a further security for their own property on the drover's
bills, provided the banker sees how to clear his own private
account, and the bills are taken up as they fall due of which he
takes care to get clear of the worst as early as possible. If the
trade is brisk, people get all paid, and the drover obtains
the further confidence of the country.' [1] So the farmers carried
the main risk of the industry on which perforce they depended,
bearing the losses if times were bad and reaping few of the
rewards.

A Parliamentary Committee in 1826 considered among other
matters measures which might be adopted to reduce the risk of
the large-scale failures among cattle dealers and the severe losses
to cattle breeders which had been experienced in the previous
few years. The evidence of the Agent to the British Linen Bank
at Dumfries following the lines of suggestions already made by
writers in the Statistical Account went to show that the only
solution lay in the drovers themselves finding security for the
accommodation which they got from the bankers, so enabling
them to pay cash to the farmers who would not then require to
resort to the discounting of bills which so frequently led to trouble.
It was pointed out, however, that such a system would certainly
mean lower prices for the farmers, and consequently lower rents
with much disorganisation and distress while the trade was
changing from a credit to a cash basis.[2]

In such a system of trading, the solvency and honesty of the
drovers were clearly of first importance. Here, too, the cattle
owners were at a great disadvantage, for while some drovers were
men of known reliability, in many cases the cattle owners were
dealing with men whom they did not know and at whose substance
and honesty they could only guess. 'Necessity, ignorance or

[1] Webster, *General View of the Agriculture of Galloway*, 1794, 25
[2] *Report of Select Committee on Promissory Notes in Scotland and Ireland 1826.* Notes of
Evidence.

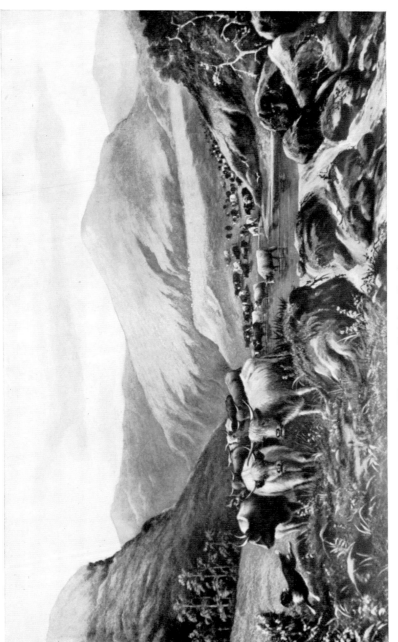

Plate 2   Driving Cattle

(From an early print)

greed of the farmers,' says a writer of the eighteenth century,
' induce them to venture their cattle at 1/- to 2/- more per head
to a man who would be ruined if he lost 5/- a head at Falkirk '[1];
but necessity and ignorance at least prevailed, and neither bitter
experience nor cruel and frequent loss sufficed to prevent the
continuance of the system until the decline of the droving industry
in the second half of last century.

The Statistical Account of 1791–99 and the Agricultural
Surveys of various parts of Scotland prepared during the last
years of the eighteenth and the first years of the nineteenth
centuries show the serious effects of the system on the cattle-
breeding areas of Scotland. From all parts come the same
complaints. The writer of the Statistical Account of the Parish
of Assynt estimates that failure among the drovers brings distress
to the district one year in every ten.[2] From Morayshire and
Sutherland come accounts of heavy losses from the same causes.
In his account of the northern counties Sir John Sinclair writes
in 1795 that heavy losses have been sustained in recent years and
recommends that cattle be sold only for ready money or good
letters of credit.[3] The writer of the Agricultural Survey of
Dumfriesshire complains of the losses suffered by the farmers and
of the stimulus given to an unsound system of finance by the
existence of small worthless local banks. He suggests that the
remedy lies in the sale by the farmers direct to England or to
English graziers in the North, so eliminating the drovers altogether. ' In view of the intelligence needed and the fact that he
has the management of property of the value of £10,000 to
£12,000,' says a writer on the Agriculture of Galloway in 1794,
' it is surprising that the drovers are often men who could not
muster £500 or men who have perhaps only 2 years back paid
10/- in the £ to their creditors. The annual loss to Galloway is
immense. In the present year several drovers in charge of large
droves had compounded with their creditors not six months
before or had narrowly escaped doing so. But possession of
confidence and a ready tongue may serve instead of great intelligence. Of these the drovers have their full share. Formerly
landed proprietors used to take cattle to England, but latterly
they stopped and the drovers took their place. These could not
buy except on credit and the country was induced to trust them

---

[1] *O.S.A.*, Abernethy, XIII, 147   [2] *O.S.A.*, Assynt, XVI, 193
[3] Sinclair, op. cit., 160

and instead of real security to rest content with a shadow.'[1]
'For almost a century,' says a Survey from the same district in
1813, 'there has not perhaps been more than one out of ten
among the drovers who have not been at least once insolvent.'[2]

While a cattle owner of the eighteenth century might well
complain of what seemed to him the one-sided nature of the
bargain by which he parted with his beasts, the drover for his
part had cause for grave thought and anxious calculation ; for
his was a complex budget in which many of the items were
unpredictable and imponderable. A drover bringing beasts from
the Outer Islands had in the first place to reckon with the cost
and risk of ferrying them to the mainland. Feeding on the
cross-country journey cost him little or nothing in the hill country,
but in the Lowland districts and near the Trysts he was forced,
increasingly as the eighteenth century wore on, to pay for his
rights of stance and nightly grazing. The rate of payment appears
to have varied considerably, depending on the district and the
quality of grazing available, but certainly tending to increase
as time passed. When the Common Land at Sheriffmuir was
divided in 1772, witnesses in the court proceedings, whose duty
it had been to collect the stance money from the drovers who
used the grazing on the way to Falkirk, spoke of the ' grass mail '
being 6d a score per night for cattle or 6s a drove. In one case a
witness's memory was sharpened by the fact that he had been
forced to follow to ' the Gowan Hills of Stirling ' a drover who
had gone off in the early hours leaving the bill unpaid.[3] At
Inveroran on the Moor of Rannoch the traditional rates were
1s 6d per score for cattle and the same for 100 sheep,[4] but old
drovers still (1948) alive, who brought cattle from the Highlands
in the last quarter of the nineteenth century, remember the rates
having risen to between 3s and 4s 6d a score for cattle and 2s 6d
or 3s for 100 sheep.

Bridges or stretches of road under the charge of Turnpike
Trustees might cost a drover 2d a beast, and while these were
avoided where possible, some, like the bridge at Stirling, might
have to be crossed. Market dues at Crieff were around 2d a

[1] Webster, op. cit., 24–5
[2] Smith, *Survey of Agriculture of Galloway*, 1813, 251
[3] Division of Commonty of Sheriffmuir, *Durie Decreets*, 2/12/1772. H.M. Register
House.
[4] *MacGregor and Others* v. *Breadalbane*, Court of Session Cases, 1846, 9 Dunlop's
Reports, 210

beast for cattle, and at Falkirk in 1834 they were 8d a score for cattle and 3d a score for sheep payable to Sir Michael Bruce, the owner of the Tryst ground who let the right of collecting the tolls to a Tacksman at a rent of £120 per annum.[1] In the absence of auctioneers at the Trysts, no commission on the sale price had to be paid, but it was not infrequent for a drover to call in a friend to act, no doubt for a consideration, as a go-between with a prospective buyer, while quite substantial payments in the form of luck-pennies, or at least extensive refreshment on the conclusion of a bargain, were almost the established practice.

Sir Walter Scott speaks of the drovers being paid 'very highly.' The wages of the leading drovers or 'topsmen' may have been considerable and commission on the outcome of a successful drove was not uncommon, but from such information as is available it seems that the ordinary working drover was not highly paid, though the much greater value of money in the droving period must be kept in mind. Early in the eighteenth century the pay of a working drover appears to have amounted to only 1s a day,[2] but gradually this increased, reaching 3s or 4s a day in the first half of the nineteenth century. Even this latter rate left little margin for any but the barest living for men who had to pay for their own food on the outward journey and return entirely at their own charges. Beyond these items, a cattle dealer who sent beasts to the markets of the South might be involved in a variety of miscellaneous costs, and the agricultural writer of 1813 already quoted, complaining of losses sustained by the drovers of Galloway, puts part of the blame on high costs incurred to bankers, lawyers, messengers and innkeepers.[3]

The total expense of a drove from the North has been variously estimated, but the cost of bringing a drove from Caithness to Carlisle, a journey of about twenty-eight days, was reckoned in the early nineteenth century at 7s 6d a head.[4] Such droving as took place in winter or early spring when the cattle required to be fed on hay was much more costly. Contemporary estimates put the cost at 10s to 15s more per head than the summer and autumn droving costs. In England costs were higher, and Youatt writing in 1834 puts the expense of the three weeks' journey from Falkirk to Norfolk at £1 to £1 4s a head. Sir Alexander Maxwell

---

[1] Youatt, *Cattle, their breeds, management and diseases.* Library of Useful Knowledge, 1834, 121.　　　[2] Macky, *Journey through Scotland,* 1723, 190
[3] Smith. op. cit., 253.　　　[4] Youatt, op. cit., 90

of Monreith in Dumfriesshire carried on a large droving trade with England in the first quarter of the eighteenth century, and his cash book records the varying success of his transactions.[1] In 1711 he pays the modest sum of fifty guineas to Pat Maxwell as droving expenses of beasts which ultimately sold for £2,372 sterling. In 1728, however, Sir Alexander incurred a big loss on a drove to England. The drove that year consisted of 746 beasts entered in his accounts as costing just over £2,677. The amount realised by the sale of the beasts as shown by the bill of sale of William Dunn the drover, was £2,711 4s 6d ' whereof to reduce of charges he gives in ain account £250 9s 11d which is a most extravagant account there being 18 of them died by the way going to the mercat of murrain which was a ly invented by him for they were killed by over-driving and all the fat heavy nolt died being driven till 10 at night and got neither water nor grasse, he constantlie drunk and never came near them and under-charged the prices he got. Soe there remains only to bear charges 702 which makes them above 7 shillings 3 half-pence per beast which must be grosse mismanadgment or dishonestie which is the same as to my losse. Losse on drove £172 2s 2d sterling which is £2,065 6/- Scots or 3,098 merks. . . .' Arthur Young, writing about 1818, quotes the same figure of 7s 1½d per head as the expense of taking cattle 112 miles from Norfolk to Smithfield. For a journey of 450 miles from Dumfries to the South he puts the cost of droving fat cattle travelling fifteen miles a day at 18s to 24s per head for the journey. The figure is quoted from Wight's *Husbandry* and corresponds fairly closely with the 1834 estimate, though the time taken for the journey is longer.[2] The popular belief in the eighteenth century that bleeding was a cure for most ills was applied to animals as well as to human beings, and one of the items noted in Sir Alexander Maxwell's account book as part of the expense of sending a drove to England is the cost of having the animals bled in preparation for the journey.[3]

In addition to the cash outlay in which the journey involved him, a drover of cattle from the Highlands had to reckon with the loss in condition which his beasts might suffer. It seems probable that this increased as the drove moved south into

[1] Maxwell, *Memories of the Months*, 5th series, 278
[2] Arthur Young, Unpublished Manuscript, *The Elements and Practice of Agriculture*, XXVIII, 355 et seq. British Museum
[3] Maxwell, op. cit.

country where facilities for wayside grazing or nightly resting-places were fewer, and where their increasing cost might tempt the drover to longer marches. The writer of an agricultural survey of Galloway in 1794 has estimated that the loss incurred through deterioration in condition, fatigue, accident or disease on the journey from Galloway to Norfolk cost the drover as much as £1 2s a head,[1] while the Statistical Account of the Parish of Sorbie puts the loss in condition suffered by a beast on the same journey at one-eighth of its original weight[2] ; but in the Highlands where the drove was moving through hill country and grazing was plentiful the loss would be much less. Some drovers even reckoned on an improvement in the condition of their beasts on the journey, and it is told of an Aberdeenshire farmer of last century that having a drove of sheep for which he had no grazing he sent them and their shepherd to travel the drove roads of the district, from which they returned a month later, the beasts in improved condition for the Tryst.

If the end of the seventeenth century brought to the drover relief from some of the political uncertainties which had harassed him, the political sky was still filled with the clouds of gathering storms. For good or ill these were to affect him no less than storms in the Minch or mists on Rannoch. The eighteenth century was hardly well begun before the first of these political storms arose. The volume of south-bound cattle traffic crossing the Borders had, as has been seen, despite all its difficulties grown by the end of the seventeenth century to large proportions. This traffic, with linen and coal, made up the bulk of Scotland's exports, and three-quarters of the total was trade to England, the Navigation Act of 1660 and Britain's foreign policy having cut Scotland off from much of her Continental trade. Scotland's growing dependence on the English markets, and the conviction among men of foresight in both countries that the welfare of each urgently demanded their complete union, had done little to offset the dislike and suspicion with which, in Scotland particularly, the idea was regarded. It was in these circumstances that the English Parliament in 1704 decided to use the threat of exclusion from England of trade in three of Scotland's most important products as a lever with which to force her to accept the Act of Union. By an Act of that year, it was provided that if before Christmas Day 1705 the Scots Parliament had not settled the

[1] Webster, op. cit., 29   [2] *O.S.A.*, Sorbie, I, 248

succession to the Crown of Scotland in like manner to the succession to the Crown of England, all 'great cattle and sheep' exported from Scotland to England should be forfeited.[1] The measure, which had threatened to prove quite as harmful to England as to Scotland, did not come into operation and was repealed before Christmas 1705. Its threat, however, had been disastrous to drovers and cattle dealers alike. The price of cattle at the West Port of Edinburgh fell in 1705 to £8 Scots, a fall of 33⅓ per cent which brought great loss to McLaren of Bridge of Turk, a notable drover of the time [2]; but one at least profited by it, for Peter Heron, a far-sighted drover of Galloway, having learned of the impending removal of the restriction, bought large numbers of cattle at Crieff Tryst at the price of £4 Scots to which they had fallen, subsequently selling them in England when the restriction had been removed for £4 sterling —a profit of 1100 per cent.[3]

The impetus given to the Scots cattle trade by the passing of the Act of Union of 1707 and the events at home and abroad in the years which immediately followed was considerable, and from then onwards a gradual increase in the trade took place; but politics were still to be a source of worry to the drovers, and the effect of the Rising of 1715 is shown in a Petition presented to the Bailies of Dumfries for compensation for the loss of customs dues suffered by the closing of the cattle markets. 'Unto the Honble, the Provest, Baillies and Counsell of Dumfries . . . that where it being evident to all and alsoe verrie weill known to your Honors that since the beginning of August last at which tyme was read the first news of the Pretender's intended invasione, all people were soe surprysed therewith that the fears of intestine troubles did not onlie during the space of those two months of August and September put such a stope to Trades and business that all Publick Mercats did verrie much faill, but lykewise, and more particularly in the beginning of October, the news of the Rebells rising in the North and the threatening of the Rebells in our own country parts to attack our Towne of Dumfries did soe arouse and alarm both Town and Countrie that all Mercats were shut and Traid laid asyde, that during the month of October

---

[1] Hume Brown, *The Legislative Union of Scotland and England*, 19 and 80. *Statutes at Large*, 4 Anne cap. 3 section 4.
[2] Ramsay, *Scotland and Scotsmen in the 18th Century*, II, 222, note
[3] Walker, *Economical History of the Hebrides and Highlands*, 1808, II, 308n

and first ten days of November, in which your petitioner was wont to collect a great deal of custom, it being the principal tyme of my Cattle Markets, no markets were or could be held by reason of the whole country being obliged to be in arms and the whole passages and entries to the town being shut up.'[1]

The Rising of 1745 seems to have had less immediate effect on the trade than might have been expected. The safe conduct granted to the Glenorchy drover in 1746 shows that even then cattle were being brought south from Kintail, and despite the Rising, Crieff Tryst was in active operation. In that same year a drover from Ross-shire took cattle to Craven in Yorkshire,[2] while a Dumfriesshire drover had nearly 1,500 beasts for sale in East Anglia. Both speculations proved unprofitable however, for in Yorkshire shortage of hay had lowered the price to 35s a head, while the drove in East Anglia fell victim to the widespread cattle disease which, combined with the shortage of beasts in the Highlands after the Rising, led to an increase in the price in the years immediately following.[3]

From 1727 till 1815 the droving trade to England benefited by the almost continuous series of wars in which Great Britain was involved, and with some minor fluctuations the price of cattle showed a gradual increase. In this the demand for salted beef for the navy played a considerable part.[4] The salting of cattle was throughout almost the whole of the droving period an English industry, for only fat cattle were suitable for salting and only England could fatten them. The agriculture of those parts of Scotland capable of fattening stock was till the early years of the nineteenth century largely an agriculture of crop cultivation, and not till then did new farming methods, based on the growing of artificial grasses and turnips, turn the attention of Scottish farmers towards stock fattening. Until that time came, the cattle of the Hebrides, the Highlands and the South Western Counties driven to market lean or at best half fattened, must seek richer grazings for the increased growth and condition which the salters demanded. Only in the South could these be found, and so from the Trysts at Crieff, Falkirk and Dumfries the Scots drovers travelled on across the Border to the grass lands of Northumberland

---

[1] Quoted by Corrie, *The Droving Days in the South-West District of Scotland*, 7–8
[2] MacGill, *Old Ross-shire and Scotland*, I, 177
[3] Letters of Thomas Bell, Dumfries (contained in Reid's *Calendar of Documents found at Dumfries*, H.M. Register House)
[4] See Appendix A (p. 225)

and the limestone dales of Yorkshire, to the pastures of North-amptonshire, Buckinghamshire and Hertfordshire, or the marshes of East Anglia. Thus the drovers profited first by the wars with Spain, Austria and France, then by the American War and most of all by the Napoleonic Wars when prices rose to high levels, reaching in the last years of the struggle a peak from which for a time they quickly fell. As the church bells of Perth rang out in 1815 to greet the peace, George Williamson, a great Aberdeenshire breeder and dealer, passing south with a big drove, heard them with dismay, ' It was a sorrowful peace for me,' he said, ' for it cost me £4,000.' [1]

The variations in the method and condition of sale and the complexity of factors which from time to time affected the cattle trade, make it impossible to do more than indicate over a period the trend of cattle prices in Scotland. When the Records of the Lords of Council and the Register of the Privy Council first start to place a value on the cattle stolen in the sixteenth and seventeenth centuries the figure appears to have been about £20 Scots (or £1 13s 4d sterling), and in 1627 the Justices of the Peace for Kincardineshire complaining of the abnormally high prices then in force quoted figures of 50 merks (£2 15s 7d sterling) for oxen and 40 merks (£2 5s 8d sterling) for cows.[2] About the time of the Union of 1707 the average price of cows in Scotland appears to have been 20s to 27s sterling,[3] and Pennant mentions that the price of cattle in Colonsay in 1736 was even then only 25s.[4] In a case before the Court of Session in 1737 reference is made to a purchase by a Yorkshire drover in Colonsay and Jura of 300 cattle at a total price of £505 sterling.[5]

By the middle of the eighteenth century an appreciable increase had taken place. In 1763 a Yorkshire drover bought Skye cattle for 2 guineas delivered at Falkirk, though 10 years later the Barra beasts only fetched £1 7s 6d.[6] Pennant in 1772 gives the price for the cattle of Skye, Islay and Colonsay as being £2 to £3 each, but those of Mull 30s to 50s,[7] and in 1786 the average price of beasts crossing from Skye was £2 to £3.[8] With the Statistical Account and the Agricultural Surveys of the end

[1] McCombie, *Cattle and Cattle Breeders*, 57   [2] *R.P.C.*, 2nd series, II, 554
[3] Ramsay, op. cit., II, 222 et seq.
[4] Pennant, *Tour in Scotland, 1772* (1790 edn.), Part I, 274
[5] *Old Session Papers*, Signet Library, F. 24.30.   1737
[6] *Farmer's Magazine*, 1804, 393   [7] Pennant, op. cit., Part I, 263, 357, etc.
[8] Knox, *Tour through the Highlands of Scotland and the Hebride Isles in 1786*

of the eighteenth century, a host of statistics of cattle prices became available ; £2 to £3 in Wick and Caithness[1] ; £2 10s in Uist[2] ; £3 3s about Lochalsh[3] and £3 15s in Islay and Aberdeenshire,[4] while the average price of beasts sold at Falkirk Tryst in 1794 was £4.[5] The lower droving costs to England from the south-west of Scotland are no doubt reflected in the prices given for cattle from Dumfriesshire and Galloway which in 1794 varied from £2 10s to 8 guineas.[6] During the next twenty years the course of Scots cattle prices was directly affected by the French Wars. Evidence given in 1826 before the Parliamentary Committee which inquired into conditions prevailing in the cattle trade during the war period, showed average prices rising to as much as £18 a head, and William McCombie, the Aberdeenshire breeder, quoting from records of his father's transactions during the wars mentions sales of Aberdeenshire cattle at £22, £23 10s and even £25 per head.[7]

A farmer of today may pertinently ask the ages at which these beasts were sold. To this question no certain answer can be given, for circumstances and practice appear to have varied at different times and in different parts of the country ; but many of the beasts were old cows and working animals past their useful life, while of the younger cattle it is probable that at least till near the end of the eighteenth century in view of the slow growth of beasts to whom each winter meant starvation, few were sold before three years and most at four years or older. Arthur Young, in his *Elements and Practice of Agriculture*, quotes from Marshall's *Norfolk* (Vol. I, p. 326). 'A Scot does not fat kindly even at three years old much less at two at which age many hundred head of cattle are annually fatted in Norfolk,' but in another passage Marshall speaks of four years as being the most common age of cattle sold in the South from Skye and the

---

[1] *O.S.A.*, Wick, X, 22   [2] *O.S.A.*, North and South Uist, XIII, 294, 306
[3] *O.S.A.*, Lochalsh, XI, 424
[4] *O.S.A.*, Kilchoman, XI, 278 and King Edward, XI, 405
[5] *O.S.A.*, Falkirk, XIX, 83
Giving evidence in 1826 before the Select Committee already quoted the manager of the Renfrewshire Banking Company referred to the prices for Highland cattle being £2, £3 or £4 a head. His evidence showed that the proportion of £5 notes to smaller notes sent by the Banks to their Highland branches largely for the financing of the cattle dealing industry was one £5 note for every £100 in smaller notes. (*Report of Select Committee on Promissory Notes in Scotland and Ireland, 1826*. Notes of Evidence)
[6] *O.S.A.*, Sorbie, I, 248
[7] *Select Committee on Promissory Notes in Scotland and Ireland 1826*. McCombie, op. cit. 101.

Highlands, some being older than this and some being old working cattle. An Agricultural Survey of Aberdeenshire in 1811 gives a table showing a calculation of the age of various classes of cattle sold from the county about the year 1770. This shows that few beasts were sold under twelve years old and many older. Most of the animals had been used in the plough for from one to four years before being put to grass.[1]

While the high purchasing power of money must be remembered in considering the relatively small prices quoted in the records of the Scots cattle trade, at least up to the end of the eighteenth century, the size of the beasts of these days must also be borne in mind. In his Analysis of the Statistical Account written about 1825 Sir John Sinclair quotes Bakewell the great English breeder as having said that he wished he had laid the foundations of his breed of cattle with Kyloes or West Highland cattle as being perfect in all but size [2] ; and all the evidence goes to show that the animals driven from the Highlands to England throughout the eighteenth century were indeed small.[3] An early commentary on the weight of cattle is contained in an eighteenth-century contract for the supply of meat for the Navy, in which it was stipulated that the carcasses should weigh not less than 5 cwt., and it should be noted that this referred to animals already fattened for killing. Even as late as 1816 a contract for meat for ships in the Downs stipulated only for a weight of 4 cwt., while a provision in a contract of 1823 requiring a weight of 6–7 cwt. is noted as unusual. Culley in 1786 says that the weight of West Highland cattle in general is from 20 to 35 stone, and an Agricultural Survey of Dumbartonshire made about 1794 refers to the cattle in the north of the county as weighing only 11–14 st. fat.[4] Sir John Sinclair in his Survey of the Northern Counties in 1795 refers to a Highland bull weighing 250 lb. as compared with a Bakewell bull of 400 lb. The cattle of South-west Scotland appear to have reached higher weights, at least by the end of the eighteenth century. The Statistical Account for Kirkcudbright mentions weights of only 20–30 st., but Webster in 1794 speaks

---

[1] Keith, *Agricultural Survey of Aberdeenshire*, 1811, 467   [2] See Appendix C (p. 235)
[3] In considering the figures given for the weight of cattle driven from the Highlands in the eighteenth and early nineteenth centuries, it may be assumed for purposes of comparison that today an average Cross-Highland bullock sold off the hills at 3–4 years old for fattening weighs approximately 8 cwt., and that the same animal when fattened for the butcher will weigh approximately 11 cwt.
[4] Ure, *General View of the Agriculture of Dumbarton*, 1794, 58

of Galloway cattle at five years old weighing 40–50 st., and
Arthur Young writing about 1818 puts the average weight in the
same district as 40–60 st., with some up to 70 st. Contemporary
estimates of the weight of cattle must, however, at least till well
into the nineteenth century be accepted with caution, for in some
cases this was reckoned in Dutch stone of 22 lb. It appears also
that in parts of Central Scotland the stone used contained 16 lb.
of 22 oz. each, while at Smithfield a stone of 8 lb. appears to have
been at one time in use.[1] The average weight of cattle sold at
Smithfield is reported as having increased by more than 100 per
cent between 1710 and 1775, and the Aberdeenshire cattle
breeder Williamson stated in the early years of last century that
during his time the average weight of cattle produced in Aberdeenshire had, from better feeding, more than doubled.[2] While the
figures available clearly do not make it possible to determine with
any certainty the rate of increase over a period in the average
weight of Scots cattle, it seems probable that until the early years
of the nineteenth century only a small proportion reached a size
which, by modern standards, would entitle them to be described
as more than ' stirks.'

If these figures seem in some respects to detract from the
achievements of the drovers, they do indeed go some way to
explain how the eighteenth-century drover solved problems of
driving and transport which, with beasts of modern size and
weight, would defy solution. They go far to explain, too, the
revolution in the cattle trade which took place during the first
half of the nineteenth century when new and better methods of
farming were so greatly increasing the size and quality of livestock, a revolution which was to prove fatal to the droving
industry.

Despite the credit so readily given by banks and financial
houses, and the light-hearted enthusiasm with which they entered
into commitments sometimes involving tens of thousands of
pounds, the cattle dealers of the eighteenth century often found
it necessary to ' engage a co-adventurer in an intended speculation.'[3] The names of Highland chieftains and Lowland lairds

[1] Robertson, *Rural Recollections*, 1829, 120
[2] Alexander, *Northern Rural Life in the 18th Century*. Youatt, writing in 1834, stated
that after careful inquiry he had arrived at the conclusion that the average weight
of a fat bullock sold at Smithfield at that time was approximately 6 cwt. (Youatt,
op. cit.)
[3] *Old Session Papers*, Signet Library, 413.8. 1800

appear little less frequently than those of graziers, cattle dealers, merchants and business-men of the cities in the story of this hazardous trade. Many of these partnerships were of the loosest and most casual nature. Accurate book-keeping was unknown, and records of transactions between drover and drover, or between partners, were kept, if kept at all, in the form of scribbled notes, intelligible at the time to none but the parties themselves, their meaning and content soon to be inextricably mixed in a maze of complex dealing. Failure to keep clear and accurate accounts was not, however, confined to the drovers of the eighteenth century. One of the leading Aberdeenshire dealers, writing in 1867, described how in the early part of the century he had at one time taken for a short time a co-partner. 'As co-partners,' he writes, 'we were not very regular book-keepers and our accounts got confused. At the wind up at Hallow fair (Edinburgh) as we had accounts of the Falkirk Trysts likewise to settle, we worked at them for days and the longer we worked the more confused they became. To this day I do not know in whose favour the balance was.'[1] In such conditions it was inevitable that disputes and quarrels should arise, and that finally the aid of the courts should be sought to unravel or, in the last resort, to cut knots in the tangled skein. That the process was slow and involved is amply shown by the records of cases decided by the Court of Session during the eighteenth century. Dishonoured bills, bankruptcies—real and assumed—liability of partners, claims by sellers and purchasers, banks and landlords, all found their way to the courts.[2] These were no easy cases. Agents and counsel too often waited in vain for instructions of clients or evidence of witnesses scattered from May to October over the length and breadth of Scotland, though as contemporary law reports show this did not always prevent the premature argument of a case in court by puzzled and ill-briefed counsel before a bewildered Bench. The drovers, for their part, ' precluded from personal interview with their Law Agents by frequent absences from home, are unable to comprehend the numerous windings and intricacies of a complicated and long protracted process.' Men who could thread their way through mountain passes and

---

[1] McCombie, op. cit., 6

[2] An English Act of Parliament passed in the reign of Queen Anne made it unlawful for drovers to evade their obligations by becoming bankrupt (1706, 6 Anne Cap. 22, sec. 8, *Statutes of the Realm*, Vol. 8, 602).

over the hill tracks of the remotest Highlands were lost among the Petitions, Answers and Objections, the Replies, Duplies and Triplies of an eighteenth-century lawsuit. Little wonder if, faced at last with the hurry and bustle of the courts in the Parliament Hall of Edinburgh, they longed for the quiet hills and the fresh uplands, for the friendly presence of their placid and slow-moving cattle.

An excellent example of the complexity of droving finance and of the litigation to which it so often gave rise occurs in a case which came before the Court of Session in 1741. The case concerns the dealings of two drovers, one from Argyllshire and the other from Dumbartonshire, who had become insolvent. With a view to recovering sums owed by them, a creditor was induced in partnership with an Argyllshire laird to lend them money to enable them to purchase a drove of 300 cattle from McNeill of Colonsay. The transaction was coupled with the most elaborate precautions to ensure the repayment of the loan from the proceeds of the cattle when sold, precautions which, as the outcome was to prove, were most fully justified. The drovers having obtained possession of the cattle, the subsequent story of their dealings soon became obscured in a fog of bills and sub-sales in which drink played no small part, an obscurity deepened by the fact that the drove became mingled with another, and that while some beasts were sold at Crieff, some were taken to Falkirk and the rest to Carlisle. The case, which did not reach the courts until three years after the events with which it was concerned, dragged on before them for at least six years, and reading today the closely printed pages which contain the pleadings of the parties, even a lawyer must feel the liveliest sympathy for the law agents who marshalled the facts, the counsel who argued the case and Lord Elchies who tried it. It was little wonder that at the end of the third year of litigation he ' made great avizandum ' [deferred judgment for further consideration] and ' circumduced the Term quoad ultra ' [declared the term for bringing further evidence to have elapsed]. It is hardly surprising to read that when nearly eighteen months later, by which time one of the parties had died, the decision of the Court was given, the unsuccessful party appealed against it. The case dragged on till March 1749, when, more than ten years after the events which gave rise to it, it was finally disposed of by a decision of the House of Lords.[1]

[1] *Arbuthnot* v. *Macfarlane*. *Old Session Papers*, Signet Library. F. 24:30. 1749.

Were an assessment of the work and character of the drovers of Scotland and of the part played by them in the commercial life of the country to be based solely on the material available in the Register of the Privy Council, the records of the Court of Session or the evidence of those who wrote of agricultural conditions at the close of the eighteenth century, the judgment must indeed go hard with the drovers ; but to base judgment on this evidence alone would be to ignore a great part of the picture. Privy Council and Law Courts saw little but the sombre side of the drover's trade, for to them fell the task of unravelling threads tangled through ignorance, misfortune or dishonesty. The parish ministers, from whom was gathered a great part of the material in the Statistical Accounts, were mainly concerned with the welfare of their parishes, and misfortunes which aggravated the hard lot of their people bulked large in their eyes. To those who wrote of Scottish agriculture in the first years of the nineteenth century, the hardships and grievances of the farmers also took first place. When Sir Walter Scott wrote in the introduction to *The Two Drovers*—' An oyster may be crossed in love . . . and a drover may be touched on a point of honour,' he was no doubt reflecting the contemporary view of the standard of a drover's honesty, and few there were to champion the drover's cause or to tell of the honest endeavour of those who successfully faced the difficulties, the risks and the hardships of the droving trade. Yet when it is considered that a system of commercial dealing calling for skill, courage and honesty of the highest order continued in Scotland through nearly three centuries marked by so much of social change and political disturbance, it is impossible not to recognise the merits and qualities of the men whose work it was. Hardship and toil were the common lot of most of Scotland's people in the droving period, and it may well be that the physical hardships faced by those who drove the cattle to the Trysts were no greater than those of the men and women who fought to win a bare existence from the soil in days before knowledge, skill and capital had made the farmer's life tolerable ; but physical hardship was perhaps the least which the drovers had to face. To them fell all the risks of accident, loss and delay on the journey, of fluctuating and uncertain prices governed by social, political and economic factors beyond their knowledge or control. Shortage of ready money but a growing abundance of credit had led to the growth of a system which put on them a heavy burden of responsibility. For many the test was too severe, and it is of those and of the distress and ruin caused by their failure that the records mainly tell ; but many kept faith whether to the men who hired their services to take their beasts to the Tryst, or to the farmers who had parted with their cattle for only the written or the spoken promise of future payment.

In the early records of these dealings few names appear, and with one or two exceptions it is not till the nineteenth century that the fuller records of the Trysts note the recurrence, year after year, of the same names showing a continuous course of honest dealing. A class of professional cattle-dealers was then arising, ' Trusty factors,' as a contemporary writer has called them,[1] whose reputation for honesty and fair dealing came to be widely recognised throughout the country. In Aberdeenshire and Galloway, names such as those of Williamson and McTurk and many another were known and respected, while in the West, Cameron of Corriechoillie in Lochaber, perhaps the greatest of all the drovers, held in the cattle-dealing world a place un-challenged for the scale of his dealings and the degree of his integrity. Cameron of Corriechoillie died in February 1856. In the year of his death he claimed that he had ' stood ' the three yearly trysts at Falkirk and the two yearly ones at Doune for fifty-five years without missing one. Mr Joseph Mitchell, the Road Engineer, has left the following description of Cameron of Corriechoillie : ' One whom I used to know and meet was a remarkable man and deserves to be noticed—Mr Cameron of Corriechoillie in Lochaber. He was the son of a crofter, who died early in very poor circumstances his only stock being a few goats. (Corriechoillie, from early association and long habit, till his death kept a stock of goats.) When quite a lad he was employed by the principal dealers to drive their sheep and cattle to market. He was so poor that his first journeys south were made without shoes, he wearing only a pair of footless stockings. Being very careful, he was soon enabled to buy a few stirks (half grown cattle), which he took to market with his employer's stock. He soon acquired a character for acuteness in the buying and selling of stock as well as being the largest sheep-farmer in the Highlands. At one time he was tenant of 11 farms and the reputed possessor of 60,000 sheep.

' He was a badly dressed little man, about five feet six inches

[1] Logan, *The Scottish Gael*, 1831, II, 65

in height, of thin make, with a sharp hooked nose and lynx eyes.
A man of great energy, he frequently rode night and day on a
wiry pony from Falkirk to the Muir of Ord, 120 miles, carrying
for himself some bread and cheese in his pocket and giving his
pony now and then a bottle of porter.   As may be supposed,
he possessed a wonderful power of organisation. . . .   Corriechoillie was in the height of his influence about 1840, but after
that period, what with cautionary obligations, said to amount
to £20,000, and heavy losses, he did not die a rich man. . . .' [1]

' Now such dealers are indeed a blessing to a country,' said
a writer of the early years of last century, ' while a King of
Prussia wilfully breaks his word, while a Monarch of Austria
pays even his ally, England, with compromise and instalments,
here are three companies of drovers, exposed to all the vicissitudes
of a most various trade, yet paying their way for thirty, forty or
fifty years without one insolvency.' [2]

The drovers of England appear to have been equally honest.
Marshall describing the scene at Smithfield in 1782 when the
drovers were settling accounts with the graziers writes :
' The room was full of graziers who had sent up bullocks last
week and were come to-day to receive their accounts and money.
What a trust ! A man perhaps not worth a hundred pounds
brings down twelve or fifteen hundred or perhaps two thousand
pounds to be distributed among 20 or 30 persons who have no
other security than his honesty for their money ;—nay even the
servant of this man is entrusted with the same charge, the master
going one week, the man the others ; but so it has been for a
Century past and I do not learn that one breach has been com-
mitted. The business was conducted with great ease, regularity
and dispatch. He had each man's account and a pair of saddle-
bags with the money and bills lying upon the table and the
farmers in their turns took their seat at his elbow. Having
examined the salesman's account, received their money, drank
a glass or two of liquor and thrown down sixpence towards the
reckoning, they severally returned to the market.' [3]

But honesty and fair dealing in the face of difficulty existed
long before the nineteenth century, as is shown by the letters of
Thomas Bell, a drover of 1745, addressed to his partner Bryce

[1] Mitchell, *Reminiscences of my Life in the Highlands*, I, 335 et seq.
[2] Cincinnatus Caledonius, *Lights and Shadows of Scottish Character and Scenery*, 2nd
series
[3] Marshall, *Rural Economy of Norfolk*, 1785, 2nd edn., II, 267-8

Blair of Annan on whom he had drawn three bills totalling £1,449 for cattle purchased. Bell had taken over 1,000 cattle south to the East Anglian markets, paying for them with the usual three months' bills. There, the cattle disease which raged that autumn throughout England attacked them, and his drove died first in scores and then in hundreds. 'God knows what we shall do,' he writes from Norfolk on 20 December. 'We cannot get money to bear pocket expenses ; all manner of sale is over . . . our conditions are such that several drovers have run from their beasts and left them dying in the lanes and highways and nobody to own them.' So bad was the disease that the drovers had been forced to guarantee the beasts for a certain time in the hands of the purchasers, and Bell reports that beasts already sold by him had died within the period of guarantee. Ten days later, the position is worse. 'All is over now. We can neither pay London bills nor nothing else. We have over £1,000 charges to pay in this country and not a shilling to pay it with.' By 7 January 1746 the disaster is complete. 'I am positive we have lost £3,000 by [the distemper] already. I shall be home at Candlemas and people may do with me as they will. They shall get every groat we have and we can do no more.' [1]

[1] Letters of Thomas Bell, op. cit., H.M. Register House
In a Note to an Article by Mr R. C. Reid describing this incident which appeared in the *Transactions of the Dumfriesshire and Galloway Natural History and Antiquarian Society* (3rd series, Vol. XXII), Sir Arthur Oliver, Principal of the Royal (Dick) Veterinary College writes : 'A serious outbreak of cattle plague (Rinderpest) occurred in Great Britain in 1745 following its extension throughout the greater part of the Continent. The outbreak was so serious that the Privy Council was compelled to take prompt action by control of movement, slaughter and provision for the disposal of carcases. It is of interest that even in those early days compensation was allowed for animals slaughtered—40s for grown beasts and 10s for calves. In all about £135,000 was paid in compensation. The outbreak lasted till 1757 and there is no record of any other major outbreak of cattle plague in this country till 1865. The mortality was exceedingly high, probably running to 90 per cent in badly affected herds. . . . This stamping out policy was effective though cattle plague existed in some parts of this country up to 1770.'

4

THE DROVE ROAD FROM SKYE AND THE WESTERN ISLES

THE descriptions of Scotland which have come down from early travellers through the country make it clear that Scotland was from very early times a cattle-producing country, the main area of supply being the mass of high ground intersected by mountain valleys lying to the north and west of that line from Dumbartonshire to the Angus glens, which later came to be known as the 'Highland Line.' This was an area little suited to any other type of farming, while the glens and the lower slopes of the hills afforded, at least in summer, ample grazing for cattle. The primitive but intensive type of cultivation practised in those limited areas of lowland country sufficiently drained for any form of agriculture, restricted stock grazing on any considerable scale to the higher ground. The Lowland areas, too, lay open to the ravages of the Civil Wars which scourged Scotland for nearly three hundred years from the end of the thirteenth century, while that part of the country lying south of the Forth and including the rich areas of East Lothian and Berwickshire were in addition at the mercy of invasion from England or raids from the unsettled districts immediately north and south of the Cheviots. For these reasons it was inevitable that the Highlands should, till more peaceful times came, be the main area of supply of cattle needed to meet the modest home demand for meat, the needs of the tanning industry for hides, or the small export demands from England and the Continent.

While these circumstances may explain why the Highlands as a whole produced Scotland's cattle in early days, it is not so clear why one of the most important supplies of cattle came originally from the remote areas of western and north-western Scotland, and particularly from the Island of Skye. The reason may lie partly in their very remoteness which, while ensuring that those areas remained for centuries the 'peccant' parts of the country so often complained of, meant that they were victims mainly of their own local troubles and were to some extent insulated by their geographical position from the troubles of their neighbours and of the country as a whole. In this, Skye and the Western Isles were peculiarly favoured, the Minch and the narrow strait between Skye and the mainland doing for them the service which for centuries the English Channel has rendered to Great Britain. The nearness of the sea gave them a freedom from frost and snow which the mainland did not enjoy, with better and earlier grass. Skye possessed much low moorland and many small glens running in from the sea, well suited for cattle to supplement the small patches of arable land, while in the Hebrides was some up-land grazing and much low ' machair ' land, too sandy and wind-swept for crops, but land where close-growing grass afforded grazing for cattle in numbers which, even by modern standards, appear to have been surprisingly large. These Western Isles had little to export, and so soon as the country passed from the most primitive stage, the need arose to send their cattle to the mainland in return for such simple products as were available, to provide money for the payment of such part of the small rents as was not paid in services, and for the landowners to pay the taxes which were levied on, and with difficulty extracted from, them. Whatever the reasons, and those suggested surely played their part, the fact is clearly established by such records as exist that behind their barriers of sea and hills, Skye, Kintail and the Western Isles from early times bred and exported in growing numbers cattle of a type peculiar to those districts and for long widely recognised as being superior to those of the rest of Scotland. ' It is in the northern and western Highlands and all the Islands and particularly the Isle of Skye and that tract of country near Kintail,' wrote George Culley in the last quarter of the eighteenth century, ' that you meet with the native breed of kyloes ; a hardy, industrious and excellent breed of cattle, calculated in every respect to thrive in a cold, exposed, mountainous country.' [1]

How early this island traffic in cattle began it is not possible with any certainty to determine, but it is known that as early as 1502 the district of Troutterness (Trotternish) in Skye was already exporting ' marts '—the surplus beasts sold off in the autumn—to the Lowlands. [2] The records of the Privy Council

[1] Culley, *Observations on Live Stock*, 1807, 70
[2] *Exchequer Rolls*, XII, 56
It is probable that these formed part of the produce rent paid by the tacksmen to the chieftain in addition to the money rent and other dues. In the first half of the sixteenth century ' marts ' handed over in part payment to the Crown of dues on tacksmen's holdings in Kintyre were driven each year to Stirling Castle, but in Morven in 1541 the ' marts ' and other produce payments were apparently resold to the tenants. (McKerral, ' The Tacksman and his Holding in the South-West Highlands.' *Scottish Historical Review*, Vol. XXVI, 10–25)

for the last years of the sixteenth century contain repeated references to thefts by men of Badenoch of cattle sent by Mackenzie
from Kintail to 'Elycht (Alyth) in the Bray of Angus' and other
markets in the east of Scotland,[1] and the number of stock already
being reared in the north may be judged by a complaint of
Alexander Bane of Tulloch in 1594 that the Laird of Raasay had
stolen 2,400 cattle from his land.[2] One of the first to engage in
the cattle trade between Uist, Skye and the mainland is believed
to have been Donald MacDonald Third of Castle Camus, Skye,
who at the end of the sixteenth and the beginning of the seventeenth centuries established a regular trade in ponies and cattle.
About 1601 he is reported to have defeated an attempt by the
MacLeods of Dunvegan and Harris to round up and ship to
Skye the cattle of North Uist.[3]

By the end of the seventeenth century, a regular trade in
cattle had grown up between Skye and the north-west districts
on the one hand and the markets of east and central Scotland
on the other. 'The Highlanders,' wrote Thomas Morer in 1689,
'are not without considerable quantities of corn, yet have not
enough to satisfy their numbers, and therefore yearly come down
with their cattle of which they have greater plenty and so traffick
with the Lowlanders for such proportion of oats and barley as
their families or necessities call for.'[4] One of the best of
the contemporary descriptions of the early drovers is contained
in Bishop Forbes' account, already quoted, of a meeting in
Drumochter Pass in 1723 with droves from Flodigarry in Skye
belonging to Macdonald of Kingsburgh on their way to Crieff
Tryst.[5] Five years later, during the short period when the
Bank of Scotland ceased payment, the Royal Bank of Scotland
cashed notes of the old Bank for a drover on his way to Skye to
buy cattle,[6] and by the middle of the eighteenth century English
cattle dealers from Yorkshire were already visiting Skye for the
same purpose. Despite the risks of the overland journey, the cattle
trade from Skye continued all through the seventeenth and
eighteenth centuries as droving traffic which only finally came to
an end in the latter part of the nineteenth century.

During the droving period Skye sent to the mainland not

[1] *R.P.C.*, 1st series, VI, 184, 459   [2] *R.P.C.*, 1st series, V, 204
[3] Angus and Archibald MacDonald, *Clan Donald*, III, 42–5
[4] Hume Brown, *Early Travellers*, 268   [5] *Bishop Forbes' Journal*, 235–7
[6] Munro, *History of the Royal Bank of Scotland 1727–1927*, 58–9

Plate 3   Loading Cattle at Kyleakin
(From an early print)

only cattle bred on the island but beasts from other parts of the Hebrides. Skye was a gathering point for cattle from North and South Uist, and in the last years of the eighteenth century the number of beasts sold annually from these islands were 300 and 450 respectively.[1] Barra sent cattle to Skye, though sometimes also to Ardnamurchan, at a transport cost of 2s 6d per head,[2] as being the nearest point on the 'continent,' and to the Ross of Mull.[3] Some Harris cattle were also landed in Skye, some being shipped direct and some going to Lochmaddy in North Uist for trans-shipment to Skye. The Statistical Account estimates the total number sold annually from Harris at only about 200. These, with kelp, are reported as being almost the only source of money to pay rents, the beasts being ferried to Skye in July.[4] Drovers from Skye sometimes went in search of beasts to the islands of Soay and Canna, but it seems that the cattle of Rum and Eigg and part of Sleat were generally shipped to the mainland near Mallaig or Arisaig, bound for Fort William and the South.

This island cattle trade was a risky and troublesome business, and the services owed by the smaller tenants to the chieftains or tacksmen in the eighteenth century often included the ferrying of cattle from island to island.[5] Between the islands of South and North Uist lies the low island of Benbecula, separated from South Uist by the South Ford and from North Uist by the North Ford. These shallow arms of the sea were till recently negotiable only at low tide, but while the South Ford could then be crossed almost dry-shod and has lately been bridged, the North Ford, which is four miles across, is intersected by deep channels which even at low tide are never dry. The main gathering-points for the cattle of the Outer Hebrides appear to have been at Ormiclate in South Uist, at Griminish in Benbecula and at Lochmaddy in North Uist, the markets taking place twice a year in late July and early September, dates which suited the Skye markets and the larger trysts at Crieff and Falkirk. When a drover attending the Ormiclate market had bought all the cattle he wanted, the beasts were rounded up and sent off on the eighteen-mile journey to the

---

[1] *O.S.A.*, North and South Uist, XIII, 294, 306
[2] According to information supplied by Mr Angus McLeod, Achgarve, Ross-shire, who started droving cattle from the Islands about 1868, the charge for bringing cattle by sailing boat from Stornoway to Lochewe at that time was 2s 6d a head.
[3] *O.S.A.*, Barra, XIII, 331   [4] *O.S.A.*, Harris, X, 356–7
[5] Buchanan, *Travels in the Western Hebrides, 1782–1790*, 53

South Ford where they crossed at low tide to Griminish. Here the same procedure was followed, the beasts from Ormiclate and the new purchases being driven across Benbecula and so over the North Ford to North Uist and Lochmaddy. The way across the North Ford is treacherous, with quicksands ready to trap men or beasts straying from the winding track. Any delay or miscalculation might mean that the inflowing tide would catch a drove in the crossing, when men and cattle would have to swim for their lives. The crossing was thus a hazardous adventure, the recollection of which lives vivid in the memories of those still (1948) alive who shared in it during the last days of the droving industry.

Lochmaddy was the main point of shipment for Skye, but Lochboisdale and Loch Skipport in South Uist and Loch Eport in North Uist were also used. In the Bay of Lòchmaddy smacks from the other islands of the Hebrides had been collecting for several days before the market. It may be that the sea transport had in some cases been arranged in advance, particularly in the case of the larger drovers who were regular buyers of the Island cattle, but it seems that in many cases the owners of the boats came at their own risk, knowing the dates of the Island markets and anticipating demand for their services. These boats varied in size from ten to fifty tons, and came from Barra, Harris and Berneray, perhaps bringing additional cattle to join the Uist beasts, while some came from as far as Coll and Tiree, for as the records of the Statistical Accounts show, in the eighteenth and early nineteenth centuries few parishes in the Islands were without their boat builders. These sailing boats were strongly built for this rough trade and for the transport at other times of slates from Easdale and Ballachulish, lime from Lismore or kelp from the Outer Isles. Some were open from end to end except for a small covered portion in the stern. Others were decked or half-decked with an open hatch-way for loading. A few were boats of forty to fifty tons, schooner rigged, and in some of these larger boats were fitted barriers at intervals to prevent the cattle falling in the rough seas of the Minch, for a fallen beast in a crowded boat seldom got up. The larger boats held up to fifty cattle and the tighter packed they were the better, for so there was less chance of beasts falling, while the drovers' profit was the greater. The method of loading was rough and ready. The boats were brought to a pier or to a convenient rock—in Gaelic a ' laimhrig '—and the cattle were driven aboard. To lessen the strain on the timbers of the boats, the stones with which they were ballasted were covered with birch branches, heather or bracken—in Gaelic a ' farradh '—which served the double purpose of protecting the timbers and affording the cattle a foothold during the voyage. According to information received from Tiree, osier twigs were also sometimes used as a covering for the floor-boards of the boats. It is suggested that this type of floor-covering served a further purpose, in acting as a filter to the dung of the beasts and so preventing it from clogging the pumps in the larger boats. The New Statistical Account of South Uist records that there were at that time (1842) four small decked vessels in the parish, chiefly employed in ferrying cattle to Skye and the mainland and in taking kelp to Liverpool and Glasgow.[1] The chief harbours then in use were Lochboisdale, Loch Eynort and Loch Skipport. The number of the crew seems to have been usually three or four. A wherry wrecked on Hyskier in 1808 while bringing cattle across from North Uist contained four men. The number of cattle on board is not stated, but all were drowned except one, on the blood of which the sole survivor of the crew kept himself alive till he was rescued.[2]

The landings in Skye were made chiefly on the shores of Loch Dunvegan, but some cattle, particularly those from Harris, were landed in Uig Bay at the north end of the island and some at Loch Pooltiel in Duirinish. When the Commissioners for Highland Roads and Bridges were considering the making of new roads in Skye in 1806, a Petition presented to them by the local people asked for a road from Dunvegan to Snizort, as ' being also the line by which the cattle from the Long Island are driven to the market at Portree.'[3] The method of landing was as rough as had been the shipment. Piers were scarce and primitive, and landing dues played little part in a drover's budget. Most of the cattle were forced overboard into the water. A rough block and tackle rigged on a yard from the mast was sometimes used to hoist them out of the larger boats, and this method was also occasionally employed for loading the cattle on to the boats, the beasts being slung aboard by means of slings attached to their horns. The practice of making the beasts swim ashore had a double merit, for it washed the cattle after what was often a rough journey,

---

[1] *N.S.A..* South Uist, XIV, 194   [2] *Inverness Courier*, 1808
[3] *H.R & B.*, 3rd Report 1807, Appendix F
Writing in 1695, Martin mentions two Cattle Fairs held annually at Portree in mid-June and early September. (Martin, *Description of the Western Islands*, ed. D. J. McLeod, 244–5)

while the salt water would be good for any gored by their neighbours in the crossing of the Minch. Some drovers carried with them Archangel tar which was useful for the rough doctoring of injured animals and also served to mark beasts bought at local markets. Various other methods were adopted by the drovers to mark their animals. Some beasts were marked on the horn, some by clipping part of the hair and some were branded. When a beast changed hands at the trysts, the new owner's mark was put on top of the old or substituted for it. This sometimes led to trouble when, as often happened, a beast strayed from one drove into another, and disputes arising between drovers from this cause found their way to the Court of Session in the eighteenth century.[1]

From Portree the cattle were driven on south, some by the route of the present road which climbs through Glenvaragill and over the moor to Sligachan, but the majority by the coast following the shores of the Sound of Raasay to Loch Sligachan and along the north side of that Loch to its head. Here at Sligachan they were joined by cattle from the grazing lands on the shores of Loch Bracadale and the glens which lie immediately to the north of the Cuillins. Midway between Sligachan and Broadford, the next important stage on the journey, the road to the South passes round the head of Loch Ainort, and here the cattle rested. It may be that the spot was chosen as a convenient half-way house between Sligachan and Broadford, but more probably because of the rich grass of the saltings at the head of the Loch. Whatever the reason, the drovers of two hundred years ago chose for their halting-place one of the most beautiful spots in the whole island. Here, sheltered from the west by the slopes of Marsco and Bheinn Dearg and from the east by the island of Scalpay, the waters of Loch Ainort mirror hills which look down on the cup of the glen into which the short River Ainort falls from the corries above. On a still September day the view of the calm loch, reflecting surrounding hills still hung with the shreds of early mist, may have gone some way to reconcile to his hard life a drover resting beside his cattle or emerging from the little change house on the north shore of the Loch, the ruins of which are to be seen today.

At Broadford, cattle from parts of Sleat and the grazings on the shores of Loch Eishort joined those from the North for the

---

[1] *Old Session Papers*, Signet Library, 134:36. 1766

market which was held where today the road from Armadale joins the main road to Kyleakin, a mile to the east of the scattered houses of the village. Here, too, would come cattle from the meadow ground at Torrin on Loch Slapin and the corries at the back of Blaven. From Broadford the drovers skirted the sandy inlets and rocky promontories of Broadford Bay. Then climbing southward through Glen Arroch they got from the watershed their last wide view back to the Bay and the Skye hills and forward to the hills of Glenelg across the Sound of Sleat.

Kyle Rhea, the narrowest point between Skye and the mainland, appears from earliest times to have been the principal crossing-place from the island. It was, no doubt, for this reason that Glenelg was chosen as a site for the barracks built at Bernera after the troubles of 1715. Telford in a report to the Commissioners for Highland Roads and Bridges in 1811 considered that Kyle Rhea would ' always remain the usual ferry for the Black Cattle of Skye,' [1] and it continued to be the main crossing-place till the construction of the railway to Strome Ferry and subsequently to Kyle of Lochalsh diverted the main traffic to the wider but easier crossing at Kyleakin. The transport of cattle across the narrow Strait of Kyle Rhea has been written of by many travellers who toured Scotland in the last years of the seventeenth and throughout the eighteenth centuries. Martin, Defoe, Knox and Pennant have all described it in some detail, and all agree substantially on the methods employed, but the most detailed account is given in an Agricultural Survey of Inverness-shire dated 1813 : ' All the cattle reared in the Isle of Skye which are sent to the Southern markets pass from that Island to the mainland by the ferry of Caol Rea. Their numbers are very considerable, by some supposed to be 5,000 but by others 8,000 annually, and the method of ferrying them is not in boats as is done from the Long Island where the passage is broad, but they are forced to swim over Caol Rea. For this purpose the drovers purchase ropes which are cut at the length of 3 feet having a noose at one end. This noose is put round the under jaw of every cow, taking care to have the tongue free. The reason given for leaving the tongue loose is that the animal may be able to keep the salt water from going down its throat in such a quantity as to fill all the cavities in the body which would prevent the action of the lungs ; for every beast is found dead and said to be drowned at the landing

[1] *H.R. & B.*, 5th Report, 1811, Appendix K

place to which this mark of attention has not been paid. Whenever the noose is put under the jaw, all the beasts destined to be ferried together are led by the ferryman into the water until they are afloat, which puts an end to their resistance. Then every cow is tied to the tail of the cow before until a string of 6 or 8 be joined. A man in the stern of the boat holds the rope of the foremost cow. The rowers then ply their oars immediately. During the time of high water or soon before or after full tide is the most favourable passage because the current is then least violent. The ferrymen are so dexterous that very few beasts are lost.'[1]

Methods similar to those employed at Kyle Rhea appear to have been used in other parts of the Hebrides, and the Reverend James Hall, writing of Barra in 1807, refers to ' the abominably cruel method ' of tying cattle and sheep to one another's tails and swimming them across a ferry often more than a mile broad, though the beasts were sometimes drowned or their tails pulled off. He speaks of this practice being then not quite abolished owing to the indolence of the people in conveying the beasts from one island to another or from the island to the ' continent,' though he adds that the shipping of half-wild cattle is certainly difficult and dangerous.[2]

Estimates vary of the number of cattle crossing Kyle Rhea annually from Skye and the Outer Islands. Pennant, who toured Scotland in 1772, puts the number at 4,000,[3] and Knox a few years later gives the same estimate.[4] Daniel Defoe in his *Tour in Great Britain*, written about 1726, gives no estimate of the total number crossing Kyle Rhea each year, but in describing the methods employed, similarly to other contemporary writers, he adds that 300 to 400 cattle can be taken across in a few hours.[5] The Statistical Account of the Parish of Glenelg puts the number at only 2,000,[6] but Youatt writing in 1834 puts it at 6,000 to 7,000.[7] A writer of the very early nineteenth century estimates that 22,000 cattle—one-fifth of the total cattle population—were

---

[1] Robertson, *General View of the Agriculture of the County of Inverness*, 1813, xxxviii–ix
[2] Hall, *Travels in Scotland*, 1807, II, 545
[3] Pennant, *Tour in Scotland, 1772*, I, 358
[4] Knox, *Tour through the Highlands of Scotland and the Hebride Isles in 1786*, 150
[5] Defoe, *Tour through Great Britain in 1724* (1762 edn.), IV, 294
[6] *O.S.A.*, Glenelg, XVI, 270
[7] Youatt, *Cattle, their Breeds, Management and Diseases*. Library of Useful Knowledge, 1834, 81.

exported annually from the whole of the Hebrides,[1] and as the cattle population of the parish of Snizort alone was reckoned in 1794 at over 2,500,[2] it seems clear that the numbers crossing Kyle Rhea each autumn for the southern markets must have been very considerable. As late as 1821, the cattle traffic crossing the Kyle was of such importance that when new piers were erected on both sides of the strait at Kyle Rhea, a sloping cobbled slipway which can still be seen was provided beside the main pier on the south side for cattle leaving the water.[3] The crossing of cattle at Kyle Rhea continued till the end of the nineteenth century, though by then the traffic had shrunk to a mere fraction of what it once had been, and latterly beasts were brought across by boat. The freedom from accident noted in the 1813 description, seems to have marked the crossing throughout, and even on one of the rare occasions when the ferry boat capsized, most of the cattle are believed to have come in the end safely to shore, though some as far away as Eileanreach on the mainland side more than a mile across the bay of Glenelg.

The difficulties of the crossing of Kyle Rhea, one of the most formidable of all the narrow straits around the Scottish coast, are to some extent reduced by a natural accident of which the boats of the local fishermen to this day take full advantage and of which the drovers no doubt availed themselves. At nearly all stages of the tide an eddy flows close inshore on either side of the Kyle, in a direction opposite to that in which the tide is flowing, and by skilful use of this a boat in the crossing may to some extent defeat the great force of the main current. For all that, the crossing of Kyle Rhea even in modern times is no light undertaking. At few stages of the tide does the current flow at less than three knots, while there are periods at each tide when the speed is seven to eight knots.[4] To one watching from the hill overlooking the Kyle how the tide sweeps like a great river northward to the junction of Loch Duich and Lochalsh, or how when the current sets south, tide and wind meet in Glenelg Bay in a welter of white and angry water, it may well seem that this crossing of the Kyle marks, as little else could do, the hardihood, the courage and the skill of the drovers of Scotland.

A drover who had successfully brought his cattle from Uist

---

[1] Macdonald, *General View of the Agriculture of the Hebrides*, 1811, 422
[2] *O.S.A.*, Snizort, XVIII, 184   [3] *H.R. & B.*, 9th Report, 1821.   Appendix Y
[4] *Nautical Survey*, 1901. Lochalsh and Kyle Rhea (New Edn. 4th December 1912)

or the north of Skye across the island and over Kyle Rhea, had before him a choice of alternative routes for the next stage of his journey south. Though the military road from Bernera to Fort Augustus by Mam Rattachan and Glen Shiel was not made till 1771, a track of some sort no doubt existed before that date if only to serve the barracks at Bernera. When James Boswell and Samuel Johnson crossed the Mam Rattachan ridge on their way to Skye in 1772 soldiers were still working on the road. It was kept in repair by military labour till 1776, after which according to the Statistical Account it was allowed to fall into disrepair. Telford reported in 1802 that ' there are just the vestiges remaining of what was once a military road to Bernera opposite the back of the Isle of Skye,' and this was one of the roads reconstructed by him for the Commissioners for Highland Roads and Bridges [1] ; but made roads had in any event little to commend them to a drover of the eighteenth century, and as he rested beside his cattle on the Skye shore before the crossing or on the mainland side with the passage of the Kyle behind him, his mind would be filled with doubts and perplexities unknown to a traveller of today. Some drovers certainly went over Mam Rattachan and up Glen Shiel, continuing down Glen Moriston and so to Fort Augustus bound for the Pass of Corrieyairack, Dalnacardoch and Crieff. A Memorial to the Commissioners for Highland Roads and Bridges in 1805 refers to the practice of sending cattle—the main source of revenue—south from Skye, Uist, Harris, Glenelg and Loch Alsh via Kyle Rhea and Fort Augustus.[2] Others, after climbing through Glen Shiel, turned southward at Cluanie, or Rhiebuie as it was then called, across the hill to reach Glen Garry and Tomdoun by way of Loch Loyne. The route by Loch Loyne and Tomdoun was chosen by Telford in 1811 for a new road to serve cattle and other traffic coming from Skye.[3] This was part of a great project, never completed, for the construction of a road from Kyle Rhea through Lochaber and across the Moor of Rannoch to Killin. The scheme was to cost about £34,500, and it was hoped that it would shorten the journey of a drove of cattle from Skye by two to three days, saving about £12,000 per annum largely in the better condition of the beasts on arrival at the Tryst ; but Telford only made his choice of this route from Glenelg after carefully weighing another alternative which may well have

[1] Telford, *A Survey and Report of the Coasts and Central Highlands of Scotland*, 1803
[2] *H.R. & B.*, 2nd Report, 1805, Appendix C   [3] See Appendix B (p. 227)

Plate 4   Looking to Glenelg from Skye
(Photo by Robert M. Adam)

been in the minds of the Skye drovers as they waited with their beasts beside the Kyle.

Behind Glenelg, leading east into the high hills, lie the parallel glens of Glenmore and Glen Beg. The two glens are connected near their head by a low pass, and near the point of connection a higher pass known as Gleann Aoidhdailean leads south-east to the head of Glen Arnisdale and so to Kinloch Hourn. This route over the Glenelg hills was one of those which Telford surveyed as an alternative to that by Glen Loyne and Glen Shiel.[1] It was a route of no great difficulty to a drove of cattle, offering the advantage of upland pasture and quiet resting-places for the night, and in his first report to the Commissioners in 1804, Telford refers to the Glen Garry road connecting with Bernera through Glenelg or Glen Shiel as a drove road ' of the utmost importance.'[2] It seems highly probable therefore that some of the cattle driven from Skye reached Kinloch Hourn by these tracks over the Glenelg hills which continued to be marked on maps at least as late as 1842.

Martin, in his *Description of the Western Islands of Scotland*, speaks of cattle sold from Skye crossing one of the *two* ferries, and while the almost unanimous evidence of other contemporary writers shows that till the railway came to Strome Ferry the great bulk of the traffic used the Kyle Rhea crossing, local recollection and tradition confirm that some droving traffic went by way of Kyleakin. The drove road on the mainland side from Kyle of Lochalsh appears to have gone by Glen Elchaig into Glen Cannich or by Glen Lichet into Glen Affric making for Beauly and Muir of Ord.

Of the drovers who reached Glen Garry by Glen Shiel and Glen Loyne or by Kinloch Hourn and Glen Quoich, it appears that many continued with their beasts down Glen Garry for only a few miles before turning south at Inchlaggan, a short distance to the west of the head of Loch Garry. Here the cattle forded the river or swam the narrow head of the Loch if the river were in flood. Then they climbed the hills on its south side, crossed the watershed and, resting at Fedden near the ridge, came by Glen Ci-aig to the east end of Loch Arkaig. This was a stage of their journey which formed part of Telford's projected road from Skye, saving nearly ten miles compared with the alternative route by Invergarry, ' nearly equal to a day's journey of a drove of cattle

[1] See Appendix B (p. 227)   [2] *H.R. & B.*, 1st Report, 1805, Appendix G

or sheep.' Though Telford's project failed, the route from Inchlaggan to Achnacarry appears to have been in common use until well on in the nineteenth century. It was the route followed by James Hogg when he visited the North-west Highlands in 1803, and in the map of Highland Roads printed in 1811 with the 5th Report of the Commissioners it is marked as 'made or under contract.' It is marked as a road in James Knox's map of 1839, and appears to have been in partial use for droving traffic till well on in the nineteenth century. From Loch Arkaig, joined by cattle from Glen Dessarry and Loch Nevis, the route of the Skye drovers was easy to the crossing of the Spean, which Wade recognised as the key-point for traffic passing at the west end of the Great Glen when he built the High Bridge of Spean in 1723.

At Spean Bridge the drovers were again faced with a choice of routes which, on the journey to Crieff and Falkirk, was so often to call for that intimate knowledge of country, of weather or of political conditions, which made their calling so difficult and so responsible. Three routes were open to them. Some drovers passed to the east of the Ben Nevis group of hills, and so to the southern end of Loch Treig, crossing the flat moorland where the Blackwater Reservoir now lies and coming down to Kingshouse at the head of Glencoe on the western edge of the Moor of Rannoch. Some might prefer the route by Fort William and Glen Kiachnish which led over the pass known as the Lairigmore to Kinlochleven, and on by the military road and the Devil's Staircase to Altnafeadh at the head of Glencoe. Others went down the east side of Loch Linnhe, crossing Loch Leven and climbing through Glencoe to Kingshouse.[1]

The first of these routes, by Loch Treig, was that considered by Telford as a continuation of his projected road from Skye to Loch Tay, though he proposed, instead of going by Kingshouse, to take his road from Loch Treig by the east end of Loch Laidon. From here it was to cross the Moor of Rannoch, passing by Glen Meran into Glen Lyon and on over the hills to Glen Lochay and Killin. It is probable that this route had long been used by droving and other less legitimate traffic. The military commander of the post at Tummel Bridge, reporting on a theft of cattle in 1749, reports that watch was kept for the thieves at the head of Glen Lyon, 'a very remarkable pass to and from the Isle of Skye.' In the following year a report from the military station at the head of Loch Rannoch refers to the practice of ' drovers returning from Crieff Fare stealing cattle from the Low Country, which they were accustomed to drive to the Highlands by the head of Loch Tay and Lion, and by the important Pass at Carn half-way between this and Augh-Chalada, a large village near Dillebegg.' [1] In General Roy's Survey 1747–55, Dillebegg (spelt Derrybeg) is marked at the east end of Loch Tulla. Telford's proposed road was never made, and in a report to the Commissioners for Highland Roads and Bridges in 1811 he refers bitterly to the failure of the project because ' the personal convenience of the proprietors is not immediately concerned.' Though his plan failed there is evidence to show that this route from Rannoch into the head of Glen Lyon continued to be used by droving traffic till the early part of the nineteenth century, the droves crossing from Glen Lyon to Glen Lochay or joining at the eastern end of Glen Lyon the drove road by Kenmore and Amulree to Crieff.

With the exception of any which went from Loch Treig across the Moor of Rannoch into Glen Lyon, it seems that by far the greater part of the droving traffic from Spean Bridge to the Trysts congregated at the head of Glencoe, the cattle resting at Altnafeadh where the military road from Kinlochleven joins the Glencoe road, or four miles farther on at Kingshouse. Here under the shadow of Buchaille Etive Mor, at the meeting-place of Glen Etive and Glencoe, of the road from Kinlochleven and of older tracks leading eastward across the moor, an inn has stood for centuries, offering such poor shelter or refreshment as it could afford to drovers, pedlars, soldiers and travellers of every sort about to face the long bleak stage southward, skirting the western edge of ' that thorofare of thieves,' the Moor of Rannoch.[2]

From Kingshouse, the next stage for the drovers was to Inveroran. Here among the woods at the head of Loch Tulla Dorothy and William Wordsworth in 1803 came on a drove southward bound, ' a stream coursing the road with off stragglers to the borders of the Lake and under the trees on the sloping ground,' [3] and a traveller in the autumn of 1818 has described the scene on this western fringe of the moor : ' Notwithstanding the wild and desolate general aspect of a great part of the tract,' he writes, ' the road at this time from the 23rd September to the

[1] *Historical Papers.* New Spalding Club (1699–1750), II, 540 and 582
[2] *Breadalbane Papers (Roads),* Box 4, H.M. Register House
[3] Dorothy Wordsworth, *Journals, 1798–1828,* Ed. Knight (1924), 322

4th October was far from being solitary. After passing on the 23rd of September the point where the road from Lochearnhead and Crief joins that from Killin to Tyandrum, the King's House and Fort William, large flocks of sheep with their drivers were met on their way to the Falkirk Tryste (Fair) ; and on the 3rd of October a considerable extent of the road through Glenurchay was almost covered with flocks of sheep and droves of cattle proceeding to the same destination from the district of Morven in Argyllshire and the Western coast and islands of Rossshire. The flocks and droves from these quarters pass the Invernessshire Lochy at the head of Loch Linnhe, or are ferried across that Lake about 10 miles further west at the Ferry of Corran and are then driven round the head of the Argyllshire Loch Leven through Glenurchay and Braidalbane by Lochearnhead to Crief and Falkirk.' [1] At Inveroran the droves rested, traditional rights of pasturage existing till 1846 when these were successfully challenged. South-east of Inveroran the route of the drovers led by the head of Glenorchy to Tyndrum. At Bridge of Orchy, or at Clifton near Tyndrum the Skye and Lochaber droves might be joined by some of the beasts from the Argyllshire coast and Loch Awe side, though it seems probable that the greater part of the Argyllshire cattle reached the markets of Central Scotland by routes farther to the south.

Till the middle of the eighteenth century Crieff Tryst was the great centre for cattle trade from the Highlands. The droves which had reached the Perthshire county boundary near Tyndrum moved on down the long glen of the Dochart, many of them reaching Crieff by way of Glen Ogle and the side of Lochearn, though according to local tradition a route from Ledchary in Glen Dochart over the hills to Balquhidder was also used. Some may have chosen the route by Loch Tay. For these, the route led along the south side of the Loch to Ardeonaig where they climbed southward through the hills and so came into Glenlednock. When Telford planned his road to the South, his description of the lines of communication from Killin contains a reference to ' the new road through Glen Lednaig to Comrie.' [2] The road through the hills from Ardeonaig to Comrie, which Telford planned, was never completed, and the route remains to this day a rough though well defined hill track, but there seems little doubt that it was much used in the eighteenth and early nineteenth

---

[1] Larkin, *A Tour in the Highlands, 1818*, 140–1   [2] See Appendix B (p. 227)

centuries. Local tradition tells of a considerable cattle traffic coming from the Loch Tay end of the Pass, crossing near Invergeldie from Glen Lednock into Glen Boltachan and so reaching the valley of the Earn. While Crieff Tryst still flourished, these droves would turn east down the river, but at a later date when Falkirk had become the main destination, the local evidence available shows that part at least of the droving traffic crossed the Earn and climbed the high ground on its south bank, reaching Doune through the hills on the south side of Glenartney.

In the second half of the eighteenth century, Crieff Tryst began to diminish in importance for reasons which will appear at a later stage, and by 1770 Falkirk had taken its place as the greatest cattle market in Scotland. From this date till the end of the droving days the principal route of the Skye and Western Isles cattle from Glen Dochart appears to have followed very much the line of the present road by Glen Ogle, Balquhidder and Loch Lubnaig to Callander and Doune. So they came to the Bridge of Stirling, though some, if the autumn were dry, avoided the toll on Stirling Bridge by crossing the Forth at the Ford of Frew six miles west of Stirling, where Prince Charles Edward's army crossed in September 1745 on their way to Carlisle and Derby. Evidence given before the Court of Session in 1783 shows the Ford to have been then in frequent use by drovers.[1]

At Stirling the Skye droves met those from the North of Scotland and from the Central and Eastern Highlands ; so here at the crossing of the Forth is a suitable point to leave them, now part of a great composite stream of beasts, plodding slowly on towards Falkirk and their unknown fate.

[1] *Old Session Papers*, Signet Library, 351:6

5

THE DROVE ROADS OF ARGYLL

WHILE the stream of cattle from Skye and the Outer Hebrides moved through the autumn days by Kintail and Lochaber to Rannoch and Central Scotland, parallel streams were flowing from the Argyllshire coast. These too had their springs in the Islands. The geographical and political isolation, mild climate and good grazing which have been suggested as reasons for the early growth in importance of the Skye trade, characterised in equal measure this more southerly district where moist airs from the Atlantic sweep across the islands and over the grass lands along the coast and bordering the sea lochs.

A trade in cattle from Argyll existed at least as early as the time of Mary Queen of Scots, and in 1565 and 1566 the inhabitants of ' Ergile, Lorne, Braidalbane, Kintyre and the Ilis,' having complained that they were afraid to come to the Lowlands for trading purposes for fear of the confiscation of their cattle, the Privy Council ordered that loyal subjects bringing cattle from Argyll to the Lowlands were not to be molested, provided, however, that goods were not taken back to Argyll.[1] Despite this, the trade remained precarious, and in 1609 the Privy Council annulled a recent Proclamation prohibiting all trade with Mull or any of the Western Isles, Maclean of Duart having protested that the sale of ' mairtis,' horses and other goods was the only method of paying taxes to the Crown[2]; but the troubles of the Mull cattle dealers were not yet at an end, and a few years later they are again complaining, this time against tolls unlawfully exacted by Macdougall of Dunollie on cattle landed from the Mull ferries.[3]

The hazardous nature of this early cattle trade from Argyll may be judged by the amount of time which during the sixteenth and seventeenth centuries the Privy Council had to devote to dealing with complaints of cattle thefts, and the key to the difficulties of which the local landowners complained may perhaps be found partly in the frequency with which these same land-

---

[1] *R.P.C.*, 1st series, I, 401, 470–1 [2] *R.P.C.*, 1st series, VIII, 757
[3] Transactions of Iona Club, *Collectanea de rebus albanicis*, I, 154

owners are cited as the guilty parties. Stewarts of Appin,
Macgregors of Loch Awe side and Campbells of Glen Orchy and
Inverawe come and go through the records, their raids taking
them as far east as Glen Isla and Strath Bran, and in 1602 the
Privy Council had before it a complaint against the Earl of
Argyll for theft by certain of his men, including Duncan Campbell
of Inverawe, of cattle from various places, including Strathbran
and Snaigow in East Perthshire.[1] In 1667 the Earl of Argyll
faced charges of theft by his tenants as far afield as Ruthven in
Strathspey, Wester Coull and Tarland in Aberdeenshire.
Acknowledging that stolen cattle had been brought to the ' wyld
rockish country of Glencoe,' he observed that ' neither the Earl nor
any landlord in the Highlands in these large mountainous countries
is able to prevent this.' [2] As late as 1682, when measures were
taken for securing ferries against the passage at night of goods
stolen from the Lowlands, the list included ' the boats on the
Watter of Aw ' and ' the ferry boats of Carranarngour, Kyllsich
Phatrick, Ardchattane and Connell.' [3]

These first references to the cattle trade of Argyll have shown
that from early times the island of Mull exported cattle to the mainland, and throughout the main droving period of the eighteenth
and early nineteenth centuries the island continued to be one of the
principal sources of the Argyllshire droving traffic. In this, Mull
played a part rather similar to that which Skye played in the
trade from the north-west, supplying not only cattle bred on
the island, but sending to the mainland those collected from the
neighbouring islands. The rich grazings of Coll and Tiree fed
considerable numbers of cattle, and it was natural that cattle
breeders there should choose routes offering the greatest chance
of grazing by the way and the shortest sea passage for the small
sailing boats then in use.

Few estimates of the number of cattle ferried to Mull from
Coll and Tiree are available till the last years of the eighteenth
century. At that time a traveller in Scotland estimates the
number sent from Coll each year at 400,[4] while a few years later
the Statistical Account puts the number ferried from Coll and
Tiree at over 500.[5] The New Statistical Account for Coll and

---

[1] *R.P.C.*, 1st series, VI, 442   [2] *R.P.C.*, 3rd series, II, 330–1
[3] *R.P.C.*, 3rd series, VII, 646. ' Caolas' ic Phatric ' was the local name of the
Ferry across Loch Leven near Ballachulish.
[4] Knox, *Tour through the Highlands of Scotland and the Hebride Isles in 1786*, 74
[5] *O.S.A.* Coll and Tiree, X, 411

Tiree records that in Tiree there were four decked vessels of 20–40 tons sometimes used for carrying country produce to market but generally looking for employment elsewhere, and 20 open or half-decked boats of 6–20 tons chiefly employed in ferrying cattle.[1] The landing place for the cattle of Coll and Tiree is vaguely described as ' at the back of Mull,' but local tradition puts the landing point at the little Bay of Kintra at the north-west corner of the Ross of Mull, and the Second Report of the Commissioners for Highland Roads and Bridges in 1805 refers to a proposed extension of the Mull road to Kintra to which Iona cattle and very frequently those from Tiree, Barra and South Uist were brought.[2] From Kintra the cattle travelled along the side of Loch Scridain and through Glen More and the Parish of Torosay where, by the second half of the eighteenth century, the birch, ash and oak woods were already being cut and burned for charcoal by the Lorne Furnace Company on Loch Etive.[3]

The Mull cattle, numbering with those from the neighbouring islands as many as 2,000 per annum, were shipped from the island at Grass Point at the mouth of Loch Don. Oban as late as the end of the eighteenth century was still, as Dr Johnson described it in 1772, ' only a small village if a few houses can be so described,'[4] and the cattle were landed on the island of Kerrera from which they swam across the narrow sound which separates the island from the mainland. According to local tradition the point on the west side of Kerrera at which the Mull cattle landed was the Bay of Barr nam Boc. This continued to be the main route till the middle of last century, but by the time the New Statistical Account of Scotland for the Parish of Torosay was compiled in 1843, the traffic was already declining, for by then many of the Outer Island cattle were being taken direct to the mainland, though the dates of the Tiree cattle markets were still fixed with reference to those of Mull.[5]

Besides the route from Grass Point, Mull possessed in the eighteenth and early nineteenth centuries another ferry of some importance to the drovers. Salen on the Sound of Mull had for long been a considerable cattle market for beasts from the north

---

[1] *N.S.A.*, Tiree and Coll, VII, 216–7
[2] *H.R. & B.*, 2nd Report, 1805, Appendix B   [3] *O.S.A.*, Torosay, III, 267
[4] Boswell, *Tour to the Hebrides*, Isham Collection, 346
[5] *N.S.A.*, Torosay, VII, 292

of the island and from the islands of Ulva and Gometra, and drovers attending that market sometimes found it of advantage to ferry their beasts from Fishnish, opposite Lochaline, to the Morven shore. There is a local tradition that the Lochaline Ferry was also used to take beasts from the Morven shore to Mull and so to the South by way of the Kerrera crossing. The fact that the local cattle sales in Morven were fixed for a date *before* the sale at Salen in Mull indicates that part of the cattle traffic went this way. Drovers who used the route to Lochaline took their beasts from Morven to the shores of Loch Sunart. At Strontian where, besides the lead mine developed by the York Buildings Company in 1730, there was a cattle market, they would be joined by droves which were sometimes landed from the Outer Isles at Kilchoan in Ardnamurchan and 'the Creek of Salen' on Loch Sunart, or at the western end of Loch Shiel by boats from the islands which entered the loch by the River Shiel for return cargoes of timber.[1] From Strontian the drove route led through Glen Tarbert in Ardgour to Corran where they were ferried, or, if weather and tide were favourable, possibly swam across the 'current of Lochaber,' as it was then called, to join the road to Ballachulish and Glencoe used by some of the Skye cattle.[2]

While the route from Mull through Morven was of some importance, the records available to us make it clear that by far the greater part of the cattle from Mull and the neighbouring islands reached the mainland opposite the island of Kerrera. There they would be joined by beasts sent to the trysts from the district immediately south of Oban, while cattle from Appin, Benderloch and Loch Etive side swelled their numbers. In tracing the paths by which these beasts reached their destinations, it is well to bear in mind the difference between the outlook of a drover of the times and that of a traveller of today. The hills and the lochs of Argyll run roughly from north-east to south-west, and to follow the shortest line from the shores of the Firth of Lorn to Crieff, Falkirk or the towns of the Clyde involves a crossing of successive barriers of hill, sea and inland lochs. To a drover these presented few obstacles, for the hills offered firm going, good grazing and resting-places for beasts at night, while the lochs could be easily crossed by ferries or privately owned boats, which contemporary records show to have been much more

---

[1] *N.S.A.*, Ardnamurchan, VII, 130, 155-6   [2] ibid.

numerous than today. In times when roads were still unmade the lochs of the Highlands were no doubt largely used for inland transport, and the shipping of beasts by boat or ferry was then a rough but familiar art. The list of boats and ferries from which bonds were taken in 1682 included the private boats on Loch Etive and the coast of Appin and Lorn. Others included in Privy Council measures of 1682 and 1684 to check cattle thieving included boats on Loch Lyon, Loch Rannoch, Loch Tay and Loch Lomond.[1]

To determine with any certainty the exact routes taken by the early cattle traffic from Argyll is now hardly possible. There is a sixteenth-century record of cattle being driven from Kintyre to Stirling,[2] and there is evidence that at least some of the Argyll cattle traffic passed regularly through or near Dumbarton in the seventeenth century ; but the exact routes at this early period must be a matter of conjecture, and it is not till the eighteenth and nineteenth centuries that the routes followed can be traced with any confidence.

For the Mull cattle which came ashore from the island of Kerrera and those from the grazings by the shores of Loch Etive and the Firth of Lorn, two possible alternative roads to Central Scotland lay open. Of these the first led through the Pass of Brander and so by Dalmally and Glen Lochy to Tyndrum, Killin and Crieff. The second led over the high ground south of Loch Etive, across Loch Awe and so to Inveraray, Loch Lomond and the markets of Stirlingshire. On the Dalmally route the River Awe was a formidable obstacle. No bridge appears to have existed till after 1755,[3] but on the large-scale survey of Scotland, associated

---

[1] *R.P.C.*, 3rd series, VII, 646 and VIII, 532

[2] McKerral, 'The Tacksman and his Holding in the South-West Highlands.' *Scottish Historical Review*, Vol. XXVI, 10–25.

[3] While it seems fairly certain that no bridge capable of carrying a drove of cattle over the River Awe existed before 1755, there is reason to think that a bridge of some sort may have been in existence at a much earlier date. In his poem *The Bruce*, written about 1487, John Barbour, Archdeacon of Aberdeen, described the skirmish between Bruce and John Macdougal of Lorn in 1308. The poem tells how the men of Lorn after failing to stop Bruce's advance through the Pass of Brander retreated down the pass :

> '. . . till ane wattir held thair way
> that ran down by the hillis syde
> and was rycht styth bath deip and wyde
> that men in na place mycht it pas
> bot at ane brig beneth thaim was.'

The Lorn men attempted unsuccessfully to break down the bridge to stop Bruce's advance. In a note to his edition of the text published in 1909, Mr W. M. Mackenzie

with the name of General Roy which was drawn between 1747 and 1755,[1] a ferry is shown near the point where the river leaves Loch Awe, and the route of an old road leading to this point, though not marked on General Roy's survey, can to this day be clearly traced on the west side of the river. According to local tradition fords over the Awe were at one time in use, including one just below the loch, but this must almost certainly have been destroyed when the level of the loch was lowered in the early years of last century for the benefit of the low-lying ground around Dalmally.[2] These fords can in any event only have been passable at infrequent intervals, and it seems probable that at least before 1755 the cattle traffic which went by this route was on a small scale. After the building of the Bridge of Awe the Dalmally route would be greatly simplified, but by then Falkirk Tryst was displacing Crieff, so tending to divert the traffic farther to the south, to the crossing of Loch Awe and to Inveraray.[3]

It seems then that it was rather to the alternative route to the south-east that the drovers from Mull and Lorn turned their eyes, to the great stretches of hill country which lie between the Firth of Lorn, Loch Awe and Loch Fyne. Through these hills run tracks traditionally believed to have been in use from the early days of Scotland's history by kings and nobles, monks and pilgrims in days when Iona was still the spiritual centre of Scotland and the burial-place of her kings. There is some evidence and much local tradition to support the view that these same tracks were extensively used by droving traffic during the eighteenth and the first half of the nineteenth centuries.

One of the chief crossing-places on Loch Awe for droving traffic was at Taychreggan. To reach this point some of the

[1] See Appendix D (p. 237) [2] N.S.A., Glenorchy, VII, 99
[3] See Appendix E (p. 339)

writes : 'The bridge was, of course, made of wood. It was probably beyond the lower extremity of the Pass, somewhere near the present bridge.'

Groome's Ordnance Gazetteer of Scotland after describing the difficult nature of the Pass of Brander adds : ' It always, nevertheless, was a point of transit or thoroughfare between the regions of Glenorchy and West Lorn ; and it is believed to have anciently had some sort of rude bridge ; yet even with aid of either bridge or boat or other contrivance, it never could be traversed without much danger, or by any but a sure-footed mountaineer ; for it was barred by a mural ascent still called the Ladder Rock and long commanded by a fortalice on the crown of the ascent.' (The Bruce by John Barbour, Archdeacon of Aberdeen ; ed. W. M. Mackenzie, 1909, 171 and 423. Groome's Ordnance Gazetteer of Scotland, new edn. 1893, Vol. I, 96) droves may have passed through Glen Lonan into Glen Nant and so by way of Loch Tromlee to the shore of Loch Awe, but the main route was more probably by way of Glen Feochan and so east through the hills to Taychreggan. This route across the hills is now deserted except for the shepherd's house at Midmuir, but it is probable that over it has passed the traffic of centuries, and at least as late as 1747–55 it appeared on General Roy's survey.

A parallel track leaving the coast near the mouth of Loch Feochan, climbs through Glen Euchar by Loch Scamadale and over the stretch of low hills known as the Sreinge of Lorn to reach Loch Awe near Dalavich. By this route would go not only some cattle from the Hebrides, but those from the pasture grounds on the south side of Loch Feochan and from the islands of Seil and Luing. Other tracks led east from Kilmelfort and from the head of Loch Craignish up the Barbreck River, both making for Loch Avich and reaching the side of Loch Awe at the narrow part of the loch near Dalavich. All these are shown on General Roy's survey, and in a Memorial to the Commissioners for Highland Roads and Bridges in 1811, the local people urged that the route from Glen Euchar to Dalavich should be improved as being necessary to develop the traffic from the coastal district to Inveraray and the South.[1]

On the south-east side of Loch Awe many tracks crossed the hills making for the south ; from Dalmally into Glenshira or into the glen of the Dubh Eas which leads to Glen Falloch ; from Cladich to Inveraray on the line of the present road ; from the farm of Braevallich, six miles east of Ford, to near Furnace on Loch Fyne, while perhaps the most important started from where the little ruined chapel of Kilneuair still stands two miles east of Ford, leading south-east across the hills through the stretch of country known at one time as the Leckan Muir to Auchendrain three miles north of Furnace on Loch Fyne. Local tradition speaks of other tracks, and others no doubt existed, for the hills between Loch Awe and Loch Fyne presented no great obstacle to a drove, and offered good going and ample pasture to travelling beasts.

On this stage of their journey, the droves were not the only traffic on the move. The woods around Loch Awe and Loch Etive supplied the fuel and the charcoal for the local smelting

[1] H.R. & B., 5th Report, 1811, Appendix D (1)

industry. Furnaces had been established before the middle of the eighteenth century to smelt iron ore brought from Ulverston in Lancashire, first at Glen Kinglass on Loch Etive side, and latterly at Bonawe. Timber cut in the woods of Glen Orchy, Glen Strae and Glen Lochy was floated down the River Orchy and through Loch Awe to the Pass of Brander,[1] and when Coleridge and the Wordsworths came down the side of Loch Awe in 1803 they found a sailing-boat in the Pass loaded with charcoal for the Bonawe Works.[2] A furnace had also been started at Goatfield on Loch Fyne in 1754, and until well on in the nineteenth century strings of ponies loaded with charcoal were to be seen crossing the hills to the south of Loch Awe.[3]

As the cattle from Mull and Lorn crossed the watershed south of Loch Awe and started the descent to the oak and hazel woods of the Loch Fyne shore, they were met by other droves coming from the west. These too were largely cattle from the islands. Off the coasts of Kintyre and Knapdale lie the large islands of Islay and Jura, with the smaller islands of Colonsay and Oronsay ten miles farther out in the Atlantic, and the nearer island of Gigha off the mouth of West Loch Tarbert. To Islay, the most southerly and one of the most westerly of the Scottish islands, nature has given a climate and a soil which have placed her from early times among the rich grazing and farming lands of Scotland. The island is described in 1549 as 'fertile, fruitful and full of natural grassing, with many great deer, many woods with fair games of hunting beside every town,'[4] and it was to bring this rich but remote part of his lands under the control of the Crown that James the Sixth in the early years of the seventeenth century directed his repeated and finally successful efforts. The grasslands of these islands fed, even in these early times, large numbers of stock. A raid by Maclean of Duart on the small island of Gigha in 1579 resulted in the theft of no less than 500 cattle and 2,000 sheep and goats.[5] As early as the latter part of the seventeenth century the sale of cattle from Islay for droving to the south appears to have been on a considerable scale. In the

[1] *N.S.A.*, Glenorchy, VII, 92
[2] Dorothy Wordsworth, op. cit., 288 et seq. The cargo would be landed in the Pass and carted to Bonawe.
[3] Macadam, *Notes on the Ancient Iron Industry of Scotland*. Proceedings of Society of Antiquaries of Scotland, 1886, Vol. 9, New Series, 130.
[4] Hume Brown, *Scotland in the Time of Queen Mary*, 30
[5] *R.P.C.*, 1st series, III, 135

spring of 1680 Sir Hugh Campbell sold to Walter Scott of Langhope ' 1,000 stots and cowes of the ile of Ila,' and a few years later he writes to his factor that owing to disturbed conditions having interfered with the normal marketing of his tenants' beasts, he will ' raise a drov on (his) own wentur and giv the tennents a resonable pryce,' though he has ' noe assurance nor probability of pryces in Ingland.' [1]

The abundance of summer grass, but the absence of hay-making, which did not become common in the islands till after 1754, made it almost inevitable that much stock should be disposed of on the approach of autumn, and it is not surprising that when the latter part of the eighteenth century brought an awakening of interest in agricultural knowledge and statistics, the export of cattle from these favoured islands was found to be large. Pennant in 1772 estimates that 1,700 cattle were then exported annually from Islay, though despite this many died in the spring from lack of food, while Colonsay and Oronsay sent 300 to market. [2] At the time of the Statistical Account, the number sold each year from the parish of Kilchoman in the south-west corner of Islay was alone estimated at 800. [3] In his *General View of the Agriculture of the Hebrides* published in 1811, James Macdonald gives figures showing the average number of black cattle ferried from Islay to Jura in each year from 1801 to 1807. These figures, kept by the tenant of the ferry at Port Askaig show that during this period the average number of beasts ferried annually was 2,640. On the conservative assumption that only one quarter of the total stock was sold off each year Macdonald estimates that this indicates a cattle population in Islay of over 10,000 head. The average price was stated to be £7 a head. [4] The *Falkirk Herald* of 27 June 1900 refers to a notice published in the *Edinburgh Advertiser* of May 1779 by the Lairds of the Island of Islay to the effect that they have in hand ' for disposal by small lots of 8 or 10, between 2,000 and 3,000 of the largest and best of the true Highland breed which have never been housed in winter or summer ; that being strangers to the gentlemen graziers of England they do not expect to be furnished with money or credit from them, but will at their own expense execute the

[1] *The Book of Islay*, 414 and 419
[2] Pennant, *Tour in Scotland, 1772*, I, 263 and 273-4
[3] *O.S.A.*, Kilchoman, XI, 278
[4] Macdonald, *General View of the Agriculture of the Hebrides*, 1811, 623

commissions given and find careful drivers with the cattle and deliver them at Glasgow or Dumfries upon receiving payment of the original purchase money, 3% commission and the net expense incurred in ferrying and driving.' The price of the cattle is not stated.[1]

The cattle owners of Islay, Colonsay and Oronsay followed the same principle as guided those of Coll and Tiree in sending their cattle to the mainland by the routes which offered the most grazing on the way and the shortest sea crossing. Colonsay and Oronsay cattle would cross to North Jura, while those of Islay were ferried from Port Askaig over the narrow Sound of Islay to Feolin at the south end of the island.[2] The *Stent Book of Islay* records the activities of the committee on the island which during the last quarter of the eighteenth and the first half of the nineteenth centuries raised and administered local assessments before the modern system of rating was established, and in it occur many references to droving from the island. In 1787, drovers coming from Islay complained of the lack of a fank for enclosing their beasts while waiting for the ferry at Port Askaig, and in that year it was decided to establish one on a site of 60 to 80 acres, an extent which shows that the droves must have been of considerable size. A few years later, James Hill in charge of the ferry was ordered to keep the paving of the slipway in good order to prevent damage to the cattle, and to regulate disputes which had arisen among the drovers about priority in ferrying their beasts to Jura.[3] John Macculloch, who toured the Western Isles in 1824, has described the scene at the crossing of the Sound of Islay : ' The shore was covered with cattle ; and while some were collected in groups under the trees and rocks, crowding to avoid the hot rays of a July evening, others were wading in the sea to shun the flies, some embarking, and another set swimming onshore from the ferry boats ; while the noise of the drovers and the boatmen, and all the bustle and vociferation which whisky did not tend to diminish, were re-echoed from hill to hill, contrasting strangely with the silence and solitude of the surrounding mountains.' [4] Macculloch's description of the noise at the

---

[1] On referring to the files of the *Edinburgh Advertiser* for 1779, the notice in question cannot be found. It is probable that a mistake has been made in the date but there seems little reason to doubt the accuracy of the reference in other respects.

[2] *H.R. & B.*, 5th Report, 1811, Appendix B

[3] *The Stent Book of Islay*, 121, 151 and 219

[4] Macculloch, *Highlands and Western Islands*, 1824, IV, 420

ferry would seem to be well-founded, for only six years earlier the local Stent Committee had found it necessary to give their attention to this very matter. Hitherto the allowance of whisky for the ferrymen had been unlimited, but a ' surplus quantity being often found injurious to the cattle and the proprietors thereof,' the allowance was in future to be fixed at one mutchkin [an English pint] for every thirty cattle ferried.[1]

After crossing to Jura, the route of the Islay cattle lay up the eastern shore of the island, some following the coast to Kinuachdrach at the extreme northern point.[2] In a note to his *General View of the Agriculture of the Hebrides* in 1811, James Macdonald wrote as follows : ' In former times the cattle exported from Islay for the mainland markets were never strong enough for the journey until the middle of June, the driest and best season of the year. They were then driven by herdsmen thro' Jura by a hill road (the shortest possible way) which went between the back of the farms, which are all on the Eastern shore, and the mountainous ridge which occupies the middle and western parts of the Island. They had freedom of pasturage, gratis, during the journey. In consequence however of the late improvements carried on in Islay, the cattle of its proprietors and tenants are much earlier ready for the market than June and indeed are exported all the year round ; and they are also much heavier and more unwieldy than they were in former time, and consequently cannot travel along the hill road. The road now making, and of which one half is made by Government, is carried along the Eastern shore, and Mr Campbell of Shawfield maintains that he is entitled to the use of it for the cattle of Islay in their passage through Jura, while Mr Campbell of Jura alledges that Islay is limited to the hill road only, which is practicable, as already mentioned, during the summer months.' [3]

From the north end of Jura the cattle crossed to the mouth of Loch Craignish, and moving up the north shore of the loch either continued up the Barbreck River towards Loch Avich and the crossing of Loch Awe, or more probably turned south-east at the head of Loch Craignish towards the west end of Loch Awe and the road over the Leckan Muir on the direct route to Inveraray. The cattle which crossed from this northern point of

[1] *The Stent Book of Islay*, 213
[2] *H.R. & B.*, 5th Report, 1811, Appendix B and *N.S.A.*, Jura, VII, 543
[3] Macdonald, op. cit., 618/9. Note.

Jura to Craignish faced a passage little less hazardous than that at Kyle Rhea between Skye and the Inverness-shire coast. On the Jura shore they were dangerously close to the tides and eddies of the Sound of Corrievrechan, while their route to Craignish took them past the north end of the perilous waters of the Dorus Mor, where the tide sweeps round the end of Craignish Point. The number of cattle which crossed by this route cannot be accurately determined, but as late as 1843 when the New Statistical Account of the Parish of Craignish was compiled, it was recorded that the parish still possessed a small vessel, chiefly employed in ferrying beasts from Jura. At that time, it was estimated that each year, 3,000 sheep and 1,000 cattle, including some from Colonsay, were ferried there on their way to the trysts,[1] and in the New Statistical Account for Jura the number of black cattle ' annually sold out of the Island ' is estimated at 1,000 to 1,200.[2]

While some drovers chose this route from North Jura, the greater part of the Islay and Jura cattle crossed to the mainland from Lagg half-way up the east coast of Jura to Keills, which lies on the north side of the mouth of Loch Sween on the coast of Knapdale. The landing jetty at Keills still stands in a little bay facing south-westward down the Sound of Jura. Sea-thrift growing among the stones and the rust of its ironwork tell of a vanished traffic ; but here on a September day of the late eighteenth century was a busy scene, and old men still (1948) living in Knapdale remember in their youth the last remnants of the traffic already shrunk to a mere shadow of what it once had been. The boats appear to have been mainly open, not decked or half-decked like some of those on the crossing of the Minch, single-masted but with heavy oars to help in calm weather. The bottom and sides were thickly lined with birch branches. These according to local evidence were often tied in bundles, the whole being secured by chains. As on the crossing from Uist to Skye, many of the beasts were thrown overboard in deep water as the ferry boats neared the mainland shore. In some of the larger boats it seems that a section of the gunwale hinged outwards to help the unloading, but cattle wearied with hours in the boat and smelling the grass of the shore would seldom linger, and once the leader took the plunge the rest would follow easily. Sometimes in calm weather the five miles crossing would take

[1] *N.S.A.*, Craignish, VII, 57   [2] ibid., Jura, 541

the full day, while the boats drifted with the strong currents of the Sound, the men laboured at the oars and the morning mist lingered on the Jura hills. In the days when the traffic was at its height, many boats would be employed and here, where the most part of the cattle of Islay, Jura and Colonsay crossed, the ferrying took several days, the cattle already landed on the mainland resting and feeding in the rich pasture along the Knapdale shore till the ferrying was completed and the drove ready to continue its long journey. Mr Joseph Mitchell, Engineer to the Commissioners for Highland Roads and Bridges from 1825 to 1853, has recorded the following description of the crossing from Lagg to the mainland :

'On arriving at the Ferry, we found every corner of the Inn crowded with drovers who had been detained by the weather for several days, and were passing their time, as was their wont, in riotous and continuous drinking.

'We felt it was no agreeable sojourn to stay in the inn with these half-intoxicated and noisy people, for the very air was impregnated with an odour of whisky.

'We appealed to the ferrymen to take us across. At first they positively refused on account of the storm, but with some persuasion, and a handsome douceur, their scruples were overcome, and they prepared for the voyage.

'No sooner had the drovers, who had been so long detained, heard that the boat was to cross at our instigation, than they got excessively angry, talked in Gaelic long and loud, and insisted that we should take at the same time a cargo of their cattle. This the boatmen could not refuse, and eighteen cattle were put on board.

'The boat was of great width of beam, and the cattle were fastened with their heads to rings on the gunwale on each side. We had also the chief drover's pony, which stood in the middle of the boat.

'The wind was quite in our favour, but it blew furiously, and the sea was high, but its severity we did not so much notice in the shelter of the harbour.

'At last we cleared the land, and got into the channel. How the wind did roar, and how the cattle struggled to get their heads free ! The extent of sail we carried was forcing the bow of the boat too deep into the sea, and there was fear of being swamped.

'The men tried to lower the sail, which, in their agitation, they could not effect, and all looked helpless.

'On this the drover seized the helm, and with sharp and decisive words took the command of the boat. By his admirable steering he relieved her a good deal, and enabled the men to lessen sail. Still the boat flew before the wind and rolled heavily ; every moment we expected would be our last. I grasped the stirrup of the saddle on the pony, in the hope that if we did go the creature might swim ashore. On we ploughed our way in the midst of this furious storm.

'How admirably the drover steered ! We had to take the narrow and rocky entrance of Lagg harbour, a most difficult navigation ; but the drover's sharp and distinct orders were promptly obeyed, and in no time he landed us in shelter within the little bay.' [1]

From Keills, 'the boating place at Keills' as it is called in the Reports of the Commissioners for Highland Roads and Bridges, the droves made their way up the north-west side of Loch Sween, skirting the little inlets and arms of the sea which are the peculiar characteristics of that loch, and past the wooded promontories where the oak and hazel grow to the water's edge. Then skirting the flat moss of Crinan they made for Kilmichael-Glassary in the valley of the River Add, a cattle tryst of considerable importance in those droving days, the memory of which is now preserved only by a pool in the river still known as the 'Stance Pool.' To Kilmichael-Glassary came also the cattle of Kintyre and Gigha, travelling up the Kintyre peninsula to West Loch Tarbert and on by routes marked in the survey of 1747–55 over the Knapdale hills by Loch Killisport and the head of Loch Sween. Those still (1948) living in Kintyre can recall the landing on the west coast of beasts brought in from Islay, Jura and Gigha for grazing in Kintyre and subsequent sale at the Tryst at Kilmichael-Glassary. The cattle were brought from the islands to near the Kintyre coast by sailing-boat and were then flung overboard to swim ashore, shepherded by rowboats which headed them off if they tried to swim in the wrong direction.

The Kilmichael market over and their cattle rested, the Kintyre, Knapdale and Islay drovers faced the first stage up

---

[1] Mitchell, *Reminiscences of my Life in the Highlands*, I, 302–3, 1883–4
Though Mitchell's description suggests that the landing was made at Lagg, it appears from the context that the crossing was from Lagg to Keills.

Loch Fyne of their long march to Falkirk.[1] Roy's map, already referred to, marks the route they followed up the valley of the Add to its head waters to join the track which crosses the Leckan Muir from Kilneuair making for Inveraray. ' By this route,' says a Memorial of 1807 urging the improvement of the road, ' the inhabitants of Knapdale, Jura, Islay, Colonsay, North Lorne and the adjacent islands take their cattle to the Low Country with hardly a single exception,' and while the statement of the Memorialists may have been coloured by a desire to prove their case, there seems small reason to doubt its substantial truth.[2] The old track, part of which is still on the list of the country roads of Argyll, is now deserted and grass-grown, and as long ago as the time of the New Statistical Account the writer of the Account for the Parish of Glassary complained of its upkeep at public expense, though it ' scarcely deserves the name of road ' ; but to follow the track as it winds uphill from the Loch Awe shore, marking how deep it has cut, is to realise that here the latter-day drovers followed in the footsteps of droves of earlier times, of pack-horse and foot traffic, perhaps dating back to a very early period in the history of the country. It was on this road among the hills above Loch Fyne, that the cattle from South Argyll and the islands met the Mull droves as they crossed from Loch Awe by the routes of the old charcoal burners.

Loch Fyne in the eighteenth and early nineteenth centuries, like many another Scottish loch, had crossing-places now gone out of use. Crossings at Otter opposite Ardrishaig, at Strachur and at St. Catherine's certainly existed, and while all the routes across the loch used by the drovers cannot now be known, it seems highly probable that the Strachur route at least was used by cattle on their way to the Clyde coast at Ardentinny and Dunoon.[3] In an action in the Court of Session in 1777, droving rights and stances were successfully claimed in North Cowal for cattle in transit from the Western Isles,[4] and in 1810 the inhabitants of

---

[1] According to information supplied by Mr McDougal, Minard, Loch Fyne, formerly tenant of Barmolloch Farm near Kilmichael-Glassary, the journey from there to Falkirk took from seven to eight days but usually a little longer was allowed for contingencies. In his early days Mr McDougal frequently drove cattle from Knapdale to Falkirk. [2] *H.R. & B.*, 3rd Report, 1807, Appendix L

[3] The cattle traffic from the north-west side of the loch was not the only traffic using the Strachur Ferry for the *O.S.A.* reports that the birch, alder and hazel woods above Strachur were made into charcoal for the use of the smelting works across the loch (*O.S.A.*, Strachur, IV, 563).

[4] *Campbell* v. *Campbell*, 1777, 5 Brown's Supplement, 599

Plate 5 Looking towards Kingshouse from Altnafeadh

(*Photo by Robert M. Adam*)

Dunoon complained to the Commissioners for Highland Roads and Bridges of the lack of a good harbour to serve the roads which brought several thousands of cattle to be shipped to the southern markets.[1]

While these routes across Loch Fyne were certainly used, the greater part of the droves from the west appear to have continued up the north-west side of the loch to Inveraray, some perhaps turning up Glen Shira bound for Dalmally and Tyndrum, while others continued eastward to the head of Loch Fyne. Till the coast road was made round the head of the loch, the route of the latter traffic probably led up Glen Shira as far as the Kilblaan Burn. Then crossing the hills by a track to the north of Dunderave, used according to tradition by pilgrims on their way to Iona and marked on Elphinstone's map of 1745, they came down into Glen Fyne at the old chapel of Kilmorich. General Roy's survey marks a route from the head of Loch Fyne to Loch Long by way of Glen Croe, following very much the line of the present road. It seems probable that this route was used by part of the early droving traffic from south and west Argyll, and the evidence of those who took part in the trade in the latter part of last century shows that by then this route to Loch Lomondside was in regular use. The 1747–55 survey, however, shows that there was an alternative route which according to local tradition was used by some drovers. This route led up Glen Fyne for several miles, crossing by the Allt-na-lairige into Dumbartonshire at the top of Glen Arnan and so reaching Glen Falloch at the head of Loch Lomond.

The north end of Loch Lomond was the meeting-place of three drovers' routes. While Crieff Tryst flourished, the quickest route for any cattle making for Crieff lay up Glen Falloch to join the route from Skye at the top of Glendochart, but after 1770 when Falkirk Tryst had taken the place of Crieff, it is probable that this route saw little traffic. A second route crossed the Falloch at the head of Loch Lomond and climbed the hills to the east of Ardlui to come into the head of Glen Gyle. James Hogg used this route in 1791 for droving sheep,[2] and those still (1948) living on Loch Lomondside remember seeing droves from Argyll climbing to the watershed from Glen Falloch. By Glen Gyle the

---

[1] *H.R. & B.*, 5th Report, 1811, Appendix R
[2] Hogg, *A Tour in the Highlands in 1803*, 15

droves passed along the side of Loch Katrine and were driven over the hill to Aberfoyle, and crossing the flat ground at the head of the Forth came by Gartmoren into the valley of the Endrick Water and so to Falkirk.[1]

The third route from the head of Loch Lomond led down the west side of the loch to Balloch and Dumbarton. The town of Dumbarton occurs early in the records of the cattle trade. In 1661 the Duke of Lennox as hereditary Keeper of Dumbarton Castle petitioned the Privy Council for an Order compelling drivers of cattle from Argyll passing Dumbarton Castle to pay a toll of 4s Scots on each beast as in the past, complaining that lately the drovers had taken a new route avoiding the castle, 'whereby his Majesty's garisons in the said castle is mightilie prejudged.' The Order was granted, but three years later the drovers protested that it was invalid and that they had a right to the road without payment 'past memory of man.' The dispute continued till 1684, when the drovers were finally successful and the tolls were abolished.[2] Four years earlier the magistrates of Dumbarton had petitioned the Privy Council for a bridge over the Leven. They claimed that 'this lying in the mouth of the Highlands and being the passe and inlett of all trade betwixt them and the Lowlands, the want of a bridge in that place does very much prejudge the trade of cowes which is one of the most considerable commodities of the nation, and which cowes are either stopt when the storme is great and so starved or in swimming over are extreamlie weakned and ofttimes drowned or in hazard thereof . . . so that they are forced to goe about by the bridge of Striveling, which is twenty-four myles of unsecure and rough gate where there is neither meat nor safety for the passingers nor cowes.'[3]

Throughout the entire droving period Dumbarton remained a cattle market of some importance for the supply of the growing population of the Clydeside towns, but from 1770 onwards an increasing proportion of the droves which came down the side of Loch Lomond crossed the Leven at Balloch, and from this point to Falkirk Tryst the route followed can be established in some detail, for it was still used in living memory by drovers from

---

[1] Information as to the use of this route has been supplied by Mr Donald McNicol whose family have for several generations been tenants of the Doune Farm, Ardlui, and by others living on Loch Lomondside.

[2] *R.P.C.*, 3rd series, I, 100, 101, 553–4 and 654; *R.P.C.*, 3rd series, IX, 86, 87, 90–3

[3] *R.P.C.*, 3rd series, VI, 498

Knapdale and Kintyre. From Balloch the route led by Gartocharn to Drymen or Killearn and then climbed the valley of the Endrick. The beasts then crossed the south shoulder of the Fintry Hills and came into the valley of the Carron Water, and so at last to Stenhousemuir and the Falkirk Tryst ; for some of them the end of all their journeyings ; for most the start of fresh travels to strange places and pastures new.

6

THE DROVE ROAD FROM THE NORTH

To one who watched from the hills behind Crieff the gathering
of the cattle for the Tryst on an autumn day of the early eighteenth
century, it would have been apparent that two main streams of
beasts were converging from different directions on the town.
While some droves were coming from the north-west down the
valley of the Earn or across the hills from Loch Tay, a second
stream was moving through the Sma' Glen from the direction of
Amulree and the valley of the Tay. Half a century later, when
Crieff Tryst had given way before the rising importance of
Falkirk, a watcher from the Castle Rock at Stirling might have
observed a similar meeting of traffic. While many droves were
approaching the crossing of the Forth from the direction of Doune
and the north-west, many more were slowly winding their way
down the track which led from Sheriffmuir into the Forth valley.

A study of the history of the cattle trade between the Highlands
and the Lowlands shows that, broadly, there were two main
routes by which droving traffic came from the north, north-west
and central Highlands to the Lowland Trysts. Of these main
streams one, and possibly the larger, had its origin in Skye, the
Outer Islands and part of the north-western districts. The other
had its source in the far north and the eastern half of the counties
of Ross and Inverness, and each was fed by tributary streams
from the country through which it passed on its way to the south.
The separate existence of these two streams of beasts is accounted
for largely by the mass of high ground lying across Scotland both
north and south of the Great Glen, which made it necessary for
much of the traffic to pass at the west or at the east end of what is
now the Caledonian Canal.[1] There were important lateral con-
nections between the streams, but in the main they remained
distinct till the markets of Southern Perthshire and Stirlingshire
and the barrier of the Forth brought them together. It is with
the stream of animal traffic which had its source in the far north,
which moved through Easter Ross-shire, Badenoch and Atholl,
and which came at last to Crieff by way of the Sma' Glen, that
we are here concerned.

[1] See Appendix B (p. 227)

Plate 6   A drove route in Wester Ross-shire : in Strathnashellag
(*Photo by Robert M. Adam*)

It has been seen that the earliest evidence of legitimate cattle traffic comes from the west and north-west where droving to the Lowlands can be traced back to the start of the sixteenth century. The reason for this would, as has been suggested, seem to lie partly in the need of the poorer north-west districts to export their beasts in the absence of feeding to carry them through the winter. In the flatter and richer districts of the east side of Scotland arable farming provided some sort of winter feeding, poor as it no doubt was, and made it perhaps less essential to market beasts on the approach of winter, while the cattle raised in the eastern half of the country seem on the whole to have been less suited for droving than those of the hardier west coast breed. Larger population and the possibility of some coastwise or export trade from the north-eastern counties meant more local demand, while it may be that the character and way of life of the people of these rather more developed areas were also less suited to the droving trade. None the less the volume of cattle traffic which used the more easterly route was by no means negligible, and the evidence available indicates that the stream of beasts which started in the far north had, with its tributary streams, reached a size rivalling the droves from the west by the time it passed through the Sma' Glen to reach the Perthshire lowlands.

In the extreme north of the country, Caithness had, at least as early as the start of the eighteenth century, an outlet for her cattle readier to hand than the markets of Central Scotland. John Brand, writing of Orkney, Shetland and Caithness in 1701 speaks of a considerable export trade with Leith in barrelled beef, tallow, skins and hides,[1] while the Dutch herring boats which came in large numbers each summer to Orkney and Shetland meant a local demand for beef; but not all the Caithness beasts were marketed at home, and the letters of Sir James Sinclair of Mey show that before the middle of the eighteenth century cattle were being sold from the county for droving to the South.[2] Defoe writing about 1726 refers to many black cattle being bred in Caithness and sold to drovers, mainly for droving to Norfolk, Suffolk and Essex,[3] and Pennant in 1772 estimated that in good years the county sold to the drovers

[1] Brand, *A Brief Description of Orkney, Zetland, etc.*, 1701, 149
[2] *Manuscript Letters of Sir James Sinclair of Mey*, Box xviii, 1738–43, H.M. Register House   [3] Defoe, *Tour through Great Britain in 1724* (1762 edn.), IV, 253

as many as 2,200.[1] By the end of the century, the annual number
driven south had risen to about 3,000,[2] and the writer of the
Statistical Account for Wick speaks of the parish being full of
black cattle which are sold to drovers for Falkirk and England
at a price of 40s to 50s.[3] He maintains that these cattle from
the north-east coastal districts drive as well as those from the
Highland districts. The general view of many contemporary
writers was, however, that cattle of the true Highland breed
from Skye and the West Highlands were better in quality and
more suitable for droving, and the relatively poor quality of
Caithness cattle for droving may well explain the important
place which barrelled beef and hides occupied in the list of exports
from the district. The beasts from Caithness moreover, faced a
four weeks journey to the South of Scotland, and a letter from
James Gunn of Braemore to Sir James Sinclair, whose beasts he
had bought in 1743 suggests that drovers of Caithness cattle
were fortunate if all their beasts 'held out to travill.'[4] An
account of a recent Falkirk Tryst contained in a letter written
from Edinburgh in October 1805 makes the following comment
on Caithness cattle : 'Large cattle from Caithness will not
answer. Sir John Sinclair's Galloway oxen, worth £14 each in
Caithness, only fetched £7 3 6d at Falkirk. The true breed
for droving to be established in Caithness is either the pure Sky
or the Argyle breed or a cross between the Argyle or Sky Bull
and the best sort of Caithness Cows. That kind of stock would
always fetch a fair price . . .'[5]

As the stream of cattle from the far north moved down the
East Coast by Helmsdale and Brora, it was augmented by
droves coming from Strath-Naver and Strath Halladale and the
glens immediately to the westward and by other cattle driven
across the hills from the north-west coast. Here in the upland
glens and on the Atlantic seaboard of Sutherland cattle rearing
had for long been the main, if not the only, industry of the country.
In the district of Reay the breeding of cattle and the inevitable
accompaniment of cattle thieving had figured in the Privy Council
records of the seventeenth century,[6] and when the Statistical

[1] Pennant, *Tour in Scotland, 1772*, III, 202
[2] *O.S.A.*, Caithness, XX, 519   [3] *O.S.A.*, Wick, X, 22
[4] *Manuscript Letters of Sir James Sinclair of Mey*, Box xviii, 22nd Oct. 1743, H.M.
Register House
[5] *Sutherland Estate Papers.* Letter from John Sinclair, 12th Oct. 1805
[6] *R.P.C.*, 3rd series, II, 566, 567

Account was compiled at the close of the eighteenth century the parishes of Reay and Eddrachillis had a combined cattle population of close on 6,000 beasts.[1] Sales to the drovers at a price of £2 10s to £4 a head were, says the Account, the main support of the people. Cattle were evidently being regularly driven to the South from the Sutherland Estates at the beginning of the century, for in a letter written from Edinburgh on 31 August 1703 addressed to the Earl of Sutherland, Mr Charles Ross asks that ' Your Lordship will be pleased to order one of your drovers to give me two fatt cows to be my winter beef.' [2]

For those cattle from Caithness and East Sutherland, the Kyle of Sutherland and the Dornoch Firth were formidable obstacles on the route to the South. Some of the beasts may have been taken across at the Meikle Ferry near Skibo, but many of the drovers appear to have preferred to cross the Kyle at Creich. The minister of that parish writing in the Statistical Account in 1794 reports that this crossing is necessary for all the cattle of Caithness and Sutherland and also for those coming from Lord Reay's country except the Assynt district. The cattle swam the Kyle, he writes, or if necessary were ferried across, the readiness with which the beasts took to the water foretelling, according to a local supersitition, whether the prices at the Trysts would be good or bad.[3]

Until the beginning of the nineteenth century there existed north of Inverness little in the way of roads save the tracks of pack-horses and cattle. There were no bridges over the large rivers, and though some of the smaller ones appear to have been bridged, Telford in his Survey and Report to the Commissioners for Highlands Roads and Bridges in 1803 reported that the lack of bridges over the Conon and the Beauly was one of the chief weaknesses of communication in the north.[4] These water barriers were a deterrent to dealers coming from the south in search of cattle, and a further discouragement appears to have been the difficulty of droving through and finding stances for their beasts in the relatively rich cultivated farming lands of Easter Ross-shire. As late as 1831 drovers were refusing to go north of Bridge

[1] O.S.A., Eddrachillis, VI, 283
[2] Sutherland Estate Papers, Bundle 19, Nos. 619–44
[3] O.S.A., Creich, VIII, 372
[4] So rapidly did the work of the Commissioners open up the country that in 1818 the Inverness Courier was able to report that ' From Inverness to John o' Groats it is now possible to travel without crossing a ferry or fording a river.'

of Conon because of the action of local landowners in confiscating cattle straying from the drove roads, particularly on that part of the route which led from Kincardine on the Dornoch Firth to Strathrusdale.[1] From the reference to this route it seems that the drovers after passing the Kyle of Sutherland crossed the high ground between the Dornoch and Cromarty Firths by the hill road past Aultnamain Inn, or possibly by tracks farther to the westward.

At intervals on the drove route from the northern counties, small local trysts had been established, at least by the mid-eighteenth century, for the sale of cattle brought from the glens and the grazings lying to the westward. Contemporary records of the cattle trade contain scattered references to Trysts at Georgemas and in the Strath of Dunbeath in Caithness, at Clashmore and Monibuie in Sutherland and at Kildary and Dornoch in Ross-shire. Some of these were certainly in existence in the first half of the eighteenth century, but the most important tryst for the droves from the north dates only from the first quarter of last century.

Midway across the narrow neck of low land which lies between the head of the Cromarty Firth and the Beauly Firth and in the direct path of traffic from north to south, the position of Muir of Ord gives to it many of the advantages which made Falkirk the great cattle market of Central Scotland. For traffic from the north and north-east reaching the Cromarty Firth about Alness the only route to the south was by the crossing of the Conon at the head of the Firth. To the west and north-west of Muir of Ord radiated Strath Garve, Strath Bran, Strath Conon and Glen Orrin, the first two affording to this day the main overland communication with the seaboard of Wester Ross. A few miles to the south lay the valley of the Beauly leading inland to Strath Glass, Glen Strathfarrar, Glen Cannich and Glen Affric. All these glens sent their quota of cattle to the Muir of Ord market. The valley of the Beauly and the road up Strath Glass offered, moreover, a route to the south by way of Fort Augustus, while the road to Inverness gave an alternative route to Crieff and Central Scotland. The Tryst at Muir of Ord was established about 1820. At first it was held near the village of Beauly and was known as ' Feill-na-manachainn.' Later it was moved to a better site about a mile to the north, and though it never rivalled in size the great Trysts at Crieff, Falkirk and Dumfries, ' Blair dubh ' as it was then called remained until near the end of last century the greatest market in the north for cattle from Caithness, Sutherland and Ross-shire.

Before the development of Oban, Mallaig and Kyle of Lochalsh, Poolewe on the West Ross-shire coast was the main port of entry for traffic from a considerable part of the Western Islands. The cattle of Skye and many of the Outer Hebrides crossed to the mainland, as has been seen, at Kyle Rhea, but for sea-borne traffic from the islands to the mainland, Poolewe was almost the only port. It seems probable that the use of Poolewe for island traffic dates back to comparatively early times. John Knox who toured in the Highlands and Islands in 1786 reported that he sailed from Stornoway to Poolewe in a small unseaworthy vessel used for the transport of cattle to the Ross-shire coast.[1] Evander MacIver, for many years factor on the Sutherland Estates, has described how as a boy he sailed from Stornoway to Poolewe about the year 1818 in a sloop laden with cattle which had been purchased at the Lewis cattle tryst. The beasts were thrown overboard in Loch Ewe and made to swim ashore.[2] At least as early as the end of the eighteenth century the route between Poolewe and Dingwall appears to have been in frequent use. James Hogg, describing a tour in the Highlands in 1803, refers to the Inn at Kinlochewe as having been built to accommodate those travelling from Dingwall to Gairloch or towards the ferry of Poolewe ' where there is a packet once each week to Lewis,' and in the same year George Brown, reporting to the Commissioners for Highland Roads and Bridges, refers to the route from Poolewe by Loch Maree and Kinlochewe to Achnasheen, Strath Bran and Garve as ' the great line of communication ' from Lewis and the West Coast to Dingwall and Inverness.

To Poolewe or to points on the nearby coast came the cattle of Lewis. The New Statistical Account for Stornoway records that near the town ' there is a square mile of moor enclosed for a cattle tryst where several thousand head are exposed for sale and 2,000 at least change hands in 2 days. From 20 to 30 drovers come from the Mainland and some from England.' [3] Some cattle from Harris also landed at Poolewe, and evidence given in

[1] Knox, *Tour through the Highlands of Scotland and the Hebride Isles in 1786,* 192–3
[2] *Reminiscences of Evander MacIver,* 1905, 6
[3] *N.S.A.,* Stornoway, Ross and Cromarty, XIV, 140

the course of litigation in 1868 by those who had taken part in the droving trade in the early years of the century tells of landings of cattle from the Outer Isles at Gairloch, Aultbea and Gruinard.[1] From Poolewe these island cattle together with those of the parish of Gairloch of which as many as 500 were sold off each year, appear to have followed the north shore of Loch Maree to Kinlochewe and Achnasheen, while many of those which landed at Aultbea and Gruinard went up the valley of the Gruinard River past Loch-na-Shellag near the head of the river and so by hill tracks to join either the road from Ullapool to Dingwall or that from Achnasheen to Garve.[2] The landing of cattle from Lewis at Poolewe and near Aultbea as late as 1880 is confirmed by Mr Angus McLeod, a retired drover now (1948) in his 100th year living near Gruinard who started droving about the year 1868. The beasts which came ashore near Aultbea at that time were, it seems, driven to Muir of Ord by way of Gruinard, Dundonnell and Braemore as being shorter than the route by Kinlochewe and Achnasheen. The hill route by Loch-na-Shellag which had been upheld as a drove road in the litigation of 1868, was apparently by that time no longer in regular use. From Braemore the beasts were driven east to Garve and Dingwall but two deviations from the main road were used by the drovers, and it appears from local information that these are still in occasional use. One of these turned due south from the main road near Altguish and crossed the forest of Corriemoillie to Garve, so shortening the distance and keeping the beasts on soft ground where grazing was available. The other short cut left the Ullapool-Garve road near Inchbrae Lodge and crossing the saddle between Ben Wyvis and Little Wyvis rejoined at Auchterneed the road to Dingwall.[3]

The Statistical Account records that in 1794 the parish of Applecross in Wester Ross-shire contained about 3,000 cattle, the annual sales of cattle being the chief means of support of the people.[4] For these, the natural route would be by Strathcarron

---

[1] *Mackenzie* v. *Bankes*. Court of Session Cases, 1868, 6 Macpherson's Reports, 936 and Notes of Evidence in *Session Papers*, Signet Library.   [2] ibid.

[3] From information collected in the Ullapool district it appears that cattle from Lewis were regularly landed at Ullapool within living memory. It is also reported that cattle from the Ullapool area were at times driven through Glen Achall into Glen Einig and so to Strathoykell by a branch road turning off at Craggan in Glen Einig which leads into Strathcarron and so to Ardgay. These routes, it seems, were regularly used for taking beasts to the late autumn sale at Ardgay.

[4] *O.S.A.*, Applecross, III, 371

and Strath Bran to the East Coast, and local tradition tells also of the regular use of droving tracks from the districts of Lochalsh and North Kintail to Glen Cannich and Glen Affric bound for the Muir of Ord market.

Many of these tracks across the North of Scotland are certainly of very early origin ; how early cannot now be determined, but when General Roy surveyed the Highlands in the years between 1747 and 1755 some of the routes, such as that from Loch Broom to Dingwall by Strath Garve were marked on the large-scale map of Scotland which was at that time prepared, and Pennant in 1772 noted that in the Loch Broom district the sale of black cattle to drovers from as far south as Craven in Yorkshire was the chief support of the people.[1] For these the only practicable route to the South was by Strath Garve to Muir of Ord and Beauly.

While the accident of a nineteenth-century litigation has established beyond all doubt the existence of droving traffic from the Poolewe area and one of the routes by which these droves crossed the country from the West Coast, it is hardly possible at this distance of time to establish with equal certainty the routes of all the other cross-country traffic in this great area of hills and glens and lochs. But if the exact routes cannot be determined the general trend of the traffic is not in doubt, and it would seem to be beyond question that to Muir of Ord came cattle not only from Caithness and Sutherland and from the many glens which drain to the Beauly and Cromarty Firths, but also from the whole seaboard of Wester Ross lying between Loch Broom and Loch Alsh.

To the south of Muir of Ord two alternative routes lay open to drovers bound for the Trysts at Crieff or Falkirk. Some part of the droving traffic from the north went by Beauly and the Aird of Lovat to Inverness, and after 1817 Inverness became the great centre for the wool and sheep trade in the North of Scotland. For cattle traffic from the north, however, Inverness appears to have been of minor importance. The town never figured in the list of important cattle markets. The *Inverness Courier* for 28 October 1824 reports that the tryst recently established at Muir of Ord has almost superseded that at Inverness, but it is on record that in the third week of May 1818 as many as 1,500 cattle purchased at the Ross-shire Trysts passed through the town.[2]

---

[1] Pennant, *Tour in Scotland, 1772*, I, 364   [2] *Inverness Courier*, 21 May 1818

The route by Inverness reaching the Spey Valley about Nethy Bridge or Aviemore passed south through the Pass of Drumochter, while it also gave access to the high passes through the Cairngorm Mountains to Deeside and the Angus glens. A Survey of the Agriculture of Inverness-shire in 1813 mentions the existence of a periodical cattle market at Kingussie and a new one established in 1804 on a date fixed to suit drovers for the South passing through Badenoch,[1] while in 1814 a Tryst was in existence at Pitmain near Kingussie for the sale to drovers of cattle for Falkirk.[2]

The alternative route to the South chosen by many drovers from Muir of Ord illustrates their preference for the less frequented ways leading them through hill country which offered greater freedom of movement with more abundant and cheaper wayside grazing for their cattle. A few miles south of Muir of Ord, the valley of the Beauly leads south-westward into Strath Glass and the hills of the Forests of Fasnakyle and Guisachan. What proportion of the droving traffic from the north chose this route cannot be accurately estimated, but it is known that many and probably most drovers preferred it. An article which appeared in the *Inverness Courier* for 26 September 1827 contains the following passage : ' We believe the great Northern Drove Road begins somewhere about the Kyle of Sutherland (at which place a number of important cattle markets are held throughout the year) and runs nearly parallel with one of the Parliamentary roads for a considerable distance, through the lands of Ardross, by Fowlis, and Dingwall to the Muir of Ord (another great market)—then branching away through the mountains towards Fort Augustus and from thence southwards—avoiding the public lines of road throughout the whole distance till it touches occasionally on the turnpike roads in Perthshire. There are other branch drove-roads leading from various points of the country into this line, but this is unquestionably the principal one as proceeding direct from two of the greatest market stances in the North of Scotland.' From the point where Guisachan House now stands near the head of Strath Glass, an easy route leads across the hills of the Guisachan Forest to Torgyle in Glen Moriston, connecting with the old military road leading to Fort Augustus, and when in 1888 a right of way past Guisachan was unsuccessfully challenged, the evidence brought in its support revealed the steady use by drovers

---

[1] Robertson, *General View of the Agriculture of the County of Inverness*, 1813, 302
[2] Elizabeth Grant of Rothiemurchus, *Memoirs of a Highland Lady*, 1898 ed., 248–9

Plate 7   A drove route from Kintail to Glen Affric : in Glen Lichet

(Photo by Robert M. Adam)

of this and other cross-country routes throughout the preceding half-century. The traffic at that time recorded was mainly a traffic in sheep, but cattle traffic too used these roads and there seems little reason to doubt that this route had long been in use for cattle droving.[1]

As these droves from Strath Glass and Guisachan descended into Glen Moriston they joined one of the routes used by the cattle which had crossed from Skye at Kyle Rhea. A Memorial of 1805 presented to the Commissioners for Highland Roads and Bridges refers to the use by cattle from Skye and the Outer Isles of the military road to Fort Augustus, and a Memorandum of about the same date among the *Breadalbane Papers* speaks of this as the alternative line for the droves which did not use the route by Glen Garry.[2] South of Fort Augustus the droves from Skye or from Muir of Ord crossed the hills to the Upper Spey Valley by the Pass of Corrieyairack, the route which Wade chose for the construction of his military road in 1731, and over which Prince Charles Edward passed in 1745. This route from the North of Scotland to the trysts was evidently in active use by stock in the early nineteenth century, for the *Inverness Courier* of 24 July 1823 reports that in the course of discussions over the Bill for the Maintenance of Highland Roads and Bridges then before Parliament, a concession had been made whereby cattle might travel from Strath Halladale in Sutherlandshire westward and southward to Fort Augustus, and so over the Corrieyairack road to Perthshire without payment of toll except 10d per score of black cattle and 5d per score of sheep and lambs payable once at the Pitmain Bridge over the Spey. This route over the Pass of Corrieyairack was almost certainly the route used by the large droves from Skye which Bishop Forbes met at Drumochter in 1723, and references to it in contemporary records show the Pass to have remained in extensive use by drovers till the second half of the nineteenth century.

At Dalwhinnie the droves which had crossed the Monadhliath Mountains from Fort Augustus joined those which had come from Inverness and the North by the more easterly route, and it seems probable that during the droving days the hills which enclose the Pass of Drumochter looked down on a concentration

[1] *Winans and Chisholm* v. *Lord Tweedmouth*, Court of Session Cases, 1888, 15 Rettie's Reports, 540 and Notes of Evidence in *Session Papers*, Signet Library, No. 98, 1888.
[2] *Breadalbane Papers* (*Roads*), Box 4, H.M. Register House

111

of droving traffic as great as was to be seen at that time in any part of the Highlands. At Dalwhinnie on 31 August 1723 Bishop Forbes found eight droves—1,200 beasts in all—bound for Crieff, and in the Drumochter Pass a drove a mile in length, with 300 more resting at the head of Loch Garry.[1] A few miles south of Drumochter Pass the drove road from the North left the valley of the Garry at Dalnacardoch, and crossing the hills by Trinafour and the head waters of the Errochty on the line of General Wade's military road, came to Tummel Bridge and the borders of the Rannoch country. Passing to the east of Schiehallion the route of the cattle then led to Coshieville near the junction of Lyon and Tay. In the 14th Report to the Commissioners for Highland Roads and Bridges in 1828 the route from Dalnacardoch to the valley of the Tay is referred to as the route by which go to Falkirk, Doune and other trysts ' almost all the cattle and sheep of the North and North-West Highlands.' [2]

From the foot of Glen Lyon part of the cattle traffic appears to have gone by Aberfeldy and Wade's Tay Bridge, while part forded the Lyon and the Upper Tay, crossing the hills to the south of Kenmore into Glen Quaich and so to Amulree on the road to Crieff. Here, at the crossing of the Tay, the drovers were on ground trodden by the feet of their less reputable ancestors. Mackintosh of Borlum, writing in 1742, refers to Kenmore as ' a very frequent and beaten Pass for driving stolen cattle from Perthshire, Stirlingshire, Kinross and Clackmannan into Glenlyon, Rannoch, Breadalbane, Glencoe, Appin and Lorn.' [3]

Until the middle of the eighteenth century Crieff remained, as has been seen, the main centre of trade for the cattle from the North of Scotland and for many of those from the West Coast and the Hebrides, but shortly after 1750 various factors undermined the importance of Crieff as a cattle market and led ultimately to the transference of the main trade to Falkirk Tryst. By the last decade of the century when the Statistical Account was compiled, though many thousands of cattle were still using the route through the Sma' Glen to Crieff, they passed the town on the day before the date fixed for the Tryst, so avoiding the market dues which were still levied.[4] By that time Crieff Tryst

---

[1] *Bishop Forbes' Journal*, 235   [2] *H.R. & B.*, 14th Report, 1828, Appendix D
[3] Mackintosh, *A Short Scheme . . . to stop depredations . . . to the Northern Counties of Scotland*, 1742
[4] *O.S.A.*, Crieff, IX, 596

had shrunk to a mere shadow of what it once had been, and a description of the cattle route from the North must follow the beasts a short distance farther to their destination at Falkirk Tryst.

A little way down-stream from Crieff the old ford of Dalpatrick crosses the River Earn. The ford is on the direct line from Gilmerton where the Sma' Glen road emerges from the hills, and the name of 'Highlandman' which the nearby railway station still bears is locally believed to date back to the days when Highland drovers in large numbers came that way. At Dalpatrick Ford the droves crossed the Earn and, coming into Strathallan by way of Muthill and the Muir of Orchil, they crossed the Allan Water about Greenloaning, and came to Sheriffmuir. Here on the north-west slopes of the Ochils, at a point immediately to the east of the site of the battle of 1715, extensive common rights of grazing for long existed. The area was a favourite stance ground, and when the common was divided in 1771 the evidence of local witnesses agrees as to its frequent use by drovers bound for Falkirk. The situation of Sheriffmuir made it peculiarly well suited for the purpose, for this was the last hill grazing available for beasts from the North on their way to Falkirk, and here drovers who were not pressed for time could rest their droves perhaps for a day or more before taking them on to the Tryst. From Sheriffmuir the droves moved down the south-west slopes of the Ochils to Bridge of Allan and the valley of the Forth, on the last miles of the long road to Falkirk Tryst.

While the extensive use of this route by Sheriffmuir is well established by a variety of contemporary evidence, it seems that some of the cattle from Crieff and a portion of those which passed through Perth from the north-eastern counties reached Falkirk by a different route. Due south of Crieff across Strathearn, Gleneagles and Glendevon provided a ready way through the low range of grassy hills which a contemporary writer called 'those verdant Downs the Ochil Hills,'[1] while to the east of Gleneagles other tracks offered an easy crossing of the Ochils and the best of upland grazing. In his *Memorial respecting the Road from Yetts of Muckhart through Glendevon and Gleneagles into Strathearn*, Sir Patrick Murray of Ochtertyre records that between July 1812 and July 1813 at the side bar on the Hillfoots road giving access

---

[1] Knox, op. cit. 11

to the Glendevon road at Yetts of Muckhart the following tolls were collected :

Cattle, 863 at 1s a score

Sheep, 13,219 at 5d a score

but it is not clear from the context whether these beasts were going south or north or both. The numbers are small, but Gleneagles and Glendevon comprised only one of several routes through the Ochils, and it must be borne in mind that drovers were adepts at avoiding tolls. For droves crossing the Ochils by any of these routes bound for Falkirk, the natural crossings of the Forth were at Alloa and Kincardine-on-Forth, and the Minute Book of the Justices of the Peace for Stirlingshire for the year 1827 shows the two ferries in active use by the drovers. In May of that year the Justices had before them a complaint that the existing rates for ferrying black cattle at Alloa were too high, and that for this reason many droves took other routes to the South. New rates were fixed at 4d. a beast up to six and 3d a beast for more, or 5s a score. In the spring of the following year a steam ferry boat was put on at Higginsneuk (Kincardine) Ferry in addition to the sailing boats used for black cattle, the ferrying rate being fixed at 6s 8d a score. The cattle traffic at the Higginsneuk Ferry appears to have interfered with the ferrying of passengers, for in the autumn of the same year it was found necessary to make special rules for dealing with the ferrying of cattle droves. It was provided that a drover coming to the ferry should have the right of using the first boat to cross, but that passengers should have the right of the next boat even if they had arrived after the arrival of the drove, and so on alternately till the whole drove had been ferried. No passengers were to cross with cattle except those in charge of them, and extra men were to be available to help with the ferrying at times of Fairs or Trysts.[1]

The crossing of the Forth behind them, a few more miles brought the tired cattle from the North to the tryst ground at Stenhousemuir, there to merge in the vast assembly of men and beasts which was gathering from every part of the Highlands and Islands of Scotland.

---

[1] *Minute Book of Quarter Sessions, of J.P.'s for Stirlingshire,* 6th December 1819

Plate 8   A drove route from Deeside to Angus : in Glen Doll

(Photo by Robert M. Adam)

7

THE DROVE ROADS OF MORAYSHIRE, ABERDEENSHIRE AND ANGUS

THE great agricultural developments which brought into the forefront of Scotland's cattle-breeding industry that part of the country which contains the valleys of Dee, Don, Deveron and Spey and the glens of Angus belong to the last years of the eighteenth and the first half of the nineteenth centuries, but long before then this north-eastern area of Scotland had figured in the story of Scotland's cattle. The long valleys of the Dee and the Don, with the passes north and south of the Cairngorm Mountains, gave ready access to the area from the wild hilly country which stretched from Badenoch to Lochaber and the West Coast, while the streams which feed the Dee on its right bank provided easy routes across the hills into the glens of Angus. The natural barrier of hills which stand round the head waters of the two rivers was thus less of a protection than a source of danger, and it was over paths trodden by centuries of raiding traffic that, when more peaceful times came, the drovers of north-east Scotland passed on their way to the trysts and their lawful occasions.

The sites chosen for the castles built at various dates on the banks of the Dee and the Don in the stormy days of Scotland's history, show how greatly the life of this area in early times was conditioned by the ready access offered by the hill passes and the valleys of the two rivers. On the Don the Castle of Corgarff guarded the upper valley of the river and the pass which leads from its head waters through the Forest of Glenavon to Speyside. A few miles down-stream Glenbucket Castle kept watch on tracks leading north-westward across the hills into Glenlivet and Lower Speyside, or northwards to the Deveron valley. Lower again the ancient Castle of Kildrummy dominated the low pass giving access to Strathbogie and the Moray coast. On Deeside, the site of Kindrochit Castle near Braemar controlled both the route leading from Badenoch and the West into the valley of the Dee and also the Cairnwell Pass which led from the Dee to the South, while down-stream the Castle of Aboyne guarded the crossings of the Dee, which gave access by hill passes to the glens of Angus.[1]

The historical records available do not make it possible to determine how early cattle breeding in this part of Scotland began, but there is no reason to doubt that on the pasture lands of what is now Morayshire, Banffshire, Aberdeenshire and Angus, cattle grazed from very early times. Certainly, by the middle of the fifteenth century, the cattle on the borders of Angus and Perthshire were of sufficient importance to attract unwelcome attention from their neighbours, and in 1454 a raid by the Munros of Foulis on Strathardle led to a fight near Inverness between them and the Mackintoshes of Moy, who had demanded a tribute or ' Road Collop' for the right of passage through their land of a large booty of cattle which the Munros were driving north.[2] By the sixteenth century, cattle trading in this area of eastern Scotland was evidently well established, for when at the end of the century the men of Skye and Kintail started to sell cattle, it was, as has been seen, to the markets of Glamis, Brechin and ' Ellit [Alyth] in the Bray of Angus' that they sent them. It was a precarious trade attended by heavy loss, for the route of the beasts took them through wild country whose inhabitants no doubt demanded some return for the right of passage, and if need be, took it by summary methods. Complaints of these cattle thefts found their way in due course to the Privy Council in Edinburgh, in common with similar tales of loss suffered by the people of Strathardle, Glen Isla and Glen Shee, for the eyes of the men of Atholl and Badenoch turned for their prey to these eastern glens.

Farther to the north, in Aberdeenshire, a regular trade in cattle had been established at least as early as the first quarter of the seventeenth century. An Order of the Privy Council in 1628 granted a weekly market a few miles north-west of Inverurie, and a further Order of the same year fixed the prices for goods, including cattle, at three fairs in the Aberdeenshire districts of Garioch and Strathbogie.[3] A description of Aberdeenshire and Banffshire compiled about the year 1662 notes the existence of a number of fairs covering the area, including fairs at Turriff on

[1] Simpson, *Early Castles of Mar.* Proceedings of Society of Scottish Antiquaries, 1928, LXIII, 102
[2] Mackenzie, *History of the Munros*, 25–6
[3] *R.P.C.*, 2nd series, II, 409, 616

Deveronside, Rayne in Garioch, Kincardine and Birse on Deeside and Deer in Buchan.[1] The contemporary description shows that horses, cattle and sheep were sold at these fairs, as well as home products and especially the webs of coarse woollen cloth in which the Aberdeenshire hand-loom weavers had established an early and prosperous trade.

While the amount of trade crossing the hills between Deeside and the South was at that time a mere fraction of what it was to become, a regular traffic over the passes certainly existed in the first half of the seventeenth century, and when about 1630 Sir James Balfour of Denmylne described ' the Chief Passages from the River Tay to the River Dee over the Mountains ' his list covered no less than eleven routes, including ' the Carnavalay [Cairnwell] from Glenshee to Castle Town in the Brae of Mar,' the Cairn-o-Mount Pass from Fettercairn to Kincardine o'Neil and routes from Glen Clova and Glen Esk to Glen Muick and Glen Tanar.[2] Sir James also listed the ' Passages over the River Dee by Boate,' and this shows thirteen crossing-places on the river between Braemar and the mouth including ferries at Braemar, Crathie, Abergeldie, Kincardine o'Neil, Banchory and Drum. Of the passes in use over the hills, the Cairn-o-Mount route was probably the most important, and in 1664 the Privy Council granted a Petition of Douglas, the Laird of Tilliquhillie near Banchory for a national contribution for the repair of the Bridge of Dee which had been destroyed by flood.[3] The Petition claimed that the bridge is the only ' hie passage mercat way ' for beasts and other traffic from north to south by way of Cairn-o-Mount, except by going twenty-four miles out of the ordinary way to Aberdeen. The use of the Cairn-o-Mount route for cattle traffic at this time is confirmed by a reference in the Acts of the Scots Parliament in 1681 to a toll on cattle passing over the Bridge of Dye.[4]

Throughout the first half of the eighteenth century, cattle breeding in the north-eastern counties of Scotland remained on a comparatively small scale. The agricultural developments which brought such big changes to the district were still to come, and in Aberdeenshire and along the coasts of Morayshire and Angus

---

[1] *Macfarlane's Geographical Collections*, II, 305
[2] National Library of Scotland, MS., 33.2.27
[3] *R.P.C.*, 3rd series, I, 519
[4] Fraser, *The Old Deeside Road*, 78-80

the farmers laboured on in a struggle to win a livelihood from land cultivated under a system whose only merit lay in its antiquity. Infield and outfield persisted, the infield in constant crop, enriched only by the manure of cattle which struggled half-starved through the winter, the outfield left fallow till the lapse of time should store enough fertility to grow a few successive crops of indifferent barley before it reverted to its fallow state. In Aberdeenshire, Banffshire and Kincardineshire, fields growing ten, fifteen or even more successive crops of grain were not uncommon as late as the closing years of the eighteenth century, and it is told of a Kincardineshire farmer that on being complimented on the good appearance of his crop he replied that it was no wonder seeing it was only the eighteenth crop since the field got dung.[1] Arable farming remained the chief activity, and with the six-, eight- and even ten-ox plough the universal method of cultivation, cattle were valued chiefly for their use as draught animals. As late as the end of the eighteenth century the minister of an Aberdeenshire parish recorded that of 953 cattle in the parish 346 were oxen for its 65 ploughs.[2] In the upland parts of these north-eastern counties some cattle breeding was carried on, and a small droving traffic passed over the old routes from Donside to Deeside and on across the hills to the markets of the Angus coast, to Crieff and the South; but this was on a small scale. Until well into the second half of the eighteenth century, though the payment of rents in money was becoming more common,[3] these continued to be paid largely in produce, a practice which forced the farmers to keep much of their land under cultivation. Moreover the risks of cattle breeding near the hills or cattle droving through them were great. Morayshire, Aberdeenshire and the Angus glens were still the hunting-ground of the cattle thieves in the country to the westward—'those wild scurrilous people among quhom ther is bot small fear or knowledge of God,' as Sir James Balfour called them, and when after 1746 the authorities set their minds to the task of bringing peace and security to the Highlands, the protection of this area from cattle raiding was one of their main preoccupations. The key to the problem lay in the guarding of a line running from Blair Atholl up the valley of the Perthshire Garry through the Pass of Drumochter to the Upper Spey, and

---

[1] Alexander, *Northern Rural Life in the 18th Century*, 23
[2] Alexander, op. cit., 71. Graham, *Social Life in Scotland in the 18th Century*, 156
[3] *O.S.A.*, King Edward, XI, 405

Plate 9   A drove route from Braemar : looking north from the Cairnwell Pass

(Photo by Robert M. Adam)

the securing of the glens and passes leading east of that line through the hills to the valleys of the Don and the Dee and the glens of Angus and Kincardineshire. Memoranda of 1744 and 1747 detail the measures proposed to check cattle thieving.[1] Small military detachments were to be posted at various points on a line between Blair Atholl in the south and Ruthven in the north, and at key-points to control such passes and inlets through which ' the thievish sett used to make their incursions.' [2] These points included Dalnacardoch and Dalwhinnie on either side of the Drumochter Pass, Glenfeshie and Glenclunie in the hills near the top of the Dee, Corgarff and Inchrory at the head waters of the Don, and Glenmuick and Glen Clova on the passes leading to Angus. In the Memorandum of 1747 the routes by which cattle were driven to the raiders' strongholds are described. From Angus and Kincardineshire the raiders passed with their stolen beasts, through Glen Clova, Glencallater and Glenclunie to Deeside and so up the south side of the Dee to the hills of the Atholl Forest, or crossing the Dee below Invercauld, they went by Glen Lui through the passes of the Cairngorms. Cattle stolen in the country between the Dee and the Don were driven through the Forest of Morven, up the valley of the Gairn and by way of Loch Builg into the valley of the Avon, and so to Speyside. The report of an officer in charge of the garrison at Corgarff in the years immediately following the Rising of 1745 described the route followed by raiders driving cattle from Banffshire.[3] Crossing the hills of the Cabrach at the head of the Deveron, they came by Glenbucket, Glen Nochty or Glen Ernan into Strathdon, then following the Don up-stream to its head waters, they passed by Inchrory into Glen Avon and so westward to the hills of Speyside and beyond. These routes which a hundred years earlier had known the hurried tread of the Macdonalds of Clanranald and Glen Garry, men from the Western Isles and men of Ulster who followed Montrose, led through high and rugged hill country calling for long forced marches with little rest or fodder for men or beasts till they reached uneasy sanctuary in the hills of Badenoch or Lochaber ; but the men who plied this trade were well accustomed to long marches and dangerous living, and it may be

[1] Spalding Club Miscellany II (1842), 85 ; New Spalding Club, *Historical Papers*, II, 490 et seq.
[2] Spalding Club Miscellany II (1842), 88
[3] New Spalding Club, *Historical Papers*, II, 506–8

doubted whether they found their lot more hard than did the English garrisons stationed after 1745 in remote outposts in the hills, and linked only by weekly patrols with other garrisons isolated in a wild and hostile countryside.[1]

The years which followed the Union of the Parliaments marked the beginning of great changes for Scotland's agriculture, and by the second half of the century an agricultural revolution was in full progress, the effects of which were nowhere more apparent than in these north-eastern counties. Hitherto arable farming had been their main activity, and even the cattle required for the heavy cumbrous ploughs which were then in use were largely imported from the counties south of the Tay. On the higher ground sheep were bred to supply the Aberdeenshire trade in woollen cloth and stockings, but cattle seem to have played a small part, and the droving traffic which crossed the hills south of the Dee remained of small proportions. ' Mr Hamilton, a steward of the Duke of Gordon's Estate of Strathbogie,' says a writer of 1811, ' was the first, it is believed, who attempted this adventurous expedition, which while then perhaps attended by advantages which exist not now, was counterbalanced also by corresponding inconveniences. The speculation was unprofitable to Mr Hamilton. He joined in the ruinous adventure with Prince Charles and in the rank of Governor of Carlisle exhibited a mournful example of the evils of revolution.' [2]

The mid years of the eighteenth century saw a great change. Improved methods of agriculture in Berwickshire and the Lothians turned the attention of the Lowland farmers from stock-raising to intensive crop-farming as a more profitable use of their rich soil, and this tended to push stock and particularly cattle-breeding farther and farther north. The trade in cloth and woollen goods which had hitherto been of importance to the north-east coast had suffered from the loss of Scotland's continental markets in which British foreign policy now involved her. The only markets now open to it were in England in direct competition with the growing English cloth industry which was

[1] A ' Memorandum concerning the Highlands,' dated 1746 pointed out that the difficulty of checking cattle thieving or of tracing those responsible lay partly in the unwillingness of witnesses to give evidence which would lay them and their goods open to the revenge of the raiders, and partly in the cost of criminal prosecution. This was estimated at £25, few of those seeking justice being themselves possessed of goods or property exceeding £40. (*Breadalbane Papers (Roads)*, Box 4, H.M. Register House)

[2] Leslie, *General View of the Agriculture of Nairn and Moray*, 1811, 303–4

stimulated by the settlement in East Anglia of immigrant workers from the Netherlands. Britain's foreign wars meant a growing demand for cattle, while the settlement of the Highlands after 1745 and the end of the long tradition of cattle thieving meant that now stock-breeding and the traffic in beasts through the hills had at last been rid of one of its main risks and deterrents. The improved methods of farming which were to spread so rapidly during the next half-century were already having their effect. The sowing of rye grass and clover was being practised in Kincardineshire by 1752,[1] and with the increase in the enclosing of pasture ground, stock-raising took a great step forward. The Rebellion of 1745 caused a shortage of cattle in the Highlands. It is said that after the Battle of Culloden the Duke of Cumberland's soldiers drove in a herd of 20,000 cattle from the surrounding districts,[2] and this, aided by serious cattle disease in England in 1746 and 1762, caused a steady rise in price, a rise which with minor fluctuations, was to continue all through the Napoleonic Wars. English cattle dealers started to come to the markets of Central Scotland in search of beasts in 1766, and Scottish drovers and dealers soon entered the trade in competition with them. This date may be taken as marking the beginning of droving on a large scale not only from the north-eastern counties but from all the cattle-breeding areas of Scotland, and from that time on the demand for Scottish cattle was steady and urgent.[3] So the farmers of the north-eastern counties came more and more to be drawn into the cattle trade, and from then on each year saw increasing numbers of their beasts brought for sale to the Tryst at Falkirk.

The north-eastern corner of Scotland now under consideration can be divided roughly into three sections. Of these, the most easterly consists of a relatively flat coastal plain stretching south from Banff and Fraserburgh on the Moray Firth to Stonehaven and the coast of Angus. To the west of this Lowland section a belt of hilly but not mountainous country extends south from Banff and the mouth of the Spey to Kirriemuir and Brechin in Angus, including in its area the valleys of the Deveron and its tributaries and the middle courses of the Don and the Dee. Westward again, from Elgin and Forres in the Morayshire plain

---

[1] Donaldson, *General View of the Agriculture of Kincardine*, 1795, 21
[2] McIan and Logan, *Highlanders at Home*, 1848, 72
[3] Keith, *General View of the Agriculture of Aberdeenshire*, 1811, 460–1

a belt of high and mountainous land stretches south to Blair-gowrie, Dunkeld and the valley of the lower Tay. Within this area are included the middle reaches of the Spey, the Cairngorm Mountains, the forests of Glenavon, Mar and Atholl and the high hills which stand round the head waters of the Don and the Dee.

The difficulties of the task of tracing today the drove roads of these several areas is determined largely by the nature of the country through which they passed. On the coastal plain the routes which linked the cattle grazings and markets of north Aberdeenshire with the markets of Central Scotland, were influenced less by the physical difficulties of the ground than by the need to avoid enclosed land. Many alternative routes were open, but with the steady growth of cultivation and enclosing in the latter part of the eighteenth century the cattle traffic came more and more to be confined to the recognised roads. Here, as the years went by, the traces and finally the memory of its passing became increasingly overlaid and obliterated by the growing traffic of a later age. In the hilly area immediately to the westward, the routes of the droves were determined to some extent by the nature of the country, by the glens and the low upland passes, but here the hills were not so high that alternative routes over them could not in places be chosen, and many of these, untouched by changing times and more recent traffic, retain the tradition and the clear record of the droving age. Only in the mountainous country on the extreme west of the area were the routes of the drovers strictly confined to mountain glens and passes, routes which remain to this day the only practicable ways through the region, used through successive centuries by raiders and soldiers, by pedlars and merchants and now by shepherds and hill walkers of a more peaceful age.

The establishment of local fairs in Aberdeenshire, which had begun to receive statutory recognition as early as 1628, continued all through the seventeenth century, and a list of fairs in the county in 1727 contains over fifty names.[1] The names, most of which commemorate festivals of the Church, cover the whole county,[2] but many were in the Lowland districts of Buchan, Garioch and Formartine ; at Fraserburgh and Old Deer in Buchan ; at Tarves, Methlick and Ellon in the valley of the Ythan, and at

[1] Smith, *The Exact Dealer's Companion*, 1727
[2] *Macfarlane's Geographical Collections*, II, 305

Rayne, Inverurie and Monymusk, where the Don and its tributaries emerge from the hills into the rich pasture land of the coastal plain. By the end of the century, a great network of small markets covered the county for the sale of cattle which were collected by the dealers into droves for the markets of the South. Of all these, the Fair of St Lawrence at Rayne dating back to the early seventeenth century was probably one of the oldest, while the market known as Aikey Fair at Old Deer in Buchan was, by the end of the eighteenth century, one of the largest in the north of Scotland. The exact routes followed on the north side of the Dee by these cattle from north and east Aberdeenshire on their way to Angus and the South, are for reasons already suggested now difficult to determine, but it is certain that these were influenced largely by the crossings of the Dee and the passes through the hills on its south bank. A bridge over the Dee had existed at Aberdeen since the end of the first quarter of the sixteenth century, and a ferry at about the same point was still in use in the seventeenth century.[1] Some cattle no doubt crossed at or near Aberdeen and followed the coast making for Stonehaven ; but dislike of tolls and thickly populated parts and a preference for hill routes no doubt influenced the drovers in Aberdeenshire as elsewhere, and all the indications are that the bulk of the cattle crossed the river farther to the west. A bridge at Banchory existed at least as early as 1664, and near Drum, ten miles down-stream, were important crossing-places either by ford or by the ferry mentioned in Sir James Balfour's list of 1630.[2] To reach these points, the route of the north and east Aberdeenshire cattle was probably by Inverurie and Kintore on the Lower Don and so south to Deeside. Cattle crossing the Dee about Drum would cross the hills on the south side of the river by the route known as the Slug Road to Stonehaven or by the old route known as the Cryne's Cross Mounth,[3] the route by which Montrose went north to Deeside in September 1644 after the Battle of Tippermuir. This route led from near Durris over the hills to Fordoun in Kincardineshire, where a tryst of some importance —the Fair of St Palladeous or ' Paldy Fair '—had long been established. Donaldson in his *General View of the Agriculture of Kincardineshire* in 1795, describes the Fordoun cattle fair as the most important in the county, as many as 3,000 cattle

---

[1] Fraser, *The Old Deeside Road*, 61n and 69   [2] ibid., 66
[3] Simpson, *Early Castles of Mar*, 123-4, 133

being sold here in July each year, mostly from the North. Traffic crossing at Banchory used the important Cairn-o-Mount Pass to Fettercairn, Edzell and Brechin, while a subsidiary route, the Stock Mounth, branched off the Cairn-o-Mount Road at the village of Strachan, and crossed into Glenbervie giving further access to Fordoun and the coast.

While a substantial part of the droving traffic from the north-east thus found its way to the South by routes crossing the Dee between Banchory and the mouth of the river, it seems probable that many, if not most, of the important drove roads passed through the belt of hilly country immediately to the west. The description of Aberdeenshire and Banffshire about 1662 already referred to and the 1727 list of Fairs in Scotland[1] show the existence at these dates of cattle fairs in Strathisla, Strathbogie and Strathdon, and in the hilly country lying between Don and Dee, and with the stimulus to cattle-breeding which came to Aberdeenshire in the second half of the eighteenth century, the rich grazing of these districts became of increasing importance. This upland country, grassy, well watered and largely unenclosed was ideal for droving, and during the years from 1750 to 1830 when droving from the north-east was at its height, a large and steady stream of cattle found its way to the South by routes which crossed the Dee at points between Braemar and Kincardine o'Neil. Till the middle of the eighteenth century, the chief crossings on this stretch of the river appear to have been ferries at Braemar, Crathie, Abergeldie, Ballater, Glentanar Church and at Kincardine o'Neil.[2] Bridges were added at Invercauld in 1752 and Ballater in 1783, while in 1814 the important bridge at Potarch, near Kincardine o'Neil, was built by the Commissioners for Highland Roads and Bridges.[3] These crossings of

---

[1] Smith, op. cit.   [2] Fraser, op. cit., 60-5

[3] H.R. & B., 6th Report, 1813

The building of the bridge at Potarch met with considerable difficulties. Two of the arches had already been completed and the central arch was nearing completion when a large part of the work was swept away by cut timber which was being floated down from the upper reaches of the Dee. The loss to the contractor was reduced by public subscription and a contribution from the Commissioners, and the accident resulted in the passing in 1813 of an Act for regulating the floating of timber during the spring and summer months. The large rivers of Scotland appear to have been extensively used for the floating of timber during the eighteenth century. The York Buildings Company who purchased woods on Speyside in 1728 are said to have introduced the practice of floating cut timber on that river in the form of rafts, and Mrs Grant of Rothiemurchus has described the floating of timber on tributaries of the Upper Spey. According to the New Statistical Account for Glenorchy, an Irish Company which leased the woods in Glen Strae, Glen Orchy and Glen Lochy in

the river all gave easy access to passes over the hills to Kincardine-shire and Angus, and it was on these points that the drove roads on the north side of the Dee concentrated.

The crossings of the Dee at Kincardine o'Neil and Potarch were important ones, giving access to the Cairn-o-Mount Pass through which the Banchory traffic also passed. To Kincardine o'Neil came cattle from the Alford district of Strathdon and the country to the north, crossing the Don at the Boat of Forbes at Alford. For cattle from Strathisla in Banffshire and much of the Deveron Valley, the route to the South was easy and direct. Ascending the valley of the Bogie from Huntly to Auchindoir, the site of an early eighteenth-century fair, they crossed the low uplands which lie between Strathbogie and Strathdon and came by Kildrummy to Donside, making for Ballater, Dinnet or Aboyne.

In the twelve miles of the Don which lie immediately up-stream from the old castle of Kildrummy were the crossing-places for a large volume of droving traffic from the North. As the river winds among the steep rounded shoulders of the surrounding hills, it receives on the north side the waters of three considerable tributaries, the Bucket, the Nochty and the Ernan. Down Glen-bucket came cattle from the Cabrach and the upper valley of the Deveron.[1] The route is shown on Roy's map of 1747. It was used by eighteenth-century cattle raiders returning from Banff-shire, and it was not till the second half of the century that the glen knew more peaceful times, for here was the home of ' Old Glenbuchat' whose implication in the troubles of 1715 and 1745 cost him his lands, his whole estate and all but his life. By Glen-bucket, too, came drovers from the Lower Spey valley, ascending Glen Livet and crossing into Aberdeenshire over the high ridge known as The Ladder. These latter drovers had a choice of alternative routes down to the banks of the Don, for from the ridge they could reach the river by Glen Nochty or by Glen-Ernan, in each case following tracks marked out by the raiding traffic of other days.

[1] *The Book of Glenbuchat*, Third Spalding Club, 1942, 39-40

the eighteenth century floated the timber down the River Orchy to Loch Awe where it was sawn and made into rafts for floating to the Pass of Brander. From there it was carted to Bonawe on Loch Etive. (Murray, *The York Buildings Company*, 60-1. Larkin, *A Tour in the Highlands*, 1818, 330. Mrs Grant of Rothiemurchus, *Memoirs of a Highland Lady*, 1807, 1898 edn., 200-5)

The immediate destinations of these drovers from Banffshire and East Morayshire were the crossings of the Dee at or between Aboyne and Ballater. To reach these points on Deeside their route lay up the glen of the Deskry Water, crossing the ridge into Deeside in the Parish of Logie Coldstone to the north of Dinnet. This, one of the busiest of the drove roads between Don and Dee, remained in active use till well on in the second half of last century, and there are those still (1948) living on Donside who remember seeing the cattle climbing to the watershed and resting at the stance at Badnogoach near the top of the Deskry Water, some distance to the west of the present road. At the top of the ridge, some may have chosen the route through Tarland to Aboyne, but it seems that many skirted the east shoulder of the hill of Morven by the old drove road, traces of which are still to be seen on the side of Culblean Hill, making for Milton of Tullich and the crossing of the Dee at Ballater.[1]

For the droves which reached the Dee at Aboyne several alternative routes were open through the hills to Angus. The old tracks known as the Fungle Road and the Firmounth Road linked Deeside with Glen Esk by way of the Forest of Birse, while farther to the west an important route led up Glen Tanar, crossing the west shoulder of Mount Keen before descending into Glen Mark at the head of the North Esk. A writer of this century has recorded that within living memory this road was much used by bands of men and women going to the south country for the harvesting.

For the droves which crossed the Dee at Ballater the main route was through Glen Muick, and so over the pass known as the Capel Mount to the top of Glen Clova and the valley of the South Esk. Glen Muick, as has been seen, was chosen in 1747 as a point for one of the military posts stationed in the hills. It seems therefore probable that this was one of the routes of the eighteenth-century cattle raiders, and the testimony of old drovers and shepherds giving evidence before the Courts in 1887 shows it in active use in the first half of the nineteenth century for droves of cattle bound for Falkirk Tryst.[2]

The survey of the drove roads from the north-east which has

---

[1] Fraser, *An Old Drove Road over Culblean*. Aberdeen Free Press, 7 June 1921.
[2] *Scottish Rights of Way Society* v. *Macpherson*, Court of Session Cases, 1887, 14 Rettie's Reports, 875 and Notes of Evidence in *Session Papers*, Signet Library, 730, 165-89.

Plate 10   A drove route from the North-east :   in Glen Fernate

(Photo by Robert M. Adam)

been attempted has covered the lowland part of the district and the upland country immediately to the west. It remains to trace the cattle routes which threaded their way through the great hills surrounding the head waters of the two rivers and the high ground lying to the south. For all this traffic the key-point was the crossing of the Dee at or about Braemar. Here was the meeting-point of the droving routes through the high hills now to be considered.

It has been seen that cattle from that part of Speyside which lies between Grantown and Craigellachie had access to the south by way of Glenavon, and that many went up Glenlivet crossing the hills to Strathdon on their way to Ballater and Aboyne ; but for these Speyside cattle a more direct route was open to the South, and there is evidence to show that, at least in the later years of the droving period, a part of the droving traffic preferred it. This route continued up the Avon to Tomintoul where, turning to the south-east, it followed the line of the military road built by the Hanoverian Government in 1754 and crossed the Don near the old castle of Corgarff, making for Crathie and Braemar. Some drovers might prefer to follow up the Avon to Inchrory, where the river turns to the west, continuing south by Loch Builg and Monaltrie Moss to Invercauld. This latter route was one of those mentioned in 1747 as in use by cattle thieves returning from raids farther to the east,[1] and an old drover still living (1948) on Donside remembers it in active use for sheep traffic, the beasts resting for the night beside Loch Builg. From the higher reaches of the Spey, about Nethy Bridge and Aviemore, led the high passes through the Cairngorms known as the Lairig Ghru and the Lairig an Laoigh, leading to the Dee by Glen Dee and Glen Lui and so to Braemar. These also are mentioned as in use by the cattle thieves of the mid-eighteenth century.[2] The Glen Dee route was in use in 1846 for bringing sheep which had come from Skye by way of Fort Augustus and Corrieyairack. According to local evidence the route through the Lairig Ghru continued to be used for cattle bound for Braemar and the South till about 1873, and people now living in the Rothiemurchus district of Speyside can recall that, until that date, men were sent up the Cairngorm passes each spring to clear from the tracks boulders moved by the winter frosts.

[1] New Spalding Club, *Historical Papers*, II, 493-4
[2] New Spalding Club, op. cit., 507

One more completes the tale of the main routes by which the droving traffic converged on Braemar. A few miles up-stream from Aviemore, the Spey receives the waters of the River Feshie running through the long glen which drains the south-west slopes of the Cairngorm Mountains. Twelve miles up the glen, where the burn divides, a low pass leads over the Aberdeenshire border into Glen Geldie and so to Braemar and the valley of the Dee, while to the south lie open the routes through Glen Tilt to Blair Atholl or by Glen Fernate to Kirkmichael. Wade planned a road through Glen Feshie after 1734 to link the barracks at Ruthven with Braemar, though this was never made,[1] and the establishment of a garrison in Glen Feshie in 1747 shows it to have been recognised at that date as a raider's route. A cattle tryst at the head of Glen Geldie is traditionally believed to have been an early forerunner of the great trysts of the eighteenth and nineteenth centuries.[2] According to local tradition the market was held on the extensive and flat top of An Sgarsoch, a grassy hill of over three thousand feet which stands about three miles to the south of the upper reaches of the Geldie Burn. The evidence of those who have visited the site bears out the existence of clear traces that the top of the hill was once used for some human purpose, though the site appears never to have been examined in detail. The position of An Sgarsoch suggests that its use for the assembling of livestock may date back to a period when freedom from surprise or attack was an important consideration.[3]

In the 1887 litigation already referred to, the evidence of drovers who appeared before the Court suggests that the route through Glen Feshie and Glen Geldie was in regular use till the middle of last century. It is probable that some droving traffic bound from Upper Speyside for Crieff and Falkirk also used the route leading from Glentromie over the Minigeig Pass into Glenbruar. In the second half of the eighteenth century this route was frequently urged as suitable for the construction of a military road. It is marked on a map of 1733 as ' The summer road to Ruthven ' and was probably one of the routes surveyed by Wade between 1723 and 1740. Evidence as to the use of the Glen Tilt route by droving traffic is not so clear. In an action which was brought before the Court of Session in 1849 to have

---

[1] Salmond, *Wade in Scotland*, 252
[2] Fraser, op. cit., 93. Salmond, op. cit., 253
[3] *Cairngorm Club Journal*, VIII, 166–9, 215–6 and 262–5

this route to Blair Atholl established as a right of way, the Pursuer's case was based partly on the use of the route by droving traffic. No hearing of evidence before the Court appears to have followed, while the statements of witnesses which were at that time taken. and subsequently lodged with the Court are now missing.[1] Such local evidence as is available seems to indicate, however, that the Glen Tilt route, perhaps owing to the narrowness and difficulty of the glen, was not extensively used for droving traffic, the route by Glen Fernate being preferred.

From Braemar the routes to the South were easy. The route up Glen Clunie and over the Cairnwell Pass to Glen Shee and Strathardle had for centuries been one of the main links between Deeside and the South, and a long chain of evidence stretching from the Register of the Privy Council, through the Statistical Accounts and the records of early nineteenth-century travellers, shows it to have been in constant use by the varied traffic of four centuries. A subsidiary, but for the drovers an important route, branches off the Cairnwell road in Glenclunie and leads by Glen-callater into Glen Clova and Angus, while near the summit of the Cairnwell road a further route branches off to the south-east and crosses the hills at an altitude of over 3,000 feet to reach the head-waters of the Isla. Though not mentioned in Sir James Balfour's list of roads over the hills to Deeside, the Glencallater route, or the Tolmount route as it was later called, was in use by cattle raiders in the early eighteenth century, and in the litigation of 1887 which finally established it as a right of way, the evidence of witnesses drawn from personal recollection stretching back to the early years of the century, shows it then carrying a steady traffic of cattle and sheep from Aberdeenshire, from Ross-shire and even from Skye.[2]

The comparative scarcity of detail available as to the routes followed by the cattle of the north-eastern counties after crossing the hills south of the Dee again illustrates the difficulty of tracing the routes of such traffic in populous or well-cultivated country. For those beasts which crossed into Perthshire by the Cairnwell Pass, it seems probable that the route most commonly used, instead of continuing down Glen Shee to Blairgowrie, branched south-west at the Spittal of Glen Shee and crossed the hills to

[1] *Torrie* v. *Duke of Athol*, Court of Session Cases, 1849, 12 Dunlop's Report, 328
[2] *Scottish Rights of Way Society* v. *Macpherson*, Court of Session Cases, 1887, 14 Rettie's Reports

Enochdhu and Kirkmichael in Strathardle. In the Statistical Account for the Parish of Kirkmichael, the writer of the Account refers to two fairs held annually at the Spittal of Glen Shee and one at Kirkmichael, of which the latter was, in the middle of the eighteenth century, one of the principal cattle markets in the kingdom, lasting for several days and sometimes a week.[1] Sir J. D. Marwick in his *List of Fairs and Markets held in Scotland*, refers to Kirkmichael as the meeting-place of two routes over the hills—the route over the Cairnwell Pass from Braemar and that through Glen Fernate.[2] Some further confirmation that this route by Kirkmichael was commonly used by beasts from the north and north-east comes from the Reports of the Commissioners for Highland Roads and Bridges. A Memorial addressed to the Commissioners had urged the construction of a road from Dunkeld to Kirkmichael, and in their Fifth Report published in 1811, the Commissioners recommended that this road should be extended to join the road from Braemar near the Spittal of Glen Shee. This proposed route would give the drovers of Aberdeenshire and the north-east direct access to Crieff through open grazing country, so saving in distance and avoiding the inconvenience of passing through enclosed and populous country.[3]

As to the route of cattle after passing Kirkmichael, the local evidence available shows general agreement that the bulk of the traffic went south-west up Glen Derby and, crossing the hills by way of Loch Broom, came into the valley of the Tummel a short distance north of its junction with the Tay. The droves are believed to have crossed the Tummel just north of Ballinluig, and the Tay by a ford called ' Stair Cham ' or ' Crooked Stepping Stones ' near Logierait, continuing in a south-westerly direction across the hills by Loch Skaich to the top of Strath Bran and Amulree. Whether many of the droves which reached the Tay at Ballinluig continued down the river is not quite certain, but Larkin, writing in 1818, speaks of six annual fairs at Dunkeld, of which the one held at Martinmas was a great market for cattle.[4]

Of the beasts which crossed into Angus and Kincardineshire by

---

[1] *O.S.A.*, Kirkmichael, XV, 514
[2] Marwick, *List of Fairs and Markets held in Scotland*, 77
[3] *H.R. & B.*, 5th Report, 16
[4] Larkin, *A Tour in the Highlands in 1818*, 350

passes farther to the east and by the great Cairn-o-mount route, some no doubt moved west by Kirriemuir and Blairgowrie, crossing the Tay at Dunkeld on their way to Crieff and Falkirk by way of Strath Bran and the Sma' Glen, but it seems probable that many, like the Aberdeenshire drover so hard hit by the Peace in 1815, continued south to Perth, entering Strathearn at its eastern end.[1] From here, those bound for Falkirk would take the route by Sheriffmuir and Stirling, or the short cut by Gleneagles and Glendevon and other routes across the Ochils used by some of the cattle from Crieff and the Sma' Glen. It may be that part of the traffic from the north-eastern counties bypassed the Falkirk Tryst, going direct to the markets of Edinburgh. For these beasts the crossing of the Ochils would be made by Glen Farg on the road to North Queensferry, and descriptions of the Forth crossing in the first half of last century refer to the number of cattle which were at times shipped across, not without accident. The Statistical Account of Inverkeithing refers to the loss of a ferry boat loaded with black cattle,[2] and a traveller in 1802 describing the crossing of the Forth recommends that ' when the boats are loaded with black cattle passengers ought to avoid them lest any sudden squall should upset them and endanger their lives.'[3]

All through the latter part of the eighteenth century, the cattle trade from the north-eastern counties grew steadily and in the early years of last century reached very large proportions. The improvement in agricultural methods which brought this about brought with it, however, other changes which were to mean the ultimate decay of the droving trade, and the first half of the nineteenth century saw in the north-east a change from cattle breeding to cattle fattening, a change which called for the

[1] About a mile to the north of Brechin in the neighbourhood of the village of Little Brechin wide trackways or ' raiks ' of turf with a ditch on either side are still to be seen. These are the remnants of drove roads leading to Trinity Tryst, an ancient tryst still held annually, which was at one time an important market on the drove road from Kincardineshire to Perth. ' This unique track, which averages a hundred feet in width, stretches for over a mile, between Findowrie and Little Brechin, and for centuries was part of the great drove road for Highland cattle coming over the Cairn o' Mounth. The once famous Trinity Tryst, on the Muir of Brechin, was the first lowland market for the distribution of these cattle, which were driven south annually in immense herds. Fifty years ago, I have seen the entire roadway of ten miles, between Fettercairn and Brechin, literally blocked for some days before the Tryst with thousands of black horned cattle, which were driven by unkempt Celts, who shouted and swore in Gaelic.' (Don, *Archaeological Notes on Early Scotland*, 42)

[2] *O.S.A.*, Inverkeithing, X, 506
[3] Campbell, *Journey from Edinburgh through parts of North Britain*, 1802, II, 82

quicker and easier forms of transport which were by then becoming available ; but consideration of the factors which meant the end of droving belongs to another chapter. It has no place in the story of how, by routes trodden in times past by Roman legions and English armies, by Highland raiders and by Montrose's men, the cattle of the north-east came to the Lowland trysts.

8

THE TRYSTS

THE holding of fairs and markets has from a very early stage
in the development of civilised life been a necessity common to
all countries and all peoples. In every part of the world so soon
as civilisation passed beyond the most primitive stage of isolation
and self-sufficiency, demand arose for goods not produced locally
or for others calling for division of labour, and with that demand
came the need for means of distribution. In an age long before
the development of adequate communication by road, the only
solution lay in the establishment by custom of convenient and
central points where local products could be disposed of, and those
from surrounding districts acquired. The development of such a
system among the early peoples of China, India, Egypt, Africa
and South America shows it to have been in every land the
outcome of fundamental needs and conditions, in no way influenced
by the customs of others, but common to all. In Europe, as
elsewhere, such a development took place and the great fairs of
Nijni Novgorod, Leipzig and Frankfurt, which have continued in
flourishing existence up to modern times, trace their direct
descent through many centuries. The sites of these great fairs
were chosen for their ease of access for buyers and sellers, by the
sides of large rivers, or at the meeting place of caravan and
trading routes. The dates, too, were determined by common
needs. Many of the great fairs were held in the late summer or
in autumn when the products of harvest were available, when
livestock nourished by the summer grazing were in a fit state to
travel, and when men must lay in goods and stores for the winter.[1]

To the fairs and markets established in these islands from
early times, the same general characteristics apply. The dates
for the holding of fairs seem at first to have been fixed where
possible to coincide with local or national festivals, but as the
influence of the Church increased fairs became more and more
associated with religious festivals and the Feast Days of the Patron
Saints, the protection and patronage of the Church being shown
in the names by which many of these fairs for long were known.

Nowhere were fairs more sorely needed than in Scotland

[1] Marwick, *List of Fairs and Markets held in Scotland*, Introd.

where mountain, river and sea and the absence of roads divided the country into isolated regions. The holding of fairs and markets had long been a monopoly of the burghs. This was a privilege jealously guarded, and the establishment of markets outside the burgh and in the remoter districts where they were most needed was achieved only gradually in the face of the bitter opposition of the burghal interests.[1] Till well on in the eighteenth century, cattle, hides, timber and salmon were the main exportable products of the Highlands, and to the cattle breeder the existence of fairs at times suited to the needs of his trade and at points convenient alike to buyer and seller, was of supreme importance. Local markets were needed where cattle from the glens, the coastal pasture lands and the hills could be collected for transport to the Lowlands, while larger markets were needed at central points nearer more populous areas.

While the origin of many of these local fairs lies far back in Scottish history, for the purpose of tracing the growth of the droving trade it is hardly necessary to attempt to follow their development back further than the latter part of the sixteenth century, when clear records of regular cattle droving make what is probably their earliest appearance. By that date, cattle from northern and western districts were already being driven to markets in the eastern half of Scotland. Fairs for their sale were then, as has been seen, in existence at Elycht [Alyth], Brechin and Forfar, while at least as early as the first half of the seventeenth century cattle fairs also existed in the Garioch and Buchan districts of Aberdeenshire [2] and at Dumfries.

In the early grants by the Crown or Privy Council conferring rights to hold annual or periodical sales, these are generally described as 'fairs' or 'markets,' and it seems that the name 'tryst,' derived probably from the old word 'triste' or 'trust,' only at a later date came into general use. The name was appropriate for the meeting-place of merchants and customers, and particularly for cattle dealers who 'trysted' the owners of beasts to meet them at an agreed place for the sale of their cattle. What is possibly the earliest known use of the word as meaning a fair occurs in a verse attributed to Thomas the Rhymer :

> 'I neither dought to buy or sell
> At fair or tryst where I may be.' [3]

[1] Mackenzie, *The Scottish Burghs*, 88–95   [2] *R.P.C.*, 2nd series, II, 409, 616
[3] Scott, *Minstrelsy of the Scottish Border*, 1st edn., 1802–3, I, xviii

While the words ' tryst,' ' market ' and ' fair ' were used somewhat indiscriminately by contemporary writers, it would seem
that as a general, though not invariable rule, ' tryst ' indicated a
market established by agreement between buyers and sellers,
while ' fair ' meant one established by public authority or Crown
grant, ' market ' probably applying to both. At least as early
as the beginning of the eighteenth century the word ' tryst '
came into fairly general use to describe these meeting-places,
and from then on though some continued to be known merely as
' markets ' or ' fairs ' many, and particularly the larger ones,
were commonly known as ' trysts.'

The early cattle markets were scattered and probably of no
great size, but till near the end of the seventeenth century they
sufficed. The Union of the Crowns in 1603 had had little
immediate effect in improving the political or commercial relations
of Scotland and England, and the trade passing between the two
countries continued to be regulated by few considerations other
than the individual and immediate needs of each. In 1669,
however, all export and import duties on cattle going to England
were abolished,[1] and the appointment in 1680 of a Commission
for the encouragement of trade between the two countries marked
the approach of new and better times.[2]

The change in the commercial relations of Scotland and
England coincides very closely with the confirmation by Act of
Parliament of 1672 to James, Earl of Perth, of the right to hold
' ane yeirlie fair and weiklie mercat ' at Crieff, a coincidence in
which it is probable that mere chance played little part.[3] For
with the steady increase of cattle traffic to the South, the need
had arisen for the concentration of the trade at some central
point where buyers and sellers could easily come together, a
need which the scattered local markets hitherto in existence could
not meet. Crieff, like Perth, lies at the gateway of the Highlands,
where the Grampians fall to the valley of Strathearn, and at the
northern edge of one of the richest and most populous parts of
Scotland. For the cattle trade Crieff possessed advantages which
Perth did not offer. The traditional route for cattle from the
North lay, as has been seen, by Dalnacardoch to Tummel Bridge
and Kenmore and so through the Sma' Glen, while cattle from
parts of Morayshire and Aberdeenshire had easy access by the

[1] *R.P.C.*, 3rd series, III, 16   [2] *R.P.C.*, 3rd series, VI, 431, 432
[3] *A.P.S.*, VIII, 65

passes south of the Dee to the valley of the Tay and thence, avoiding the more populous districts, through Strath Bran to join the same route at Amulree. For cattle from Skye and most of the Outer Isles the route across the western edge of the Moor of Rannoch led them easily to Crieff by Loch Tay and Loch Earn, while drovers from Argyll could, if they wished, reach the same point by way of Glen Dochart and Loch Earn. Here, then, was a natural gathering point for beasts from the Highlands, while affording easy access to dealers coming from the South or to those returning with stock for the markets of England. It was for these reasons that at the end of the seventeenth century Crieff became the greatest cattle market in Scotland, a position which it retained for well over half a century.[1]

The growth of the Crieff Cattle Tryst must have been rapid, for when Macky visited it in 1723 the number of cattle reported by him as having been sold there that autumn was 30,000, the total price being about 30,000 guineas,[2] many of the beasts being driven on to England by Highland drovers who, according to Macky's description, hired themselves at 1s a day for the southward journey, returning at their own expense. The market took place in the second week of October each year, a date which forced those bringing cattle from the north and west to dispose of them or face the hazardous alternative of driving them on, so late in the year, to seek other markets farther south. The market was under the control and patronage of the Earl of Perth, who held a court for the purpose of regulating disputes which might arise and for keeping order. Certain of his feuars were bound by their charters to act as guards for policing the market, and as late as the time of the New Statistical Account, though Crieff Tryst had come to an end nearly eighty years earlier, these services had not long since ceased to be exacted.[3] While the Earl of Perth's court may have been effective in preventing trouble on the tryst ground itself, it appears to have had a very limited jurisdiction. The writer of the New Statistical Account of the Parish of Monzie, describing the past glories of Crieff Tryst, reported that when the market was at its height the inhabitants

---

[1] The position of Crieff at the border of Highlands and Lowlands which made it so suitable as a centre for the cattle trade in the early eighteenth century made it also a potential centre of political trouble and intrigue. Despite the presence of Hanoverian troops at the Autumn Tryst of 1714 quarrels occurred which only the close of the market prevented from anticipating by one year the troubles which were so soon to overtake Strathearn. (Millar, *History of Rob Roy*)

[2] Macky, *Journey through Scotland*, 1723, 190   [3] *N.S.A.*, Crieff, X, 525

of the surrounding country went in fear of their lives from the Highland drovers who broke into their houses, forcibly billeting themselves, and often carried off part of the household goods.[1] Yet despite this, the passing of Crieff Tryst was a cause of local regret, and the Rev. Robert Taylor, who compiled the Statistical Account of Crieff in 1794, reported that ' The old people here sometimes speak with deep regret of the glorious scene displayed to view when 30,000 black cattle in different droves overspread the whole adjacent country for several miles round the town.' [2] In return for his patronage of the market, the Earl of Perth was entitled to the market dues amounting to 2d per beast, but the right of collecting these was let by him for a yearly sum of £600 Scots (£50 sterling) to a tenant who made what he could on the transaction.[3] Much of the trade was done by means of bills, and during the second quarter of the century Crieff came to be regarded as one of the main financial centres of Scotland. Considerable sums, however, also changed hands in the form of gold as Macky has described, and an entry in the Minute Book of the Royal Bank of Scotland in 1730 shows that tellers were that year sent from Edinburgh to Crieff with £3,000 in notes to put into circulation in return for cash.[4]

The Rising of 1745 seems not to have affected Crieff Tryst seriously, for a Dumfriesshire cattle dealer writing to his partner in 1746 refers to a rival having gone to Crieff to buy several thousand beasts,[5] and references by the commanders of English garrisons stationed in the Highlands immediately after the Rising to thefts of cattle on their way to Crieff show that the troubles of the times had not deterred some at least of the drovers.[6] The Rising had, however, a more serious if less immediate effect on Crieff Tryst. Hitherto the trade with England in Scots cattle had been largely in the hands of Scotsmen. The more peaceful times and the higher cattle prices which followed the failure of the Rising brought English dealers increasingly to the Scots cattle markets after the middle of the century to share directly in the trade. This in turn meant the need for a market more convenient to them, and in conjunction with the increasing cost of droving and the need to adopt the quickest routes to market, led to the

[1] *N.S.A.*, Monzie, X, 270   [2] *O.S.A.*, Crieff, IX, 596   [3] ibid.
[4] Munro, *History of the Royal Bank of Scotland, 1727–1927*, 105
[5] Letters of Thomas Bell, in *Reid's Calendar of Documents found at Dumfries*, H.M. Register House
[6] New Spalding Club, *Historical Papers*, (1699–1750), II, 524, 540 and 582

eventual eclipse of Crieff by Falkirk, which remained till the end of the cattle-droving industry the greatest cattle tryst in Scotland.

The early history of the cattle market which came to be known as the ' Falkirk Tryst ' is obscure, but in the complex legal proceedings between 1761 and 1772 which led up to the division of the Commonties of Whitesiderigg and Reddingsrigg near Falkirk, where the market was originally held, the evidence of witnesses traced it back to the years immediately following the Union of 1707.[1] The Tryst at Falkirk was never a statutory fair. The process in connection with the division of the commonties states that it ' was originally constituted and has since been kept up by advertisements in the newspapers or other notices given to the public that a tryst was to be held at Falkirk upon such a day to which all dealers in cattle, buyers and sellers, are invited, the proprietors of the land to give a proper stand for the cattle, security and protection as far as they can and that all comers will have entertainment at reasonable rates. . . . It stands confessed and is proved that these trysts have uniformly been kept upon these muirs immediately above the town of Falkirk at least from 1716.' The documents in connection with the division also show from 1717 the names of the tacksmen who collected on behalf of the Duke of Hamilton tolls from cattle coming to the market, and in writing of his tour of Scotland in 1747 Pococke tells of having been turned off the road by droves on their way to Falkirk.[2]

Shortly after the division of the commonties the market was moved to a site called Rough Castle to the west of Falkirk. ' From time immemorial,' wrote Nimmo in 1777, ' the Highlands of Scotland which in few places are capable of culture have produced great quantities of cattle ; these though of a small size when fattened upon richer pastures are reckoned superior to English beef. By transporting them into England large sums of money were brought back in return, insomuch that before the establishment of manufactures this was almost the only branch of trade which conveyed specie into the country. After the Union, the Scots had still greater advantages for carrying on this article of commerce ; and in order to settle a regular method of transacting it the dealers of both Kingdoms agreed to fix certain convenient places where at proper seasons they should meet for

---

[1] Division of Commonties, Reddingsrigg and Whitesiderigg. Signet Library, *Old Session Papers*, 135, No. 30, 1768 ; and *Durie Decreets*, 19/12/1807, H.M. Register House　　　　　[2] Pococke, *Tours in Scotland, 1747, 1750 and 1760*, 295

the purpose of buying and selling the cattle. A large muir called Reddingridge a mile southward of Falkirk was pitched upon for that purpose. This continued to be the place where these stated markets were held till a few years ago when on account of the division of that Muir which was formerly a commonty they have been removed to another Muir westward of that town. At one of these trysts which usually last two days, sometimes above 50,000 head of cattle have been assembled and all sold off.'[1] The site at Rough Castle continued to be used till 1785 when, possibly in consequence of the construction of the Forth and Clyde Canal which interfered with easy access from the north, the market was again moved, this time to an extensive site at Stenhousemuir near Larbert, where, still known as Falkirk Tryst, it remained till its final disappearance in the last years of the nineteenth century.

Originally the market appears to have been held twice a year, but in consequence of the decline of Crieff between 1760 and 1770, the Falkirk Tryst came to be held three times a year—in August, September and October—the October Tryst being possibly the largest as offering practically the last chance for Highland drovers to dispose of their beasts. By 1770, though market dues were still levied at Crieff, to the annoyance of the drovers from the north, Crieff had almost come to an end as a cattle market, all the business being done at the Falkirk Tryst[2]; and Pennant,

---

[1] Nimmo, *History of Stirlingshire*, 1st edn., 1777, 456–8

[2] In October 1770 a Petition signed by twenty-seven ' dealers in black cattle from the North of Scotland for themselves and in name of all the other dealers ' was presented to the Commissioners for the Annexed Estates in Scotland. It narrates that ' whereas in former years the Michaelmas mercat at Crieff was annualy the Great Mercat for black cattle and the meeting place for that purpose betwixt the English buyers and the Petitioners, yet that now too true it is that for several years past this mercat hath been dwindling away ; and that this year the Petitioners and others are laid under the necessity of carrying on their cattle at great expense to Falkirk, there to meet with the English buyers, few or none of them have at this time appeared at this place. That by this means the Village of Crieff hath now become and probably will continue to be only a resting place for the Petitioners and their cattle.' They complained that customs were still levied at Crieff though they had no opportunity of selling their cattle there, the market stance having been almost wholly enclosed and that a further toll was exacted from them at Stirling Bridge ; that if the customs dues at Crieff were continued they would be forced ' to take some proper method for elideing the payment thereof by taking another road with their cattle ' to the prejudice of Crieff which ' would suffer greatly through the loss of money that would be there necessarily spent during their stay.' (*Forfeited Estates Papers*, Perth, Ptfo. 21F, 21 January 1771, H.M. Register House.) It appears that the customs dues complained of were not then abolished, for the writer of the *O.S.A.* for the Parish of Crieff reports that in 1792 cattle from the North were forced to pass through the town before midday on the day preceding the market to avoid the dues, though by that time the sales of cattle had fallen to only about 1,000. (*O.S.A.*, Crieff, IX, 596)

writing in 1772, estimates the number of cattle sold there that year at 24,000.[1] At the time of the Statistical Account the numbers had reached 20,000 to 30,000 at the October sale alone,[2] and the writer of the Agricultural Report for Stirlingshire of 1812 puts the numbers sold at the October Tryst at between 25,000 and 40,000.

' The central situation of Stirlingshire,' he writes, ' with regard to the breeders of cattle in the northern and western counties on the one hand and the buyers or dealers from the southern and eastern parts of the island on the other, has for a long period rendered it the theatre of the principal fairs or cattle markets in Scotland. Of these, the Falkirk Trysts, as they are called, are the most distinguished. These trysts were originally held upon a large common in the vicinity of Falkirk which is at present in the course of being brought under cultivation ; they are now held on that account upon a field in the Parish of Larbert, but though the site be changed the ancient name remains. They were formerly held upon a fixed day of certain months but on account of the inconvenience which often arose from these days falling too early or too late in the week they have been lately fixed to a certain Tuesday of these months. The first Falkirk Tryst is held upon the second Tuesday of August. There are generally exhibited there from 5,000 to 6,000 black cattle. The second tryst is held upon the second Tuesday of September. There are generally exhibited about 15,000 black cattle and 15,000 sheep. The third tryst is held upon the second Tuesday of October when there are generally exhibited from 25,000 to 30,000 black cattle ; even 40,000 have been known to have been exhibited at this tryst. There are also at an average 25,000 sheep exposed to sale.' [3]

The original selection of Falkirk for a cattle market and its subsequent removal to the site at Stenhousemuir may have been a matter of accident and expediency rather than of conscious judgment, but however it came about, the outcome proved it to be a fortunate choice, and for over a century this broom-covered field near Larbert and the land immediately around it was to be the scene of one of the most important yearly events in the commercial life of Scotland. For here, midway between the rich

[1] Pennant, *Tour in Scotland, 1772,* II, 230
[2] *O.S.A.,* Larbert and Dunipace, III, 335
[3] Graham, *General View of the Agriculture of Stirlingshire,* 1812, 332-3

areas of the eastern Lowlands and the fast-growing population of Clydeside was a natural centre for cattle traffic from the north, already concentrated by the passage of the Forth, while it was a convenient centre for the drove roads from the west which passed to the north and south of Loch Lomond. For the cattle dealers of Southern Scotland and of England, too, it was a convenient point, saving them from arduous and often hazardous journeys into the Highland districts, while to the south led easy routes across the Southern Uplands to Dumfriesshire, to the Border and to England.[1]

Contemporary descriptions of Falkirk Tryst show it to have presented a scene of rare animation.[2] Here came dealers from Yorkshire, the north of England and the Border counties to meet the drovers of Uist, Skye, Lochaber, Ross-shire, Angus and Argyll. The Gaelic of the west and the speech of Aberdeenshire mingled with the dialects of Yorkshire, Cumberland and the Borders as men strove and argued over the merits of black and dun, red and brindled, collected from every district of Highland Scotland. The numbers of beasts brought to the tryst were such that the tryst ground itself was quite inadequate to hold them. As the tryst days approached, the gathering droves spread over a large area of the surrounding country, moving into the tryst ground for the actual sale. Here the cattle congregated in the centre of the ground. On the outskirts were the tents of those who provided 'the elements of conviviality in immense abundance,' while fires lit in the open cooked huge pots of broth for men chilled by autumn rains or flagging markets. There were, of course, during the greater period of the tryst's existence no auctioneers, and though a friend might intervene to break the deadlock between a Skye drover and a Yorkshire dealer arguing over the merits of Highland stirks, business at the tryst was done largely by the dealers threading their perilous path among the parcels of cattle and striking their own bargains direct

---

[1] The view that the choice of Stenhousemuir may have been arbitrary is rather strengthened by a passage which appears in the *O.S.A.* for the Stirlingshire Parish of Kippen: 'It is the opinion of many of the graziers and dealers in cattle that Kippen is one of the most convenient places perhaps in Scotland for a cattle market; and that in the late fluctuating state of the trysts it might not have been difficult to transfer to it a great part of the spring and autumn markets. There is a spacious moor near the village which lies very convenient for that purpose. With a view to encouraging their resort to it Mr Graham of Gartmore, the proprietor, offered it to the dealers in cattle free of custom for 90 years.' (*O.S.A.*, Kippen, XVIII, 351)

[2] See Appendix F (p. 240)

with the owners. The deal made, the two parties retired to a refreshment tent to seal the bargain, or to the booths set up by the Royal Bank of Scotland, the British Linen Company, the Commercial Bank or the Falkirk Bank for the benefit of those who wished to deposit money, or to get notes of the Scottish banks in return for the Letters of Credit from English banking houses with which the dealers from the South had supplied themselves. Through the motley crowd went sharpers, thimblers and gamblers, ballad singers, fiddlers and beggars, to make up a concourse which for variety, bustle and noise must have been almost without parallel in contemporary Scotland. The number of beasts for sale was such that the business was not completed in one day, the October Tryst in particular lasting for several days, while the drovers fought to get the last penny of price from dealers equally determined to get bargains of beasts which they knew must, so late in the year, ultimately be sold.

'At times,' writes a contributor to the *Stirling Journal* of 27 September 1844, 'when the market is densely crowded and there is danger of the separate lots being mixed, the Celt is seen in all his fury and excitement ; his Highland blood is up and he screams himself hoarse in shouting to his dogs, ordering his neighbours or assistants and threatening with the infliction of his cudgel those who show a disposition to encroach upon his stance or throw his lot into confusion. The maledictions between the herdsmen are exchanged in Gaelic and as the colleys seem to catch the spirit of their masters the contention is generally wound up by a regular worry, presenting altogether a scene of the most admired disorder and of no little amusement to those who have nothing else to do than to look on and enjoy it.'

The constant vigilance of the drovers was nowhere more necessary than in the neighbourhood of the tryst ground, and here, as in the northern hills they slept beside their beasts. A writer of the early part of last century [1] has so described the scene :

'In the latter part of the day when the tryst is over, to see every spot not only of the flat muir but of the beautifully undulating ground above, covered with cattle asleep and herdsmen in their characteristic Scottish dress either stretched in their plaids or resting for a while their wearied limbs—but still watchful —or gathered in groups and telling of the occurrences and bargains

---

[1] Youatt, *Cattle, their Breeds, Management and Diseases.* Library of Useful Knowledge, 1834, 121n

of the day ; this is a scene which the agriculturist will not soon forget and to which no one can be insensible.'

All through the first quarter of the nineteenth century the importance and popularity of Falkirk Tryst steadily increased. Each autumn saw more and larger droves coming from the Highlands across the old bridge leading to Stirling, where a dispute with the tollsman once held up the traffic till the whole road back to Bridge of Allan was ' one dense mass of cattle, sheep and ponies.' Before the middle of the century the total number of cattle sold each year at Falkirk Tryst is reported in the local Press to have risen to close on 150,000 besides sheep in great and increasing quantities.[1] But the years after 1860 saw a rapid change, and railways, steamships and auctioneers combined with changing methods of agriculture to rob the trysts of their former glory.

The streams of beasts which fed the great Trysts of Crieff and Falkirk had, like the Highland rivers which they crossed, passed through pools and eddies before reaching their final destination. On most of the cattle routes from north, east and west were smaller local markets, where droves on the main routes swelled by tributary streams from the surrounding hills changed hands, some to local graziers in need of fresh stock, but most to dealers collecting their purchases into composite and larger droves for the great markets. A list of fairs covering the whole of Scotland in 1727 contains over 500 names spread over the whole year.[2] Not all of these are described as cattle fairs, but the list includes the names of almost all those fairs known to have been cattle fairs, and from an examination of the districts and the dates of the remainder, it seems clear that the great majority were at least partially for the sale of cattle. Despite the number of these local markets, however, it appears that few of them offered the local cattle proprietors an opportunity of selling to big dealers from the South, not many of whom came far north. Marshall, writing in 1794, urged the establishment of regular cattle markets in the Central Highlands,[3] while Hogg considered that markets should be set up along the line of the proposed Caledonian Canal for the benefit of the farmers of the North who were forced to take what price was offered by the drovers at their

[1] *Stirling Journal*, Sept. and Oct. 1827
[2] Smith, *The Exact Dealer's Companion*, 1727
[3] Marshall, *General View of the Agriculture of the Central Highlands*, 1794, 68

doors or face the long drove to Falkirk perhaps with only a few beasts.[1]

The route from Skye and the Islands had its markets at Portree, Sligachan and Broadford. Robertson reports that ' at Portree there is an annual fair but in other places of the Isle of Skye some fluctuating meetings are held by concert among the dealers which are called " trysts ".' [2] The Portree Market had from its origin, probably in the early seventeenth century, grown to such proportions that John Macculloch, who visited it in 1824, found the place too crowded for his liking. ' Do not pay it a visit,' he writes, ' when all sorts of cattle come to be bought and sold ; when horn is entangled in horn, and drover with drover.' The inn that year was little better. ' Have I not sat over the fumes of tobacco amid the steam of hot whiskey to listen to prices and bone and rib and weight and pedigree till I could almost have bought and sold a stot myself. . . . And therefore I took refuge from the Lairds and Chiefs in the opener element of the Fair itself. And then the cows and the queys and the stots and the stirks began to bellow and roar and whisk their tails, and the sellers of cows and the buyers of cows began to compete for the mastery and all the town began to look like a stable, and I had nothing to do but to leave them to poke about their horns and bellow down the Highland drovers if they could, or remain to be daubed by the whisking of cows' tails in Portree itself.' [3] In a map of Portree in 1766 the tryst ground is marked slightly to the north-west of the town, and the Statistical Account complains of the damage done to grass and corn by cattle brought to the tryst.[4]

At Broadford, cattle from Dunvegan and the Outer Isles, their numbers swelled by many from the south of Skye, passed through their second market on the journey to the Lowlands. Though not so old as Portree Market, that of Broadford was of some importance, and as late as the third quarter of last century a traveller in Skye found the scene a busy one.[5] Here too were the noise of cattle and the shouting of drovers, the quarrelling, bargaining and courting of the crowd, the tents in the hollow where food was cooking for weary drovers, and in the background the steep stony sides of Ben-na-Cailich looking down on the

[1] Hogg, *A Tour of the Highlands in 1803*, 48
[2] Robertson, *General View of the Agriculture of Inverness-shire*, 1812, 302
[3] Macculloch, *Highlands and Western Isles*, 1824, III, 366 et seq.
[4] *O.S.A.*, XVI, 159   [5] Smith, *A Summer in Skye*, 138

bay and the river and the old farm buildings at Coirechatachan where Dr Johnson stayed in 1772. In his *Tour to the Hebrides* Boswell has recorded that MacKinnon of Coirechatachan had made so much money by droving and selling meal in his earlier days that the interest on the money sufficed to meet the rent of £50 which he paid for the holding.[1]

'These markets,' wrote Joseph Mitchell in his Journal for September 1837, 'are of much importance in Skye. They are held at Portree, Sligachan and Broadford at stated periods. The south-country drovers attend and purchase from the breeders and farmers. The large farmer here generally disposes of his stock, the cottar his cow and stirk, or two or three sheep. The debts that are contracted at other periods of the year are here generally discharged and there is thus a most heterogeneous collection of people—tacksmen, farmers, drovers, cottars, factors, shopkeepers, innkeepers, many women and gillies great and small. There are besides the extensive droves of cattle and sheep that are driven to these places to be sold and sent forward to the South.'

'At Sligachan the road was lined with tents. It was about 11 o'clock of the second day and the tent-keepers were engaged in cooking broth, mutton and potatoes for the country people inside with the only drink, mountain dew. The tents, if they could be called such, were temporary, formed of blankets and most miserable. The whole aspect of the place—a lone and barren mountainside—was wild and savage. It had been raining all night, and as most of the people had been either up drinking or sleeping on the bare ground during the night, they had a dirty and dishevelled appearance. The gentlemen had a bleary, unshaven aspect, the horses were ungroomed, and there being no stables little gillies with kilts, bare heads and bare legs were mounted and with much glee were riding backwards and forwards along the road.'

'The cattle and sheep extending over an immense space were standing quietly looking at each other while the gillies, their drovers, were leaning on their sticks or lying on the damp ground, their faithful collies at their feet, panting for employment. Such was the fair at Sligachan which I viewed with no very favourable impression of the civilisation of the people.'[2]

[1] Boswell, *Tour to the Hebrides*, Isham edn., 125
[2] Mitchell, *Reminiscences of my Life in the Highlands*, 219–20

The drove road from the north of Scotland also had its local markets. Those of Caithness, like that held in the Strath of Dunbeath, were probably little more than gathering places for cattle bought locally for driving to the South, but Muir of Ord in Ross-shire was an important market, and in the second quarter of last century was probably the largest tryst in the north of Scotland. South of the Great Glen on the moor near Kingussie a cattle market was, by long-standing custom, held each September to suit the convenience of drovers coming from the North. This was something of a social gathering, and Mrs Grant of Rothiemurchus in 1814 described the gathering of drovers, lairds and farmers for this 'Tryst of Pitmain' where Lord Huntly presided after the morning market at a dinner for which he provided a stag from his Forest of Gaick.[1]

Of the Aberdeenshire trysts, some were of very long standing. A weekly fair at 'The Chapel of Garioch' near Inverurie had been granted by the Privy Council in 1628,[2] and St Lawrence cattle market in the same district was, as early as 1684, of such a size that the Privy Council changed the market day from Monday to Tuesday to avoid Sabbath-breaking by drovers coming to it.[3] Aikey Fair, held on Aikey Brae in the parish of Old Deer in Buchan, was one of the largest of the Aberdeenshire fairs, and at the beginning of last century was probably the most important in the north-eastern counties. At that time beasts in their thousands were to be seen moving south in one continuous drove after the fair ended, and Aikey was said to be one of the only cattle fairs in the North to which English buyers regularly came.[4] The fair continued to be held till the last quarter of the century, though by then the cattle sales had shrunk to a mere shadow and the main business was in horses. Besides the fairs which existed in the eastern and north-eastern parts of the county, important fairs were also held each year in Strath Isla, Strath Bogie and on Deeside at least as early as 1662,[5] and it is estimated that by the early years of the nineteenth century no fewer than 180 fairs and markets took place annually in various parts of Aberdeenshire.[6]

[1] Elizabeth Grant of Rothiemurchus, *Memoirs of a Highland Lady*, 1807 (1911 edn.), 273 and 300
[2] *R.P.C.*, 2nd series, II, 409
[3] *R.P.C.*, 3rd series, VIII, 380
[4] Alexander, *Northern Rural Life in the 18th Century*, 79–82
[5] *Macfarlane's Geographical Collections*, II, 305–6
[6] Fraser, *The Old Deeside Road*, 100

Plate 11   All-Hallow Fair, Grassmarket, Edinburgh—about 1800

(From a print in Edinburgh Central Library)

At most of these the main trade was in cattle to be driven across the Don and the Dee and through the hill passes to Angus and the South. Those drovers who took their beasts south by Braemar and the passes at the head of the Dee might make further purchases at Kirkmichael in Strathardle, where a market was held each autumn a few days before the September Tryst at Falkirk. The Kirkmichael market is described in the Statistical Account as one of the main cattle markets of the kingdom.[1] Here, says a traveller of the early nineteenth century, used to come not only sellers of black cattle but shoemakers from Atholl and sellers of bog-oak from Badenoch.[2]

Argyll had its local markets at Salen in Mull and Strontian in Ardnamurchan, at Duror in Appin and Kilmore and Kilchrennan in Lorn, while to the large tryst at Kilmichael-Glassary near Lochgilphead came dealers and drovers from all parts of Scotland to buy the cattle of Islay, Jura, Kintyre and Knapdale.

Farther to the east, Doune in Perthshire was the scene of an important cattle market for beasts coming from Skye and north-west Scotland, and it was from Doune Tryst that Robin Oig set out on the ill-fated journey to England described in Sir Walter Scott's tale *The Two Drovers*. This market long remained of considerable importance, and at the time of the Statistical Account, though Falkirk Tryst was steadily growing in size, 10,000 cattle were sold here at the Autumn Tryst. In the course of the proceedings in 1768 leading up to the Division of the Commonties of Whitesiderigg and Reddingsrigg, reference was made to ' the tryst lately set up at Down . . . which is now in a flourishing way. . . . The town of Stirling, judging this tryst would be hurtful not only to its fairs and markets but also to duty upon black cattle passing along their bridge, as by coming to the Tryst at Down they could have passage (over the Forth) duty free by the other fords,' took legal advice as to their right to stop Doune Tryst but were advised they could not do so.[3] ' Snowy Doune,' as it was called, had the distinction of being the last important cattle sale of the year, and here in November, drovers late for Falkirk or disappointed with prices there found a last chance of selling before approaching winter put a stop to cattle trade. Cattle brought to the Tryst at Doune appear not to have been

[1] *O.S.A.*, Kirkmichael, XV, 514
[2] Larkin, *A Tour in the Highlands in 1818*, 35
[3] Signet Library, *Old Session Papers*, 135, No. 30, 1768, 24

subject to the customs dues levied on those sold at Crieff or Falkirk, and as late as 1845 the New Statistical Account refers to cattle for Doune Tryst being allowed to graze free for a week before it. Nimmo, writing in 1777, describes how at Stirling too in the month of November another of these trysts was formerly held, but of late the drovers had 'relinquished that station on account of the enclosures which now everywhere surround the town and assemble with their cattle at Down in Menteith where they have more room and are likewise exempted from sundry tolls and customs which they were obliged to pay at the former place.'[1] Despite these advantages, Doune Tryst seems to have been unpopular with the drovers, probably because the weather was often bad and the tryst ground cut up by the trampling of the beasts, while the late date resulted in forced sales and bargain prices in a buyer's market.

Dumbarton was an old and important market for cattle from Argyllshire, while in the uplands of southern Scotland, a market which met with only moderate success, replacing one of much earlier date, was set up at Hawick in 1785 near one of the main drove roads to England, on a date between Falkirk Tryst and St Luke's Fair at Newcastle.[2] In the south-western counties a number of cattle markets existed for the sale of animals locally bred or imported from Ireland. Of these the market held on the White Sands at Dumfries was by far the largest, rivalling in importance all but Falkirk Tryst itself.[3]

So over the whole of Scotland spread a network of fairs, markets and trysts, where the local people sold the homely products of farm and hand-loom, buying in return the goods of pedlar and packsman. To nearly all came cattle from the surrounding hills and grazing lands for sale to the dealers and drovers, and for many of these fairs in the Highland areas it was the cattle sales chiefly which justified the existence and ensured the continuance of the market. Geography had determined the sites, custom and convenience the dates ; but Crieff and, later, Falkirk Trysts were the central points in the cattle dealer's year, and as the local cattle markets developed, they came less by conscious design than by necessity to form integral parts of one great continuous enterprise, by means of which cattle collected

[1] Nimmo, op. cit., 458   [2] N.S.A., III, Hawick, 402
[3] For a fuller account of the cattle trade of the south-western counties, see Chapter 9

in early summer from the Outer Islands, the far North, Aberdeen-shire and the Central and Western Highlands came at last to the markets of Perthshire, Stirlingshire and southern Scotland. To serve this end, from May to October in all parts of the country men met, argued, quarrelled and bargained, for, as a writer of last century has said : ' If there's ocht in this warl' the farmer breed prides itself in, its in ha'en ta'en in somebuddy most desperately wi' a beast.'

9

THE DROVE ROADS OF SOUTHERN SCOTLAND

In the attempt which has been made to trace in some detail the routes through the Highlands used in the eighteenth and nineteenth centuries by the drovers of Scotland's cattle, it will be seen that the task has been made possible by the existence of certain sources peculiar to the district and to the period. The years which followed the Union of the Parliaments saw a steady growth in England of interest in Scottish affairs and an increasing realisation of the urgency of solving the many problems affecting Scotland, of which those relating to the Highlands were among the most acute. The political and economic instability of this area had concentrated attention on the question of Highland communications, and the selection of the routes of the military roads and the measures taken to bring order and peace to the Highlands before and after 1745, provides evidence of the routes and methods then in use by cattle drovers both within and without the Law. The task of Highland road construction reached its fullest development in the work of the Commissioners for Highland Roads and Bridges in the first quarter of the nineteenth century. The duties and functions laid on the Commissioners were based largely on the principle of assisted self-help in road-making, and to this is due the considerable body of local evidence in support of applications for assistance brought before the Commissioners, which is contained in their reports and which includes valuable material bearing on the economic life of the country. From the growing interest in Scottish affairs resulted also the increasing popularity among Englishmen of travelling in all parts of the country and particularly in the Highlands. Their experiences and observations have been recorded in detailed journals, some written in the fashion of the times in a verbose and philosophical strain tedious to modern ears, but many containing fine descriptive writing and much valuable information. The last decade of the eighteenth and the early years of the nineteenth centuries saw too in the Statistical Account and the County Agricultural Reports a comprehensive survey of Scotland which provided a wealth of detail relating to the social and economic life of the country, equalling if not surpassing, that available for any other part of these islands.

For the south of Scotland these sources are not available, or where they exist, as in the case of the Statistical Account and the Agricultural Surveys, contain less detail bearing on the work of the cattle breeders and drovers. With the notable exception of the south-western counties, breeding and dealing in black cattle was in the south of Scotland of far less importance than in the north. From a very early date the Lothians and the lower parts of what are now the counties of Berwick and Roxburgh, were among the most highly developed and closely cultivated parts of the country. In the pastoral and upland areas of Peeblesshire, Selkirkshire and Roxburghshire cattle were indeed bred and grazed in substantial numbers, but the emphasis from early times was rather on sheep rearing, an emphasis which became more marked as time went on, encouraged in the eighteenth century by the English demand for wool and mutton and finally by the growth of the cloth industry in the towns of the Southern Uplands. For the southern counties, other than Dumfriesshire, Kirkcudbrightshire and Wigtownshire, the Statistical Account and the Agricultural Surveys contain comparatively small reference to cattle rearing, while the evidence on the subject which is available for the Highlands through the work of the road-makers is largely lacking. The great cattle trysts of Ross-shire, Aberdeenshire, Perthshire and Stirlingshire on which the livelihood and interest of the Highland farmer of the eighteenth century so largely centred, had, save in the south-west, no parallel south of Falkirk, and the material and colour available from this source for reconstructing a picture of the drover's work is to this extent limited. The place of the southern counties of Scotland in the story of Scotland's cattle industry is indeed, with the exceptions mentioned, less that of a breeding and gathering ground than of an area of passage for beasts in transit to markets across the Border.

A further difficulty presents itself in attempting to trace the history and course of the droving trade in southern Scotland. The general trend of the droving routes of the Highlands was towards two fixed points—Crieff and Falkirk. South of Falkirk the course of the animal traffic was subject to no such concentrating influence. Between Falkirk and the Cheviots lay the wide grassy tableland of the Southern Uplands, offering a variety of easy routes with few obstacles of river or hill worthy of the name to men who had brought their cattle from the farthest parts of the Highlands, and such information as is available seems to indicate that for at least part of the journey to the Border a variety of routes were in fact used. Among the Cheviot Hills themselves, there were from Yetholm to Kershopefoot few points at which the crossing could not be made, while the destinations of the cattle on the English side were as yet too distant or too diversified to impart to the traffic more than a general southward trend. It is subject to these difficulties and limitations that the attempt is made to reconstruct the droving routes from Central Scotland to the Border.

The early history of the Scots droving trade has shown that at least as early as the fifteenth century Scots cattle were being driven to England in a traffic which, despite many changes of fortune, grew slowly but fairly steadily in volume in the centuries which followed. The Union of the Parliaments and the political and economic changes of the eighteenth century brought a great expansion of this south-bound trade. It will be recalled that the Tryst at Crieff was rising to importance in the early years of that century and continued in existence till about 1770. While there seems little doubt that many of the cattle which changed hands at Crieff found their way to England, there is little direct evidence as to the extent at this period of the traffic to the South. It seems probable that only a few English buyers at that time ventured even as far as the borders of the Highlands, and while Highland drovers were no doubt regularly taking beasts to the South it was probably not until Falkirk Tryst began to take the place of Crieff after the turn of the century that English buying in Scotland assumed large proportions. By then the demand for beef in Scotland itself was growing. There is evidence of buying in the eighteenth century at Falkirk by Scots graziers who fattened the animals in Stirlingshire and Dumbartonshire for the growing towns of Central Scotland,[1] and as early as 1777 Nimmo had referred to the increase in manufacturing in Scotland and the consequent increasing demand for beef as tending to lessen the export of meat to England.[2] The greater part, however, continued their journey to England by drove routes which led though the Southern Uplands to the Border.

[1] Belsches, *General View of the Agriculture of the County of Stirling*, 1796, 45 and 58
[2] Nimmo, *History of Stirlingshire*, 1st edn. 1777, 457–8

In his description of the Parish of Morvenside (Muiravonside), written about 1723, Alexander Johnstoun mentions the crossing of the West Lothian Avon at the Bridge of Dalquhairn by ' the Highland cattle from the markets at Falkirk in their way to the Borders of England.' [1] Johnstoun was, of course, writing at a time when the Falkirk market, as yet in its infancy, was still being held on its original site at Reddingsrigg to the south of Polmont. All the evidence available suggests, however, that even after the tryst had been moved to Rough Castle and later to Stenhousemuir the drove routes from it to the Border continued to lie as Johnstoun had indicated, to the south-east rather than due south, and there is little indication in contemporary sources that cattle from Falkirk used to any large extent the routes leading to the Border by way of Lanark and the valley of the Upper Clyde. The exact route from the crossing of the Avon is uncertain. Some drovers may have preferred to pass by Bathgate on the south-west side of the high ground lying to the south of Linlithgow. Others appear to have chosen the route through Linlithgow itself, and according to an old tradition in the district these drovers after passing through Linlithgow turned south making for Ecclesmachan, Uphall and Mid Calder.[2] Whatever the exact route, and in this cultivated country it can hardly now be definitely established, there is general agreement that the aim of the south-bound droves was the pass known as the Cauldstane Slap which crosses the Pentland Hills between the East and West Cairn Hills.[3] In Armstrong's and Thomson's maps of Peeblesshire drawn in 1775 and 1821 respectively, the pass is shown as a drove road and is still so shown on the maps of today. Both Armstrong's map and Thomson's were prepared at a time when cattle droving to England was in steady operation, and since the marking of drove roads as such in contemporary maps was by no means usual, there seems little reason to doubt that this route through the Pentland Hills was then in active use, and that the continuation of these routes through the Southern Uplands, marked by both these map-makers as drove roads, can be accepted as authentic. To this day the marks of animal traffic through the Cauldstane Slap can be seen in the soft broken ground

[1] Macfarlane's *Geographical Collections*, I, 317
[2] Miller, *The Origin of The Falkirk Trysts*. Falkirk Archaeological Society Transactions, 1936
[3] Chalmers, *Caledonia*, IV, 940. The road through the Cauldstane Slap to Peeblesshire is described as having been ' established by custom and continued by use.'

to the east of the small burn which feeds Harper Rigg Reservoir at its south-eastern corner. The tenant of Harper Rigg Farm, whose family have been in the farm for several generations, recalls having seen a few droves using the route by the Cauldstane Slap as late as the end of last century, and of having heard his father and grandfather speaking of heavy droving traffic in their day. According to their account the beasts crossed the Water of Leith a short way to the east of the present reservoir and passed to the east of the farm-house. The farm tenants tried, if possible, to get their meadow hay cut before the arrival of the droves, for the beasts went pretty much as they chose, and the drovers were none too careful in herding them. The cattle ' stanced ' for the night in the meadow or beside the drove road all up the slope of the Pentland Hills towards the pass, the drovers sleeping beside them, the ' topsmen ' or the owners sleeping in the farm-house. The present tenant can remember his father telling him of having seen the snow in an early autumn reddened from the feet of the beasts, presumably worn by the hard roads which they must have used for part of their journey from Falkirk Tryst.

South of the pass the line of the road as indicated by Armstrong followed the Lyne Water to West Linton, and thence to Romanno Bridge from which point it crossed the hills in a south-easterly direction to Peebles. Romanno Bridge was evidently a point of some importance on the drove route to the South, and in 1832 a dispute, which came before the Court of Session, arose between the trustees for the 1st and 2nd Districts of Turnpike Roads for Peeblesshire over the erection of tollbars. A statement to the Court by the Clerk of the 2nd District claimed that the annual revenue of the tollbar at Harestanes, two miles south of Dolphinton, was £262 and of that at Romanno £193, and that a large portion of this revenue and in particular that from the Romanno Tollbar arose from toll ' paid by Highland cattle passing through the County of Peebles from the North, partly by drove and partly by Turnpike roads on their way South to the English and other markets, which cattle have been in use heretofore to enter the County of Peebles at the Cauldstane Slap and to pay the first toll within the County at Romanno Tollbar. That these cattle pass that tollbar on their way South and never return, yielding an annual revenue to the 2nd District varying between £80 and £100.' [1] At Peebles the drovers were liable

---

[1] *Williamson* v. *Goldie*, Signet Library, *Old Session Papers*, 1832, 236, No. 218, 5

to payment of customs duty but had in return the right of grazing their beasts on a stretch of common land beside the Tweed on a site known as the Kingsmuir, rights of common pasture dating back to a Charter of James IV in 1506.[1]

South of Peebles, Thomson's maps of Peeblesshire (1821) and Selkirkshire (1824), show various alternative routes, all marked as drove roads. Of these one led from Peebles by way of Kirkhopelaw and Stakelaw into the glen of the Douglas Burn and so to Dryhope at the east end of St Mary's Loch. This route, which is still marked on modern maps as a drove road, is easily traced as it climbs the hill to the south of Peebles, enclosed by drystone dykes. Crossing Yarrow the road came by Tushielaw into the Ettrick Valley. From Tushielaw the route led south up the Rankle Burn by Buccleuch, crossed the high ground by Kingsmoor Loch and Girnwood to reach Deanburnhaugh on the Borthwick Water ; and so to the valley of the Teviot. Another route shown on Thomson's maps led south-east from Traquair, crossing the hills by Minch Moor and Broomylaw to the top of Long Philip Burn to reach the Ettrick Valley to the west of Selkirk. This was the route which Montrose's defeated troopers had followed north in September 1645 after the Battle of Philiphaugh, and it was the Minch Moor route which was followed by the droves under the charge of Robin Oig and Harry Wakefield, described in Sir Walter Scott's tale *The Two Drovers*. Yet another route, marked on Thomson's maps as a drove road, branches off the road from Selkirk to Hawick some three miles south of Selkirk and passes by Akermoor Loch and the Shaws Lochs to Gildiesgreen and Buccleuch.

It is clear that droves using these routes to the South would pass within a comparatively short distance of Hawick. The town of Hawick appears to have been of some importance in the cattle trade, at least as early as the second half of the seventeenth century. In 1669 the King and Parliament had before them a Petition of William, Lord of Drumlanrig for himself and the inhabitants of Hawick, which stated that the town and village of Hawick being situated near the English Border ' wherethrow diverse persons doe repair thither for buying and selling of bestiall, victuall and other commodities propper to be bought and sold ther,' the inhabitants are prejudiced ' throw the want

[1] *Charters and Documents relating to Peebles, 1165-1710.* Scottish Burgh Records Society, 38

of the liberty of two other frie Fairs . . . besides the Fairs which they presentlie have.' The Petition was granted and by an Act of that year two free fairs were established for the sale of 'horse, nolt, sheip, etc.' to be held on 6 May and 10 September.[1] Till 1777 there existed at Hawick a common where beasts could be rested, but in that year the common was divided, and since at that time, despite the grant of 1669, no cattle market of any size appears to have existed in the town, Hawick ceased to be a point of importance on the drove route to the South. The Burgh Records of Hawick contain the following reference : '1777. June 3. The which day the Magistrates and Town Council being convened heard ane advertisement read to be published in the "Edinburgh Courant" against Drovers of Cattle to rest in Hawick Common, now allotted to the Burgesses and Inhabitants of the Town of Hawick, which was approven of and ordained to be published.'[2] The lack of an established resting-place here for their beasts seems to have been felt by the drovers, for in 1785 they proposed to the Hawick authorities that they be allowed to rest their beasts for three days on condition that they offered them for sale. In support of their proposal, the drovers argued that all the cattle that are driven from Crieff and Falkirk to Newcastle and most of those bound for Carlisle passed through Hawick or within twelve miles of the town. This was the year when Falkirk Tryst was moved to its new ground at Stenhousemuir, and it is possible that the Hawick people saw an opportunity of developing their town as a centre of the cattle trade. However this may be the Hawick authorities appear to have welcomed the proposal which was adopted.[3] The Statistical Account for Hawick records that 'there is a weekly market and four Fairs besides a Tryst established within these few years for black cattle, etc. in October between Falkirk Tryst and Newcastle Fair, which promises to succeed,'[4] but the writer of the New Statistical Account for Hawick half a century later referring to the October cattle tryst there mentions that 'it has not been so successful as was expected.'[5]

The doubts thrown by the New Statistical Account on the success of Hawick Tryst lend some support to the view that the route shown on Thomson's map of Selkirkshire (1824) as reaching the Teviot Valley some way to the west of the town, was largely

[1] *A.P.S.*, VII, 661–2
[2] Johnman, Transactions Hawick Archaeological Society, 1917, 33
[3] ibid.   [4] *O.S.A.*, VIII, 527   [5] *N.S.A.*, Hawick, III, 402

used by the drovers. Local tradition, and the evidence of those still living in the district whose memory reaches back to the last days of droving add confirmation.[1] According to this evidence the droves reached the valley of the Teviot below Commonside some seven miles up-stream from Hawick. Here they were on the direct route to Langholm and Carlisle, and it is at least highly probable that some droves went that way. Well defined droving tracks are still plainly visible on the west side of the Limiecleuch Burn, one of the head waters of the Teviot, at a point which suggests that droves bound for Langholm and the Esk Valley may have left the main Carlisle road at Teviothead rejoining it by way of the valley of the Eweslees Burn about three miles south of Mosspaul Inn. Local evidence however leaves little room for doubt that while the route by Langholm was probably used by some of the drovers, it was not the main drove route to England.

Almost opposite the point where the drove road from Dean-burnhaugh reaches the Teviot Valley below Commonside, the Northhouse Burn joins the river from the south side, and the local evidence available is to the effect that this was the route more commonly used. Following a short way up the Northhouse Burn this route crossed the head of the Allan Water and the Dod Burn, making for Peelbraehope. The next point on the route was the shepherd's cottage at Hawkhass, from which, crossing the flat ground at the head of Longside Burn, the droves are believed to have crossed the ridge which lies between Greatmoor Hill and Scaw'd Law. Marks of droving traffic are clearly to be seen near Hawkhass and again on the south slope of the ridge where they may be easily traced on the east side of the Sundhope Burn, and on the first edition of the 6-in. Ordnance Survey of Roxburghshire published in 1863 the route is clearly marked as a drove road. The route crosses the Whitterhope Burn up-stream from the old tollbar near Whitterhope which was thus avoided, and today the tracks are to be seen climbing the low shoulder of the hill known as the Ninestone Rig. Here the tracks divide. One branch leads by Riccarton and Saughtree to the top of the Liddel Water and so to England and the valley of the North Tyne. The other turns due south from the Ninestone Rig and keeping to the east side of the Hermitage Water, where the tracks are still in places to be seen, crosses the Liddel Water some three miles above Newcastleton to reach the English Border at the Kershope Burn.

[1] Curle, *The History of the Berwickshire Naturalists' Club*, XXIX, 195

Of the routes to Carlisle from the North which passed farther to the west or north-west of Hawick, there is evidence that at least the one which led through Annandale was used. The writer of the Statistical Account for the Dumfriesshire Parish of Dryfesdale, referring to the road which led to Lockerbie, reports that ' along this road in the spring, but especially in the end of harvest, vast droves of black cattle from the North and West Highlands pass into England to the number of about 20,000 annually, prices from £3 to £7 each, in order to be fatted in the Norfolk fens and other places and supply the London and other markets, making the most delicious meat, vastly preferable to the large and rancid Irish horned bullocks.' [1]   It may well be that some beasts reached Annandale by way of Ettrick and Eskdalemuir or by St Mary's Loch, Birkhill and the Moffat Water.   There is little direct evidence, however, that these routes were used, and the reference in the Peeblesshire litigation already quoted, to cattle traffic at the tollbar of Harestanes near Kirkurd, suggests that some of the traffic which crossed the Pentlands at the Cauldstane Slap reached Annandale by Broughton and the head waters of the Tweed.

It will be recalled that the argument used by the drovers in asking for pasturage rights at Hawick in 1785 was that all cattle bound for Newcastle and most of those bound for Carlisle passed through the town or within twelve miles of it.   Now if this statement be accepted as approximately correct, it is consistent not only with the use of the route to the west of Hawick by Deanburnhaugh and Commonside which has been described, but with the existence of other routes to the east of the town crossing the Border by way of the Jed Water and Carter Bar, or by the ancient Dere Street and the top of the Kale and Oxnam Waters.   The list of routes across the Border which was compiled in 1597 [2] includes many to the east of Hawick, and the use of Duns and Kelso as customs posts for controlling cattle traffic in the sixteenth century would seem to show beyond reasonable doubt that some cattle at that time crossed to England by way of the East as well as the Middle and West Marches.   It seemed therefore a reasonable assumption that two centuries later when the cattle traffic to the South had increased so greatly some at least of these routes would still be in use, and when the present inquiry was taken in hand it was anticipated with some confidence,

[1] *O.S.A.*, Dryfesdale, IX, 428   [2] *Border Papers*, II, 1595–1603, 469

that despite the limitation of sources already referred to, clearer evidence to this effect would emerge than has in fact become available.

An examination of the ground at the head of Bowmont Water reveals the existence of a number of well-defined tracks, some of which have very much the appearance of drove roads crossing the Border to the south of Cocklawfoot, and at Windy Rig and Windy Gyle slightly to the west, leading down into the head-waters of the Coquet. On Stobie's map of Roxburghshire which is dated 1770, a road is marked crossing the Border from the head of Bowmont Water. Neither on that map, however, nor on later maps of that area up to and including the first edition of the 6-in. Ordnance Survey in 1863, is there any indication that this route was in fact a drove route, nor does there appear to be in the district any tradition of droving traffic from the North having used the valley of the Bowmont at least during the main droving period in the eighteenth and early nineteenth centuries. It is not possible to determine with any certainty the age or even the exact character of the traffic which caused the tracks now to be seen near the top of Bowmont Water, and all that can be said of them is that they have all the appearance of having been made by animal traffic. It may be that such droving traffic as passed that way was of a purely local character and of comparatively recent date. Some of it may, however, be much older, dating back to the fifteenth, sixteenth or seventeenth centuries, to a time when cattle trade from the North, legal and illegal, was using every byway over the Cheviots, when frequent cattle raiding or stock movement across the Border was causing 'brode waies or rakes' like those which Sir Robert Bowes and Sir Ralph Elleker observed in this district in 1542.

As to the routes which crossed the Cheviots near the head-waters of the Kale and Oxnam Waters the state of the evidence is rather similar. Here, too, occur many tracks still clearly visible on the ground which appear to have been made by animal traffic. The first edition of the 6-in. Ordnance Survey (Sheet XXXV) shows indeed three routes marked specifically as drove roads crossing the Border immediately to the south of Nether Hindhope Farm and in the vicinity of the Roman camp at Chew Green, but these routes are not continued on the adjoining sheets to the North. There are, indeed, many traces of droving traffic visible on the ground to the north of this point, but it is not possible to say whether these were made by through traffic or merely by the movement of stock from grazings in the neighbourhood. Pennymuir Fair which took place annually near Tow Ford on the Kale Water was an important local sheep market. It continued in existence into the last quarter of the nineteenth century, and from it considerable numbers of stock were regularly driven south across the hills to the top of the Coquet and Redesdale. There is little evidence that droving traffic used the route by Carter Bar, but many traces suggestive of droving traffic are to be seen on the high ground between the Jed and the Rule Waters, possibly making for the Wheelcauseway and the North Tyne. In the absence of direct evidence all that can be said is that while heavy droving traffic by this route within the last two centuries seems unlikely, it is hard to believe that no droves used it, at least during the early years of last century when the total numbers of cattle driven to England are believed to have reached figures in excess of 100,000 per annum.

To attempt to draw, from the scraps of evidence available, any definite conclusion as to the large numbers of tracks across the Cheviots to the south-east of Hawick would clearly be unwise and quite unwarranted. In an upland district of this nature over which has passed the varying traffic of many centuries, it is only possible to guess at the age of the tracks which are still today so plainly visible, or at the precise type of traffic which caused them. There is, however, one consideration which is not without relevance. A study of the map will show, that while the route from the Cauldstane Slap by Peebles and Tushielaw crossing the Teviot west of Hawick, leads almost directly south to the Border from the West Lothian plain, any route to the Border hills passing between Hawick and Coldstream would entail a wide detour to the east of the direct line. Had such a route led through country more attractive for droving than the direct route it might well have been chosen ; but the reverse is the case. Any such route would entail the crossing of the lower part of Teviotdale or the Merse of Berwickshire, districts which from early times were closely cultivated and thus less suitable for droving than the upland country to the westward which offered all the conditions which the drovers sought. When this factor is considered in conjunction with the absence of satisfactory evidence to the contrary from maps or printed sources, local recollection or tradition, it may at least be said to support a tentative but reasoned conclusion that during the eighteenth and nineteenth centuries the bulk of the droving traffic from Falkirk to the Border passed to the west rather than to the east of Hawick.

If the part played in the story of Scotland's cattle trade by the south-eastern counties would seem to have been rather that of a passage-way to England than of a breeding ground, the role of the south-western counties was very different. Here from an early date cattle breeding had been of prime importance. In the reign of William the Lion (1165–1214) the penalties fixed by the justices of Galloway for breaking the King's Peace was 12 score cows and 3 bulls, a fine which could only have been paid in districts where the cattle population was considerable.[1] Hector Boece in 1527 wrote of Annandale, Nithsdale and Galloway as having ' store of bestiall '[2] grazing in a countryside which half a century later Bishop Leslie described as abounding in ' nobill pastorall,'[3] and it seems probable that cattle breeding in this south-west district on a scale of some importance dates back at least as early as in any other part of the country. The unsettled state of the Border up to 1603 no doubt acted as a severe check on the activities of the earlier cattle breeders of the south-west, but there is little reason to doubt that at least a part of such cattle trade with England as persisted during the two or three centuries preceding the Union of the Parliaments came from Wigtownshire, Kirkcudbrightshire and Dumfriesshire. The choice in 1612 of Gretna as a customs post for taxing livestock traffic crossing the Border[4] was no doubt made partly with a view to traffic from these south-western counties, while the construction of a drove road from Annan to Gretna in 1619,[5] and the appointment in 1625 of Commissioners in Nithsdale and Annandale to prevent the export of cattle to England,[6] seem conclusive evidence that an appreciable droving traffic from these districts already existed. Taylor ' The Water Poet ' reported having seen numerous herds grazing in south-west Dumfriesshire in 1618, and in Annandale alone he counted 1,100 beasts on ' as good grasse as ever man did mowe.'[7]

The full extent of this seventeenth-century livestock traffic from the south-west is uncertain. Customs dues levied on

[1] A.P.S., I, 378
[2] Hume Brown, Scotland before 1700 ; from Contemporary Documents, 70
[3] Hume Brown, op. cit., 117   [4] R.P.C., 1st series, IX, 267 and 394
[5] R.P.C., 1st series, XI, 633–4   [6] R.P.C., 2nd series, I, 138
[7] Taylor, Works, 1630, 128

livestock crossing Dumfries Bridge in 1655 only amounted to £573 6s 8d Scots,[1] so the numbers paying toll can hardly have been large, but the changing attitude of Crown and Parliament towards the cattle trade to England, which marked the latter part of the seventeenth century, no doubt benefited the drovers of the south-west. When in 1697 a drove road from New Galloway to Dumfries was marked out on the instructions of the Privy Council, the route was described as ' the line of passage taken by immense herds of cattle which were continually passing from the green pastures of the Galloway Hills into England—a branch of economy held to be the main support of the inhabitants of the district and the grand source of its rents.' [2]

The first attempts at improving the methods of rearing and management of cattle appear to have taken place in south-west Scotland, and in the last quarter of the seventeenth century Sir David Dunbar of Baldoon in Wigtownshire started the practice of enclosing land on a large scale for grazing. The cattle park which he formed is said to have been two and a half miles long by one and a half miles broad capable of holding 1,000 beasts, of which some were bred at Baldoon and some collected from the neighbouring country. From this enclosure it is reported that Dunbar sold yearly to the drovers or sent to the markets of England as many as eighteen to twenty score of cattle. The beasts bred at Baldoon appear to have been so large that in 1683 a number of them were seized in England and slaughtered under the belief that they were Irish cattle, the import of which was at that time, and for many years to come, prohibited. The mistake complained of was perhaps not altogether surprising, for it appears that in 1670 Sir David had been fined for importing Irish cattle for sale in England.[3]

The enclosing of land in Galloway by stone dykes for the improvement of cattle breeding and the enlargement of farms was to lead to serious disorders. Many small tenants who had hitherto enjoyed grazing rights in common over the ground enclosed were evicted in favour of a single farmer renting the enclosed land at an increased rent. In the spring of 1723, when much enclosing had already been completed, many of the evicted

---

[1] *Minutes of Dumfries Town Council.* Quoted in McDowall's *History of Dumfries,* 838 et seq.

[2] Chambers, *Domestic Annals of Scotland,* III, 153

[3] *R.P.C.,* 3rd series, III, 105–6, 129

Plate 12　A drove route south of Peebles

(*above*) Between stone dykes near Kirkhope Law.　(*below*) Climbing from the
Tweed Valley

(*Photos by the Author*)

tenants met at the Fair of Kelton Hill and organising themselves into companies of fifty, set to work systematically to overturn the dykes. The movement soon assumed the aspect of a riot, and troops were sent from Dumfries, Ayr and Edinburgh to deal with it. The authorities appear to have acted with moderation, and of 200 'levellers' rounded up and taken to Kirkcudbright, many were allowed to escape and only a few of the ringleaders were imprisoned or sent to the Plantations. The movement is said to have materially retarded the progress of improvement in the south of Scotland, and the factors which gave rise to it are in many ways parallel to those which were to cause distress in the Western Highlands and Islands half a century later.[1]

The part played by these south-western counties in the Scots cattle trade depended not only on their importance as a breeding ground but on the export through them of cattle brought in from overseas. As early as 1627 the Earl of Annandale had obtained from the Privy Council permission to land at Portpatrick and take to England cattle belonging to his Irish tenants, to enable them to pay their rents.[2] The import of Irish cattle appears to have continued, for Thomas Tucker writing of Galloway in 1655 speaks of Portpatrick as having a trade with Ireland in horses and cattle.[3] In 1667 and 1668 the Privy Council made orders prohibiting the landing of Irish cattle,[4] and in 1684 a Commission was appointed with the object of preventing it.[5] There is no evidence to show how successful were these efforts to check the trade, but the import of Irish cattle remained at least in theory illegal till 1765. The ban was then withdrawn, and it is on record that five years later Portpatrick possessed six vessels of fifty tons each which were mainly employed in shipping cattle from Ireland.[6] The Statistical Account for the Parish records that between 1786 and 1790 over 55,000 head of Irish cattle were imported,[7] and in 1812 as many as 20,000 were landed.[8] 'This trade,' says the Statistical Account, 'depends so much upon the quantity of grass, of hay, or of turnips in England, and sometimes even upon the prospect of large crops of these articles that there is much speculation in it. Great gains and great losses

[1] Mackenzie, *History of Galloway*, II, 393–403
[2] *R.P.C.*, 2nd series, I, 591   [3] Hume Brown, *Early Travellers*, 180
[4] *R.P.C.*, 3rd series, III, 147   [5] *R.P.C.*, 3rd series, VIII, 411
[6] *N.S.A.*, Portpatrick, IV, 152   [7] *O.S.A.*, I, 43   [8] *N.S.A.*, IV, 153

are therefore sudden and frequent. Hence the import is unequal. Some people suppose the trade is favourable to smuggling and hostile to the revenue. Others object to it, as in a peculiar manner detrimental to those districts in Scotland where black cattle are bred ; and there seems to be rather a hardship in permitting such numbers of cattle to be imported into North Britain or even carried through it in order to rival the productions of that very country in the only market to which it has access. Without entering, however, into these speculations it may be sufficient at present to remark that the import will probably diminish of itself in consequence of the rapid progress which Ireland is now making. The time is fast approaching when that Kingdom will be in the same state in which England is at present, having a market within itself sufficient for the consumption of its own production.' [1]

From the Wigtownshire coast to Dumfries stretched a series of cattle markets or trysts. Some of these appear to date back at least as early as the end of the seventeenth century and owed their existence to the importance of the local cattle-breeding industry, but some, of later date, no doubt owed their rise and growth largely to the Irish trade. The position of these trysts gives a fair indication of the route by which the Irish beasts and those of local breeding passed eastward to Dumfries, to Carlisle and to England.[2] The main trysts appear to have been held at Glenluce, Newton-Stewart, Gatehouse, New Galloway, Kelton Hill, Crocketford and Dumfries. The market at New Galloway dates back to a Royal Charter ratified by an Act of Parliament in June 1633 which conferred on the Provost, Bailies and Council the privilege of holding ' one market on Wednesday weekly with three fairs yearly, each one to last for the space of three days. . . .' [3] In a description of the market in 1778 reference is made to the town as being a gathering place for all the cattle in the Stewartry on their way to England, and Heron in 1792 speaks of it as a stage on the road to Rhonehouse or Gatehouse of Fleet.[4]

The market at Kelton Hill was at one time described as among the largest in the south of Scotland. According to an old tradition its selection as a site for a market came about by an

[1] O.S.A., Portpatrick, I, 43
[2] Further detail regarding the drove routes from Portpatrick to Dumfries is given in J. M. Corrie's *The Droving Days in the South-Western District of Scotland*, 91 et seq.
[3] *Reg. Mag. Sig.*, 1620–33, 458–9 ; *A.P.S.*, V, 101
[4] Heron, *Journey through the Western Counties of Scotland*, II, 157

accident somewhat similar to that which is said to have determined
the site of Aikey Fair in Aberdeenshire. A passing pedlar had
occasion to spread his goods out to dry on the side of the hill.
The local folk, attracted by the display, collected, and bought
up the whole contents of the pack with a readiness which induced
the pedlar to promise to return at the same time in the following
year, so giving rise to a custom which continued year after year.[1]
Though the date when the Kelton Hill market originated is not
known, it seems probable that it was in existence at least as early
as the middle of the eighteenth century, for a writer in 1825
describes it as dating back far beyond the reach of any living
recollection. Heron gives a description of it which corresponds
very much to the contemporary descriptions of Falkirk Tryst :
' From Ireland, from England, and from the most distant parts
of North Britain, horse dealers, cattle dealers, sellars of sweet-
meats and of spirituous liquors, gypsies, pickpockets, and smugglers
are accustomed to resort to this fair. Every house in the village
(of Rhonehouse, which owes its origin to the fair) is crowded, and
all become on this occasion houses of entertainment.'

' The roads are, for a day or two before, crowded with comers
to this fair. On the hill or park where it is held tents are erected
in rows so as to form a sort of street. . . . Through the whole
fair day one busy tumultuous scene is here exhibited of bustling
backwards and forwards, bargaining, wooing, carousing, quarrelling, amidst horses, cattle, carriages, mountebanks, the stalls of
chapmen, and the tents of the sellers of liquors and of cold victuals.
The village also holds high festival during the week, and besides
the peasantry, the neighbouring gentry are spectators for a short
time of the confusion, the tumult, and the rude festivity which it
displays.' [2]

But of all the cattle markets in the south of Scotland none
appears to have equalled the Tryst at Dumfries. The natural
centre for an extensive and rich grazing area, Dumfries lay on
the direct road to Carlisle and the South. Weekly markets and
three Autumn Fairs at Dumfries date back at least as early as the
seventeenth century, and during the last quarter of the eighteenth
and the first half of the nineteenth centuries, the White Sands at
the mouth of the Nith saw each year a growing number of cattle
exposed for sale. Pennant in 1772 records that ' the great weekly

[1] Alexander, *Northern Rural Life in the 18th Century*, 79
[2] Heron, op. cit., II, 129 et seq.

markets for black cattle are of much advantage to the place and vast droves from Galloway and the Shire of Air pass through on their way to the Fairs in Norfolk and Suffolk.'[1] The fortunes of the Dumfries Market were naturally and directly affected by the demand from the South, and the largest sales appear to have been those in September, which fitted in with the big Fair at Brough Hill in Westmorland later in the same month or the October Market of St Faith's near Norwich, while at the Dumfries sales in the middle of October cattle changed hands on their way to the Market at Hempton Green in West Norfolk held on 16 November. Indeed the importance of the English trade to the Dumfries sales was so great that the market held there in mid-October came to be known as ' Hempton Wednesday,'[2] while the great composite drove collected in September for the Norwich sale was locally known as the ' St Faith's Drove.'[3] An Agricultural Survey of Dumfriesshire in 1794 reports the sale in one year of 20,000 head of cattle to the four main drovers at a price of £130,000.[4] All through the first quarter of the nine-teenth century the local Press records a growing trade at the Dumfries Market. In 1829 and 1830 the number sold in the last week of September was reported to have risen as high as 6,000[5] ; but by that time changes in farming methods in Scotland were already far advanced, and with the growing diversion of the Irish cattle trade to the direct sea passage to England the droving traffic which passed through Dumfries entered on a period of gradual decline.

For the cattle which crossed the Nith at Dumfries bound for the English markets, the natural routes lay by way of Annan and Gretna, crossing the Esk and the Eden by fords near their mouth. In addition to these routes, fords across the Solway Firth itself were at times also used.[6] The most important were those known as the Dornock Wath and the Stoney Wath or Bowness Wath, and in his life of George Moore, a Cumberland merchant, Samuel Smiles has described the crossing of the Bowness Wath in the first quarter of last century. Moore in his early youth

[1] Pennant, *A Tour in Scotland, 1772*, I, 115
[2] Bryce Johnston, *General View of the Agriculture of the County of Dumfries*, 1794, 11
[3] Signet Library, *Old Session Papers*, 1798, 392, No. 14, 6
[4] Bryce Johnston, op. cit., 19   [5] *N.S.A.*, Dumfries, IV, 20
[6] For a fuller description of the fords of the Esk, the Eden and the Solway Firth, see *The Fords of the Solway*, McIntire. Transactions Cumberland & Westmorland Antiquarian and Archaeological Society, 1939, XXXIX, new series, 152–70

Plate 13   Cattle crossing the Solway Firth

(*From the painting by Sam Bough, R.S.A.*)

had been sent by a Cumberland banker to take cash to a client who had bought cattle at Dumfries, and had been persuaded to help in driving the cattle south. 'They drove the cattle by unfrequented routes in the direction of Annan. At length they reached the shores of the Solway Firth. The proper route into England was by Gretna, though the road by that way was much longer. But the cattle dealer declared his intention of driving his cattle across the Solway sands. . . . The tide was then at low ebb. The waste of sand stretched as far as the eye could reach. It was gloaming by this time and the line of the English coast— about five miles distant—looked like a fog-bank. Night came on. It was too dark to cross then. They must wait till the moon rose. It was midnight before its glitter shone upon the placid bosom of the Firth. The cattle-dealer then rose, drew his beasts together and drove them in upon the sands. They had proceeded but a short way when they observed that the tide had turned. They pushed the beasts on with as much speed as they could. The sands were becoming softer. They crossed number-less pools of water. Then they saw the sea-waves coming upon them. On, on ! It was too late. The waves which sometimes rush up the Solway three feet abreast were driving in amongst the cattle. They were carried off their feet and took to swimming. The horses upon which George Moore and his companion were mounted also took to swimming. They found it difficult to keep the cattle together—one at one side, and one at the other. Yet they pushed on as well as they could. It was a swim for life. The cattle became separated and were seen in the moonlight, swimming in all directions. At last they reached firmer ground, pushed on and landed near Bowness. But many of the cattle had been swept away and were never afterwards heard of.' [1]

[1] Smiles, *George Moore, Merchant and Philanthropist*, 42 et seq.

10

BEYOND THE BORDER

I will bring you, my kine,
Where there's grass to the knee :
But you'll think of scant croppings
Harsh with salt from the sea.

The Drover

PADRAIC COLUM

THE story of Scotland's cattle trade from its first discernible beginnings in the fourteenth and early fifteenth centuries has shown how closely its varying fortunes were, from the first, bound up with the markets south of the Border. Now encouraged, now restricted, and at times entirely prohibited, the trade was, at least up till the Union of 1603, always conditioned by the political and economic relations between the two countries and by the state of the Border lands ; in short, by the presence or absence of factors which interfered with the free flow of cattle to the English markets. As the seventeenth century drew to a close, the barriers which had divided the two countries began at length to give way. The Union of the Parliaments saw the final end of the customs and tariffs against which the cattle traders had for so long fought by protest or by evasion, and from 1707 dates the steady increase in their trade with England, which gradually brought the volume of south-bound droving traffic to its peak in the second quarter of last century. From first to last the most powerful magnet drawing cattle from the glens of the Highlands lay south of the Border, and as the years passed, buying for England came more and more to determine the prosperity of the markets at Crieff, Falkirk, Dumfries and many smaller trysts. A full account of the cattle trade to England forms no part of the present purpose, but no attempt to describe or understand the droving trade in Scotland can be complete or fully intelligible which ignores the fate of the Scots cattle, their routes and their final destinations south of Berwick and Carlisle, and the watersheds of the streams which drain the Cheviots.

The volume of southbound cattle traffic in the centuries prior to the Union of the Parliaments is hard to gauge. Such references to the trade as are available occur mainly in the complaints of those, on one side of the border or the other, whose object lay in controlling, taxing, or preventing it, in Acts of Parliament or Orders of the Privy Council passed with a similar purpose, the wording of which, to modern ears, suggests exaggeration. 'Vast,' 'universal' and 'in great numbers,' phrases frequently used, give little real indication of the volume of traffic, and it is not till the second half of the seventeenth century that the references become more specific. One of the earliest estimates is that already referred to from the Tax Records of Carlisle in 1662 when it was reported that 18,574 cattle passed through the town paying toll,[1] a total which would, no doubt, include, and may well have been made up largely of, cattle from the important cattle-breeding districts of Galloway and the south-west. Pococke, in a letter dated 6 May 1760 describing his tour in Scotland, wrote : ' I came to the Downs of Wigtown. . . . Here they graze a great number of small oxen which they send to a Fair near Norwich and they are fattened for six months in Norfolk, Suffolk and Essex for the London Markets,'[2] and a Note to Pococke's *Tours in Scotland* quotes Agricultural Reports of 1794–5 for the statement that in 1675, 20,000 to 30,000 cattle went south each year from Galloway.[3] Had the Scots beasts sent to London from Norfolk been as numerous as is indicated by the eighteenth-century writers they would have accounted for a very large part of the total consumption of London, leaving small place for the cattle of Wales and the south-west and Midland counties. It seems probable that the estimates are too high. Nathaniel Kent put the fat bullocks sent from Norfolk to London at 20,000 per annum, three-quarters of which he estimates were Scots cattle.[4] It is known, however, that during the first half of the eighteenth century the number of cattle sold at Smithfield alone for the London market was between 75,000 and 80,000,[5] and that a high proportion of these came fat from the Norfolk grazings. Whatever the true figure of Scots cattle driven to England before 1700, it was certainly considerable. The important part played by the cattle trade in the negotiations for the Union of 1707 shows that cattle were already among Scotland's main exports, and in

[1] *State Papers. Domestic.* Charles II, 1663–4, p. 226
[2] Pococke, *Tours in Scotland, 1747, 1750 and 1760,* 18   [3] ibid., note
[4] Fussell and Goodman, *18th Century Traffic in Livestock.* Economic History (Supplement of Economic Journal) Feb. 1936, III, No. 11
[5] McCulloch, *Dictionary of Commerce,* new edn., 1856, 271

contemporary records there seems to be general agreement that by then at least 30,000 Scots cattle crossed the Border each year.

The century which followed the Union of the Parliaments was marked for Scotland and England alike by changes so great that the two countries which then came together in complete, if unwilling, union are hardly to be recognised in the nation which fought Napoleon. England, at the start of the eighteenth century, was still almost entirely an agricultural country. The vast majority of her people lived in districts still completely rural. Roads, their neglect or upkeep a matter of purely local responsibility, were still in a primitive state, and communities divided one from another by difficulties of transport were, of necessity, largely self-supporting. Such industry as existed was carried on mainly in small villages or country cottages, and the larger towns were little more than markets for the products of the country districts which they served. Norwich, Bristol, Leeds and Halifax distributed the cloth and woollen goods of East Anglia, the Cotswolds and the Dales. Newcastle carried on a coastal trade with London and some export trade with the Scandinavian ports, but the great stimulus of the coalfields of the north-east coast was yet to come. Only London, with one-fifth of the entire population of 5½ millions, was already showing clear signs of possessing those magnetic qualities which were to transform her out of all recognition in the coming century.[1] Outside London, the population of the country was fairly evenly spread. The most populous districts lay in a belt extending north-east from the Bristol Channel to Northamptonshire and Buckinghamshire. Over the great part of the remainder of the country the density of population was generally uniform, only Cumberland, Westmorland and the North Riding of Yorkshire falling much below the average.

By 1800 the picture was very different. The London area was still by far the most densely peopled, but outside it the greatest centres of population now lay in Lancashire and the West Riding of Yorkshire, in Staffordshire and the North Midlands, with a lesser degree of concentration along the Bristol Channel and in Durham.[2]

These movements of population are significant of a great social and economic change which, by the end of the century, was already far advanced. At the beginning of the eighteenth

[1] Trevelyan, *English Social History*, 341, 343
[2] Grant Robertson, *England under the Hanoverians*, 337, 338

century as many as four-fifths of the population were engaged in agriculture, tilling by traditional and unscientific methods land little developed and occupied at the will of the landlord, or at best on short tenancies. As the century progressed, increasing wealth seeking profitable investment in a time when opportunities for investment were scarce, and the demands of an expanding population, turned the attention of the landowning classes more and more to the development of their estates, while growing knowledge of scientific methods of farming made available to them the means of turning their land to good account. It is estimated that in the hundred years between 1696 and 1795, two million acres had been added to the agricultural land of England and Wales.[1] Townshend, the retired Secretary of State of George II, Coke on his Norfolk estate at Holkham and Jethro Tull in Berkshire had shown the benefits of crop rotation made possible by the sowing of clover and artificial grasses and the cultivation of the turnip, while Bakewell in Leicestershire had pointed the way to better livestock by improvement in the methods of breeding. The enclosure of land for crop cultivation and the consolidation into economic units of the mosaic of small patches cultivated under the old system, was a necessary outcome of the new agriculture. In the first half of the century enclosure of land by agreement had made substantial progress, and by 1800 a further area of over 4,000,000 acres of land had been enclosed by Act of Parliament,[2] a development partly responsible for and partly facilitated by the drift of population to the growing towns. By the end of the century, though the standard of English livestock and arable farming had enormously improved, the proportion of England's population engaged in agriculture is estimated to have fallen from four-fifths to one-third.

The revolution through which England's agriculture passed in the course of the eighteenth century was, as in Scotland, complementary to the great Industrial Revolution which started about 1760 and gathered momentum all through the remaining years of the century. The rapid growth of Britain's colonial empire and the expansion of her overseas trade supplied for industrial development the necessary markets and raw material, while the discoveries and inventions of the second half of the century provided the means to profit by them. Cargoes from the American plantations fed through Liverpool the growing mills of Lancashire,

[1] Trevelyan, op. cit., 374n.   [2] Grant Robertson, op. cit., 331

where Arkwright's invention was transforming the cotton industry, as those of Hargreaves and Compton were transforming the spinning industry of the West Riding. In Staffordshire Wedgwood was laying the foundations of the pottery trade, while perhaps most important of all was the discovery that coal and coke could be used in place of charcoal for smelting iron. This was a development which more than any other influenced the movement of population in Britain, bringing industry and wealth to those areas where coal and iron were to be found close together, to South Wales and South Yorkshire, to Tyneside and the Clyde basin. The end of the century found the Industrial Revolution little more than well under way, but already the movement of population to the new industrial areas had gone far in defining the lines of later development. These changes in eighteenth-century England have a close bearing on the Scots cattle trade, and in their light it is possible to assess with some certainty the factors which, during the century following the Union of 1707, led to the steady increase in the cattle traffic to the South, freed from the burden of tariff restriction or national prejudice.

Throughout the whole of the period of upward of four centuries covered by the records of the droving trade of Britain, a large and steadily growing portion of the traffic made its way to the London market. Here, throughout, was by far the greatest concentration of population and wealth. Meat and bread were the chief foods. Defoe says that as early as the sixteenth century it was the common practice to send beasts to London to have them killed there, and by the time of Queen Elizabeth great cattle fairs in Northamptonshire and Leicestershire were already supplying through Smithfield the needs of the taverns, the coffee-houses and the private households of the capital. As has been seen, no reliable figures are available for the period before 1700, but it is known that long before that time the trend of cattle movement to market was more and more towards south-east England. During the eighteenth century this trend continued and the numbers grew despite the growing demand of the new industrial areas of the Midlands and the North. From Wales, following traditional routes, cattle were driven to the Midlands, to Essex and to Kent for fattening for the London market. From the south-western counties, by way of the Wiltshire Downs and the valley of the Kennet, they crossed the country to Hertfordshire and Buckinghamshire to the same end, while the destination of the Scots cattle was the grass land of the

Home Counties and of East Anglia, which fattened much of London's beef.[1] From 1732 to 1794 the number of cattle sold each year at Smithfield Market alone rose from 76,000 to 109,000.[2] How many of these were Scots beasts cannot be determined, but in view of the high proportion of Scots cattle which found their way to East Anglia for fattening or to the great market at Barnet in Hertfordshire, it would seem beyond doubt that the demand of the London market was throughout of the first importance for the Scots cattle trade. ' Often at great distances of two or three hundred miles or more from the collossal emporium of men, wealth and intellectual power,' wrote de Quincey in the early years of last century, ' have I felt the sublime expression of her enormous magnitude in one simple form of ordinary occurrence, viz. in the vast droves of cattle upon the Great North Road all with their heads directed to London and expounding the size of the attracting body together with the force of its attracting power by the never-ending succession of these droves and the remoteness from the capital of the lines in which they were moving.' [3]

The movement of population and the rise of the industrial towns of the Midlands and the north of England in the second half of the century created new demands, second only to the needs of London. Cattle for the new markets must, like those for Smithfield, be fattened in areas within easy reach of the consumers. Graziers in Northumberland now supplied the growing population of Tyneside and the north-east ports, those in north-east Yorkshire the needs of Whitby, Scarborough, Hull and the Yorkshire coast, while the grass lands of Cumberland, Westmorland and the Craven district of Yorkshire fed the cloth workers of the West Riding and the mill workers of Lancashire.[4]

---

[1] Fussell and Goodman, op. cit.

[2] The Smithfield figures show a marked decline in the totals for the years between 1745 and 1750. As the figures relate to all cattle brought there for sale, it is impossible to tell to what extent this was due to the Rebellion and the unsettled state of the Highlands immediately after it. It may well be that the widespread cattle disease in England in 1746 was a more important factor, though evidence given in the course of the division of the Commonties of Reddingsrigg and Whitesiderigg already quoted referred to few cattle being brought there for sale in 1746. A marked increase in the Smithfield figures after 1760 corresponds closely with other evidence as to the growth of the Scots droving trade. (Macculloch op. cit., 1856, 271. *Report of Select Committee on Cultivation etc. of Waste Lands*, 1795)

[3] Thomas de Quincey, *Autobiographical Sketches*, Vol. XIV of Works (1863 edn.), 179

[4] Fussell and Goodman, op. cit.

While the demands of the English home market were thus steadily growing, the cattle trade was being called on to meet another urgent need. From the early years of the eighteenth century till the Battle of Waterloo the armed forces of Britain were almost continuously on a war footing, engaged first in maintaining the balance of power in Europe and latterly in the growing struggle with France. From first to last the part played by the Navy was of supreme importance, whether in the Narrow Seas, the Baltic, the Mediterranean or on the American coast, and it was on the possession and maintenance of sea power more than on any other factor that the issue throughout depended.

Beef, fresh or salted, was among the traditional foods of the Navy, and agents of the Naval Victualling Board were constant buyers of fat cattle to meet the growing demands of Britain's expanding fleet. From the main victualling depot and ' cutting house ' at Deptford, the smaller depots at Chatham, Dover, Portsmouth and Plymouth were fed, and they in turn supplied ships lying at these ports, in the Downs, and at Margate, New Romney, Falmouth and Weymouth and at other ports of the south and south-east coast.[1] Among the Minutes of the Victualling Board in the Public Record Office are preserved the contracts for the supply of a great variety of naval victualling stores. Here are contracts for the supply of flour, bread and ' bisket stuff'; of rum, beer and lime juice ; of sugar and molasses ; of lemons, onions and vinegar ; and beef was one of the chief items.[2] The main salting season lasted from the end of September to the end of March, and many of the contracts for the supply of H.M. ships required that beef be cured between these dates with a sufficient quantity of Saint Ubes Bay Salt ; ' that it be full of pickle ; good sound, sweet, well fatted and of the best quality.' [3] No ' bull stags ' must be supplied ' nor any ox which dropped upon the road.' Despite the conditions in the Supply Contracts as to the quality of the animals and the methods of salting, complaints about the meat issued to the Fleet were frequent. From the beginning of the eighteenth century to the end of the Napoleonic Wars the records hold many references to inquiries into complaints lodged, but these seem generally to have ended in a finding

---

[1] *Select Committee on Finance,* June 1798. House of Commons Committees, XIII, 509
[2] *P.R.O.,* Admiralty, 111/73
[3] *Select Committee on Finance,* op. cit., 534. Setubal, a bay on the coast of Portugal was known by British sailors as St Ubes, or St Ives Bay.

Plate 14 Smithfield Market in the early 19th century
(*Drawing by Thomas Rowlandson. By permission of the Trustees of the British Museum*)

that the meat is 'good, sweet and fit for the service.'[1] The small size of the cattle of the eighteenth century, even when fattened for killing, is shown by a condition in a contract of 1798 that the beasts must weigh not less than 5 cwt.[2] A contract of 1816 requires a weight of only 4 cwt.,[3] while a stipulation in one of 1823 that the beasts must weight 6 to 7 cwt. is described as unusual.[4]

The purchases of cattle by the Victualling Board were on a large scale. The Board Minutes for the early years of the eighteenth century frequently record the supply of up to 200 fat cattle by one contractor in a single transaction, and a Minute of 1 October 1746 records that this being the day when contracts were made for the supply of beef, contractors were notified that the Board would require during the next six weeks 1,600 cattle for the Deptford stores, 600 for Portsmouth, 500 for Plymouth and 300 for Dover.[5] By the closing years of the century the needs of the Navy had greatly increased. Victualling Board Minutes of 1794 show payments in that year totalling close on £18,000 for the supply of beef, much of it described as 'Scotch beef,' for ships lying in the Thames, and over £15,000 for fresh meat supplied for Chatham,[6] while one of October 1804, typical of many at the time, records the payment to John Grant of over £1,000 for fresh beef supplied during five months of that year to ships lying at Norwich.[7] In the year of Trafalgar payments to contractors who supplied salted beef to the stores at Deptford, Chatham, Dover, Portsmouth and Plymouth show that for these alone the number of cattle slaughtered was over 16,000,[8] while local purchases of fresh meat were made at every port from Newcastle to Margate, from Dover Roads to Dartmouth and from Milford Haven to Greenock.[9] As the French Wars neared their end the purchases of cattle for the Navy appear to have reached still higher levels, and an entry in the Victualling Board's ledger for the year 1812 shows payments to Wm. Mellish, one of the principal naval contractors, totalling no less than £455,397 for beef and suet supplied between 1 October 1811 and 30 September 1812.[10] The average price appears to have been approximately £15 a head.

[1] *P.R.O.*, Admiralty, *passim*
[2] *Select Committee on Finance*, op. cit., 509
[3] *P.R.O.*, Admiralty, 112/85
[4] *P.R.O.*, Admiralty, 109/78
[5] *P.R.O.*, Admiralty, 111/32
[6] *P.R.O.*, Admiralty, 112/180
[7] *P.R.O.*, Admiralty, 111/173
[8] *P.R.O.*, Admiralty, 112/191
[9] *P.R.O.*, Admiralty, 112/84
[10] *P.R.O.*, Admiralty, 112/198

The extent to which the naval demand for beef was affected by the political situation is shown by a series of communications between the Victualling Board and the Admiralty in 1771.[1] Fresh as well as salted beef was supplied to the Fleet on certain days in the week, and in the spring of that year when the calls on the victualling stores were heavy, that department asked the Board of Admiralty to direct that fresh meat be issued only twice a week to enable the stores of salted meat to be built up. Two months later they reported to the Admiralty that the Convention with Spain [2] having been ratified, the demand for meat would be much less than had been expected and that a great quantity of salted beef was in store. They asked that salted beef only be issued, the surplus in store being sold to the public, and the records for the next few months show public sales to the extent of over £4,000.[3] The end of the Napoleonic Wars brought a great contraction in the scale of naval buying, and for Plymouth alone the number of cattle supplied fell from over 5,000 in 1812 to less than 700 in 1820.[4]

What proportion of the cattle supplied to the Navy were Scots cattle cannot be exactly determined. It has been seen that some of the beef supplied to the Thames in 1794 was specified as Scots beef and there is no reason to consider this an isolated case, but as a rule the contracts did not distinguish Scots meat or Scots beasts from English. The demand was for fat beasts which had already passed from the hands of the drovers to those

---

[1] *P.R.O.*, Admiralty, 110/25

[2] In 1770 relations between Great Britain and Spain, already strained over the question of Louisiana and complaints of contraband trade with the Spanish colonies, became further embittered by a dispute over the possession of the Falkland Islands, where a Spanish expedition from Buenos Aires had forced the British to evacuate Port Egmont. Great Britain demanded reparation and both countries prepared for war. Spain looked to France for help, but this was refused and, faced with a naval war in which her fleet would be no match for that of Great Britain, Spain gave way. The Spanish forces were withdrawn from the Falkland Islands, and on 22 January 1771 a Convention was signed which provided for the restoration of Port Egmont to Great Britain. (*Recueil de Traités*, Martens, 1st series (2nd edn.), XI, 1)

[3] Confirmation of the fall in cattle prices in England in 1771 may be found in a Petition of William Robertson to the Commissioners on the Forfeited Estates for the tenancy of the farm of Wellhouse in the parish of Kilmorack in Inverness-shire, previously rented by his brother Duncan. Duncan in that year had driven to England some 1,600 or 1,800 cattle from the Trysts at Crieff and Falkirk, but the prices fell and he suffered great loss, spending the whole winter driving the beasts from place to place at great expense in an attempt to market them ' whereby he lost more of his health and effects than he has since that time been able to recover or make up again.' (*Forfeited Estates Papers*, Scot. Hist. Soc., 1st series, 57, 140)

[4] *P.R.O.*, Admiralty, 112/206

of the English graziers. The records show, however, that much of the naval beef supplies came from East Anglia where a large proportion of the Scots beasts found their way, while the total volume of the demand disclosed by the Admiralty Victualling Records shows beyond doubt that during the whole period from 1700 to the end of the French Wars naval buying was a factor of major importance to the droving trade. The War Office Records do not show so clearly the extent of Army purchases of beef as do those of the Admiralty, but some idea of the scale of the purchases of meat for the Army may be got from correspondence which passed between Lord Palmerston, at that time Secretary for War, and the Duke of York in 1812. Lord Palmerston had advocated that in the interests of economy bulk contracts should be made for the supply of the Army's meat. In support of his argument he wrote to the Duke in September 1812 that he estimated from figures available to him that if bulk contracts were entered into the saving alone in the course of one year would amount to between £60,000 and £80,000.[1]

Founded then, at its outset, on a demand from the South, and freed at length from political obstacles, the Scots droving industry derived from 1707 onwards stimulus and growing incentive from many sources; from the change in farming methods which developed cattle feeding in England nearly half a century earlier than in Scotland; from the growing wealth of the industrial areas; from demand for the Navy and the Merchant Fleet and, always and above all, from the growth of London.

The difficulties which until 1707 drovers of cattle from Scotland to England faced in crossing the Border hills were political and economic rather than physical. At few places in the whole stretch of the Cheviots is the ground so rugged or the hills so steep as to present a serious barrier to travelling cattle. The route by the east coast entailing passage of the rich Berwickshire plain would have relatively few attractions, but to the south-west a succession of easy passes lay open across the hills offering to the droves grass, water and quiet stances; by the valleys of the Bowmont, the Kale and the Jed into the head waters of the streams which feed the Coquet and the Rede; from the top of Liddesdale to the source of the North Tyne, from Eskdale and Annandale to the valleys of the Eden and the South Tyne. The exact routes followed by the Scots cattle in England up till the

---

[1] *P.R.O.*, War Office, 4/442

time of the Union must remain a matter for conjecture, for few detailed records have survived. The figures given for the Carlisle cattle traffic in 1661 indicate that the west-coast route into England was extensively used, but since London was already by far the greatest market in the South, it is probable that a large proportion of the traffic at that time kept down the east side of the Pennines by Corbridge and Northallerton. That some of the beasts were sold in Yorkshire is apparent from the complaint of the local graziers about 1660 that the Scots were underselling them, but it seems probable that many of the Scots beasts travelled straight on to East Anglia and the Home Counties.

By the middle of the eighteenth century the volume of cattle traffic from Scotland had reached great proportions, one contemporary estimate putting the total as high as 80,000 head each year.[1] By now the movement of population in England was having its effect in changing the routes and destinations of the Scots beasts. More of the traffic now entered England by way of Carlisle, from Eskdale and Liddesdale, or across the shallow estuary of the Solway to the Cumberland shore, a traffic swelled by imported Irish cattle. From Carlisle the routes of the Scots beasts led up the Eden Valley to Appleby and Kirkby Stephen or to Brough Hill near the borders of Westmorland and Yorkshire. At Brough Hill, towards the end of the century, as many as 10,000 Scots beasts were sold annually at the great fair at the end of September.[2] Some of these went to drovers from the South, some to graziers from Yorkshire and Cumberland, and some stayed in Westmorland for fattening.

From Westmorland a variety of routes led to the South. Some crossed the country by Richmond or Ripon to join the eastern drove route at Northallerton or Boroughbridge, while others led south to Kirkby Lonsdale, to Settle or to Skipton. These drovers' routes in the northern counties of England are in many places still to be seen, some as tracks crossing bare and open moorland, some enclosed between dry-stone dykes, but nearly always keeping so far as possible to the higher ground. The period of the main growth of the droving traffic to the South after 1750 corresponded with the period of the greatest extension of the Turnpike Trusts, and the choice of routes for the droves was dictated very largely by the need to avoid the tolls which the Trusts exacted. A

---

[1] Postlethwaite, *Britain's Commercial Interest Explained and Improved*, 1757, I, 57
[2] Fussell and Goodman, op. cit.

178

Broadsheet printed in 1753 urging a Turnpike Trust in Craven says : ' It is well known that the graziers in driving cattle from the North and other places where they buy them, keep constantly to the moors and never come on any road at all.' [1]

The Craven district of Yorkshire in which Skipton lies occupies an important place in the story of the Scots droving trade. The rich grazing of this limestone area, well suited to the fattening of cattle, was equally well placed for the supply of the English markets. To the west and south were the growing industrial areas of Lancashire and Yorkshire, while cattle fattened here could be readily driven across the low passes of the Pennines to supply the ports of the Yorkshire coast, or to join the main routes down the east side of the country to Northamptonshire, Buckinghamshire and East Anglia. During the first half of the eighteenth century the cattle trade from Scotland to England was, as has been seen, largely in the hands of Scotsmen, but after the turn of the century English dealers started to go north in increasing numbers. Graziers from Craven were among the first English dealers to come to Scotland in search of cattle. As early as 1745 Birtwhistle, one of the largest and most successful Yorkshire dealers, undeterred by political events around him, travelled through the Hebrides and the Highlands buying lean stock.[2] Moorhouse, another Craven grazier, bought the Skye and Raasay cattle in 1765.[3] A few years later Pennant reports dealers from the same district buying as far north as Ullapool,[4] and soon English dealers were attending the trysts at Crieff and Falkirk and penetrating far to the north and west in search of beasts. In 1767, the same year in which he was financed by the British Linen Bank,[5] Birtwhistle was pursuer in a Petition to the Court of Session against the factor for Mackenzie of Seaforth. The dispute was over a bill given by Birtwhistle for cattle purchased in Lewis. ' Of late years,' says the factor in his ' Answers ' to the Petition, ' it has been usual for the dealers in black cattle in our neighbouring country to come or send to the remotest parts of Scotland to purchase cattle.' [6] Birtwhistle was for many years tenant of the limestone grazing around Malham

---

[1] Brigg, *The King's Highway in Craven*, 59
[2] Hurtley, *Natural Curiosities in the Environs of Malham in Craven, Yorkshire*, 1834
[3] *The Farmer's Magazine*, 1804, 393
[4] Pennant, *Tour in Scotland, 1772*, I, 364
[5] See Chapter III
[6] *Old Session Papers*, Signet Library, 150, No. 24, 2

Tarn in Upper Wharfdale, ' a prodigious large field of enclosed land, being upwards of 732 acres in one pasture, a great part of which is a fine rich soil and suitable for making cattle both expeditiously and uncommonly fat.' Here ' you might frequently see 5,000 head of Scotch cattle at one time. As soon as these were a little freshened, notice was dispersed among the neighbouring markets and villages that a fair would be held in this field on a particular day. . . . As soon as these were disposed of a fresh drove succeeded, besides sheep and horses frequently in great numbers. Mr B. has had 20,000 head of cattle on this field in one summer. . . . To say the truth, when fattened on these rich old pastures, there is no beef equal to them in fineness either of grain or flavour.' [1]

While the route from Scotland down the west side of the Pennines saw yearly an increasing traffic, the more easterly route continued to be extensively used. Some of the Scots cattle lingered in the grazing lands of Northumberland to supply the needs of the small towns and the shipping of the north-east coast. Others grazed their way down through the hills which drain to the Coquet and the Tyne passing through Northumberland and Durham to North Yorkshire. From Northallerton their road lay by Boroughbridge to Doncaster and on by Gainsborough and Newark to Grantham and Peterborough, following roughly the route of the Great North Road which a traveller of the middle of the eighteenth century described as having wide stretches of turf on either side perpetually roughened by the passage of great droves of cattle.[2] Some, turning east about Grantham, went by Spalding and Wisbech into Norfolk, and a record of 1750 reports 20,000 Scots cattle as passing along the Wisbech road.[3] The routes of the drovers through Yorkshire and Lincolnshire, as in other parts of the north and Midlands of England, are marked by the names of the wayside inns, some of which still survive. The Drover's Inn at Boroughbridge and Wetherby, the Drover's Call between Gainsborough and Lincoln and the Highland Laddie at Nottingham and St Faith's near Norwich, recall the droving traffic to East Anglia and the Home Counties, as the Highland Laddie at Gretna and the Drover's Rest at

[1] Hurtley, op. cit.
[2] Fletcher, *The Making of Modern Yorkshire*, 17
[3] Thompson, *Cattle Droving between Scotland and England*. Journal of Archaeological Association, 1932, 87 (new series, 37), 181.

Kirkandrews in Cumberland recall that bound for Cumberland and the West Riding.[1]

In his *Tour through Great Britain 1724* Defoe described the meadow land between Norwich and Yarmouth : ' In this vast track of meadows,' he wrote, ' are fed a prodigious number of black cattle which are said to produce the fattest beef though not the largest in England. . . . The gross of all the Scots cattle which come yearly to England are brought thither, being brought to a small village lying north of the City of Norwich called St. Faiths where the Norfolk graziers go and buy them. These Scots " runts " as they call them, coming out of the cold and barren mountains of the Highlands of Scotland, feed so eagerly on the rich pasture of its marshes that they thus in an unusual manner grow monstrously fat, and the beef is so delicious for taste that the inhabitants prefer them to the English cattle which are much larger and fairer to look at. . . . Some have told me and I believe with truth, that there are about 40,000 of these Scots cattle fed in this country every year and most of them in the said marshes between Norwich, Beccles and Yarmouth.' [2]

Writing of the Norfolk grazings, half a century later, a writer of 1769 says : ' Here besides the cattle of the country numerous herds of starved cattle from the Highlands of Scotland find their way. Here they lick up the grass by mouthfulls, the only contention is which can eat the most and grow fat the quickest. When they have gotten smooth coates and swagging sides they continue their journey to the Capital and present themselves to Smithfield where they find many admirers.' [3]

The Fair at St Faith's which Defoe describes had existed since the twelfth century, and throughout the 150 years during which detailed records of Scots cattle droving to England are available this was the principal market for cattle from the North. To it came not only cattle from Skye and the Central Highlands but from Galloway. It started on 17 October each year and seems to have continued so long as there were cattle left for sale —usually a period of several weeks.[4] The woollen industry

---

[1] Thompson, op. cit., 180, 182
For certain of the information regarding the cattle trade and the drove routes in the northern counties of England I am indebted to an unpublished manuscript by Mr Kenneth J. Bonser, Leeds.
[2] Defoe, *Tour through Great Britain in 1724*, 6th edn., 1762, I, 59–60
[3] Gilpin, *Observations on Several Parts of the Counties of Cambridgeshire and Norfolk, etc.*, 1769   [4] Marshall, *Rural Economy of Norfolk*, 1795, I, 340–4, II, 49–52, 361

around Norwich which flourished through the greater part of the eighteenth century provided a local demand for fat cattle, but the greater part having been finished off on turnips after the autumn grazing were driven to the fat market at Smithfield in the following spring. Besides the great market at St Faith's, smaller but important ones existed in other parts of East Anglia, particularly at Hempton Green in West Norfolk, held on 16 November each year, and at Bungay, Hallisworth and Harleston near the borders of Norfolk and Suffolk.[1] Most of these were, like St Faith's, autumn markets, but some were held in the spring and early summer for the sale of stock from Scotland and the north of England for the summer grazing. Farther to the east in Hertfordshire, Barnet was the scene of a great market mainly for the supply of London, and here came cattle from Scotland, from the west of England and from Wales.[2]

The droving traffic from Wales affords a close parallel to the Scots droving traffic with which it must often have been in competition. Droving of Welsh cattle to England appears to be at least as old as the Scots traffic. As early as 1312, 700 cattle from North Wales were sent to Windsor for the supply of the King's household kitchen, and throughout the fourteenth century Welsh cattle were regularly bought for the supply of the Court or the houses of the great nobles. Welsh cattle were used in the fifteenth century for the provisioning of the army in France, and in the reign of Henry V there is a record of the salting of ninety-three Welsh cattle for the supply of the troops at Calais.[3] Disorder on the Welsh marches and the activity of cattle thieves hampered the traffic to England just as the state of the Borders affected the traffic from Scotland, and during the early years of the Civil War Welsh drovers petitioned the King for a safe conduct through the royal armies for the cattle traffic on which they depended for their livelihood and the payment of taxes.

From the records available it seems that the Welsh drovers fulfilled a function for which there is little parallel among the drovers of Scotland. In the seventeenth and early eighteenth centuries, when banking facilities were still unknown and travel was still precarious, the Welsh drovers started to act as agents for

---

[1] Smith, *Survey of the Agriculture of Galloway*, 1813, 249–50
[2] McCombie, *Cattle and Cattle Breeders*, 1867
[3] Skeel, *Cattle Trade between England and Wales from the 15th to the 19th Centuries*. Royal Hist. Soc. Transactions, 1926, 4th series, IX, 137–8

people in Wales who wished to transfer money or pay debts to correspondents in London. In some cases the money appears to have been carried to its destination, and there is a record of the transfer by drovers to London of the Denbighshire ship-money in 1636,[1] but latterly the drovers took to leaving the money at home and discharging the commission from their receipts in England at the end of the drove. This led to a primitive form of banking, and in 1799 the Black Ox Bank of David Jones and Company was started at Llandovery by one of the principal Welsh drovers with a picture of a black ox engraved on its notes, one ox for each pound of the note's value.[2]

Despite the drovers' difficulties, the Welsh cattle trade prospered, and during the seventeenth and eighteenth centuries reached large proportions. An estimate of the number of cattle driven from the three counties of Carmarthenshire, Pembrokeshire and Cardiganshire about the end of the eighteenth century puts the total at 30,000 per annum.[3] The routes from Wales are known with rather more certainty than those from Scotland. From South and Central Wales the main route appears to have taken the drovers across the Radnorshire border into Herefordshire and thence by Ross, Ledbury and Tewkesbury bound for the grazings of Leicestershire and Northamptonshire or as far east as Essex and Kent, but it seems probable that few Welsh drovers went as far east as Norfolk. From North Wales they passed through Kenilworth and Castle Bromwich into Warwickshire making for Barnet Fair and Essex.[4] A substantial part of the North Wales traffic came from Anglesey, and Aikin, in his *Journal of a Tour from North Wales in 1787*, has described the scene at the crossing of the cattle to the mainland in words which might well have been written of the crossing of Kyle Rhea by the Skye drovers :

' They are urged in a body by loud shoutings and blows into the water and as they swim well and fast, usually make their way to the opposite shore. The whole herd proceeds pretty regularly until it arrives within about 150 yards of the landing-place, when, meeting with a very rapid current formed by the tide eddying and rushing with great violence between the rocks that

---

[1] Skeel, op. cit., 151   [2] Skeel, op. cit., 143
[3] Lloyd, *Historical Memoranda of Breconshire*, 1903
[4] Fussell and Goodman, op. cit. Skeel, op. cit. Hughes, *Wales and the Drovers*, 1943

encroach far into the Channel, the herd is thrown into the utmost confusion. Some of the boldest and strongest push directly across and presently reach the land ; the more timorous immediately turn round and endeavour to reach the place from which they set off ; but the greatest part, borne down by the force of the stream, are carried toward Beaumaris Bay and frequently float to a great distance before they are able to reach the Caernarvonshire shore.'

Aikin records that as in the case of the Skye cattle, 'an instance seldom, if ever, occurs of any being lost.'

If the risks of droving from the Highlands to the trysts of the Scottish Lowlands were great, the drover who crossed the Border was launched on an enterprise fraught with risks and uncertainties even more varied and more serious. In the easier country of the South a longer day's march was possible, and stages of fifteen to twenty miles seem to have been not uncommon ; but charges for grazing and stance rights were higher. Shortage of hay or failure of the English turnip crop might spoil markets. Cattle disease, like that which ruined Thomas Bell in 1747, was a constant menace, while the cattle trade was always at the mercy of the issues of peace or war which were never far from men's thoughts in eighteenth-century Europe. As the droving trade developed and competition among the dealers grew more keen, it became the custom for those in charge of southbound droves to maintain with the dealers in Scotland a regular correspondence.[1] Some of these letters were honest appreciations of the situation from which the dealers in the North could judge the state of markets and the prospects for further droves, but some, less honest, were intended to convey to a wider circle such information as the drovers judged it wise and profitable to let them have. On any good news from the South, further droves would be sent off from Scotland with an optimism characteristic of the droving profession, which took little account of the risk that bad weather or political changes might, while the droves were on the long road, produce conditions ruinous to their owners. Evidence given before the Parliamentary Committee in 1826 already quoted, shows that in the autumn of 1801 severe losses were suffered by the drovers owing to the fact that news of the negotiations for the Peace of Amiens was only received

---

[1] Webster, *General View of the Agriculture of Galloway*, 1794, 25

after the Scots cattle had started on the journey to the English markets.[1]

Part of the droving traffic to England was spring droving. For this there were ready markets and good prices, though the losses among beasts driven in spring were often heavy. The number of beasts marketed in the spring was relatively small, and with the whole of the summer grazing ahead there was little of the autumn pressure to sell ; but most of the traffic took place in autumn when financial losses were more frequent. The writer of the *General View of the Agriculture of Galloway in 1794* has described the dangers of the trade to England :

' In September it is chiefly the best cattle that are bought to be fed on turnips and if the crop of turnips in England be plentiful, the prices of cattle in Galloway are generally high. Of consequence they must also be high in the Hempton Market, and if the first sold there are got off to advantage, then instant orders are sent down to hurry up every beast that can be purchased. At the approach of winter it is plain that every person will wish to dispose of all he can. . . . The English dealers, well acquainted with the former practices of the drovers and expecting plenty to be sent up, keep off from buying. Drove follows drove, no sales are made but at losing prices ; keeping gets up to an extravagant rate and perhaps the season becomes late, is rainy, the road becomes bad and numbers of cattle must be left at every stage, the greater part of which pay little more than for their skins. Such a practice as this may seem unaccountable but it must be considered that the drovers are in such a situation that it becomes unavoidable ; for while they are selling in England their bills are running on in the country, and thus their credit is constantly at stake, of which the banker takes care to advertise them.' [2]

In his account of St Faith's Fair in 1781, Marshall observes :

' The drovers do not bring their whole stock upon the " Bullock Hill " at once, but let them remain in the pastures until they are wanted ; nor do they bring any large droves at once into the country, but keep them back in Lincolnshire or

---

[1] *Report of Select Committee on Promissory Notes in Scotland and Ireland, 1826.* Notes of Evidence.
[2] Webster, op, cit., 26

perhaps in Scotland until they see how the demand is likely to prove. I did not learn the annual demand on a par of years but was told that Tate (one of the principal drovers) alone brings some thousands every year into this country.' [1]

Despite the risks and constant losses, the trade to England continued on an increasing scale. What they lacked in capital the drovers made up in courage and optimism, some secure in the knowledge that they had in fact little to lose, and that their losses if they failed would fall on others, but many relying in all honesty on their skill, knowledge and fortune. In the course of evidence given before the Select Committee on Promissory Notes in 1826 covering the preceding quarter century and the end of the Napoleonic War, witnesses drawn largely from officials of the Scots banks referred to bankruptcies involving £30,000 to £55,000, and in one case £70,000, on which dividends as low as one shilling in the pound were paid. William McCombie the Aberdeenshire cattle breeder, who was in the trade during the first half of last century, has recorded that when prices were at their height during the French Wars as much as £4 was sometimes made or lost on each beast driven to England.[2] In some cases the loss fell on the farmers, but in others on the bankers who had too readily given advances to the drovers, or had departed from their prudent rule of requiring two good names on a bill before it could be discounted. But such disasters appear to have acted as small deterrent, and the droving trade to England continued to flourish until a change in the farming practice in Scotland and the development of other means of transport led to the rapid decline of the industry in the second half of the nineteenth century.

[1] Marshall, op. cit., 52   [2] McCombie, op. cit., 99

11

THE COMING OF SHEEP

THE story of the origin and growth of the droving industry in Scotland is to a great extent the story of Scotland's cattle. The traffic which from early times traced out the routes of the drove roads, was largely traffic in the small black cattle of the Highlands with which these roads will always be associated ; but sheep too played their part, and in the first decades of the nineteenth century when stock traffic from the Highlands to the Lowland Trysts was at its height, sheep and cattle were equal partners.

The descriptions of Scotland, which have come down to us from travellers through the country in the thirteenth, fourteenth and fifteenth centuries and the records of the Privy Council in the sixteenth and seventeenth centuries, on which in the main must be based our knowledge of the livestock of contemporary Scotland, lay the main emphasis on the cattle rather than the sheep population. In Scotland, as in many other countries in primitive times, the ownership of cattle was the accepted measure of wealth, and cattle rather than sheep formed the common currency of the thieving traffic of the Highlands and upland districts of Scotland, with which so many of the early records are concerned. To men engaged in a perilous trade, the most valuable stock alone could justify the risks they ran, and when success depended on rapid escape with their booty, it was of vital concern to them that only those animals should be taken which could face hard forced marches across hills and rivers and mountain passes. Cattle alone supplied the answer to the reivers' problems, and save in island raids where boats were used or occasionally where large-scale expeditions gave leisure and opportunity for carrying off more cumbrous booty, cattle were the reivers' main prey.

For all that, there is no lack of evidence of the existence in Scotland from early times of a considerable sheep population. John of Fordoun in the fourteenth century, John Major, Hector Boece and Bishop Leslie in the sixteenth century all agree as to the large numbers of sheep in Scotland at the times of which they wrote. The grazing rights from which the early monasteries derived much of their wealth were not confined to cattle alone, and the Chartularies of the Abbeys of Arbroath, Newbattle, Melrose and Kelso fully confirm the descriptions of these early travellers.[1] The Exchequer Rolls for the year 1378 put the number of fleeces exported at 1,473,586.[2] The surprisingly high figure is possibly to be explained by the fact that until the latter part of the sixteenth century export trade from which the Crown derived its revenue was encouraged rather than home industry. It seems probable that for this reason the early export trade in wool was considerably greater than at a later date.[3] Ayala and Perlin writing of Scotland in the sixteenth century refer to large numbers of sheep as well as cattle in the country, and in 1591–92 the Privy Council had before it a complaint against the Scotts of Harden and Quhitslaid for the theft from Drumelzier and Dreva in Upper Tweeddale of 4,000 sheep.[4] Major in 1521 wrote of 10,000 sheep in the ownership of one man,[5] and in the confusion of Orders, Statutes and Regulations which reflect the changing and uncertain policy of the Crown to the livestock traffic of the sixteenth and seventeenth centuries, sheep are mentioned little less frequently than cattle.

At the start of the eighteenth century, the woollen industry in Aberdeenshire was one of the few prosperous industries in the country. Here a trade in rough plaiding had been gradually built up by the farming folk working their hand-looms to eke out the bare livelihood which their small farms or meagre daily wage afforded them. By the early years of the century as much as 400,000 ells of cloth were reported as being exported from Aberdeen each year, and while much of this appears to have been made from wool imported from the south of Scotland, some would no doubt come from the sheep of the North-eastern and Central Highlands. Before the end of the seventeenth century woollen cloth had taken its place with linen yarn and salt among the main exports of Scotland,[6] and the woollen industry was among those which were intended to benefit from the 'equivalent' payment arranged to compensate Scotland for the joint obligation for the National Debt which the Union of the Parliaments imposed on her.

---

[1] Cosmo Innes, *Sketches of Early Scottish History*, 99, and *Liber Sancti Marie de Melros*, xiv and xv
[2] *Exchequer Rolls*, II, xc   [3] Davidson and Gray, *The Scottish Staple at Veere*, 87
[4] *R.P.C.*, 1st series, IV, 709
[5] Hume Brown, *Scotland before 1700 : from Contemporary Documents*, 48
[6] Hume Brown, *History of Scotland*, III, 50

Little in the way of contemporary description of the sheep in Scotland before the eighteenth century has come down to us, and it was not till the middle of that century that the introduction of new and better breeds drew comparisons with the old native sheep, which tell what these were like. These eighteenth-century descriptions, while differing in small details, agree in the main that the old breed of sheep in Scotland was small in size, mainly white or dun-faced with wool fine in texture but meagre in quantity, a contemporary writer estimating that the fleeces of the old native sheep weighed no more than from twenty to twenty-eight ounces.[1] One writer described the sheep as having coats of short down, with some long straight hair like the coat of the beaver or other furred animals.[2] The small size of these native sheep is hardly to be wondered at in a breed which, like Scotland's cattle, had seen little change in blood for centuries, while lack of wool would naturally follow from the prevailing practice of keeping the sheep indoors throughout the winter. William Mackintosh of Borlum in 1729, advocating as a means of improving livestock the enclosing of farm land in Scotland by the planting of hedges, pointed out that such enclosing would not only make possible hay for winter food but would give some shelter for sheep in winter. 'Why may they not keep them unhoused,' he writes, 'which housing is certainly an enemy to the sheep and the staple of their wool.'[3]

There was indeed at that time little incentive to improve the breed of sheep in the country. There was little demand for mutton even at $1\frac{1}{2}$d or 2d a pound, and till the great expansion of the woollen cloth trade, which took place after the middle of the eighteenth century, the crop of wool from the native sheep of the old breed would be sufficient to meet home demands or such cloth export trade as had survived the loss of the continental market and the competition of England. It seems, too, that the practice of smearing the skins of the sheep in autumn with a mixture of tar and butter, which was considered necessary to destroy parasites and to protect the sheep against the cold and wet of the winter, not only lowered the value of the wool but raised the cost of home-produced woollen cloth by the added labour which the cleaning of the wool entailed.

---

[1] Alexander, *Northern Rural Life in the 18th Century*, 71
[2] Marshall, *General View of the Agriculture of the Central Highlands*, 1794, 46
[3] Mackintosh, *Essay on Enclosing*, 1729, 257–8, 263

Until the middle of the eighteenth century the farmers of Scotland continued in the belief that the weather of a Scottish winter would be fatal to sheep in the open, but about 1750 the discovery was made in Perthshire that sheep wintered out of doors not only survived but prospered. The discovery came at a time when the agriculture of Scotland was entering on that long period of change and improvement, which in the course of the next century was to raise it from a static condition of hopeless apathy till it rivalled, if it did not surpass, that of any other part of the British Isles. The defeat of the Rebellion of 1745 had brought with it the final disappearance of the clan system. Hitherto the main feature of land tenure in the Highlands had been the existence of large numbers of tenants and sub-tenants occupying their land with no fixity of tenure under a tacksman, often a relation of the chieftain from whom he held the land at a low or nominal rent. It was a system which had little to commend it, either as a social system or as a method of sound land management. The small tenants, with no security of tenure, struggled under the weight of burdensome services to make a bare living from such grazing rights as they had, or from the tiny patches of land which poverty and traditional methods of bad farming made them unable to improve. The land was over-peopled [1] and much of it over-stocked, and, in the absence of turnips, hay or potatoes, only the most rigid economy, the barest of living and the sale of surplus stock in the autumn, enabled the people to emerge from the winter months with enough starving beasts or sufficient seed to start the weary round when the spring came. The rents in money, in kind or in services paid by the smaller folk to the tacksmen greatly exceeded the nominal rents which the latter paid to the chieftain, and for the tacksmen, often with little real interest in or feeling of obligation towards their land or their tenants, the arrangement was highly profitable. For the chieftains, the main benefit lay in the fact that their lands were peopled by large numbers of tenants owing allegiance to them at a time when the ability to call on the services and loyalty of a strong following carried with it prestige and political advantage.

The years immediately after 1745 brought widespread changes.

---

[1] Sir Walter Scott quoting from the *Gartmore Manuscript* records that in the first half of the eighteenth century in the country round Inversnaid 150 families lived on an area rented at a total of only £90 per annum. (*The Highland Clans*, Sir Walter Scott, 1856, 30)

Of these, some were the direct result of the defeat of the Rebellion, others the outcome of the Union with England, the benefits of which to Scotland were only then coming into full effect. The loss of Scotland's continental markets through England's wars with France and Holland was only slowly made good by the opening of wider markets and trade opportunities in Britain's growing colonial possessions, and, for a time, it seemed to Scotsmen that their country had at the Union surrendered much and received little in exchange ; but when they came the changes and the benefits came quickly. Expanding trade abroad and growing industry at home meant a greater flow of money into circulation, fed by increasing commerce and stimulated by the activities of the growing banks. Nowhere were the changing times more felt than in Scotland's agriculture, and the years which followed the Rebellion saw the beginning of an agricultural revolution which was in its outcome to prove as complete as the Industrial Revolution of the first half of the nineteenth century. The growing towns of the Lowlands and a rising standard of living meant more demand for the products of Scotland's farming lands, and as the lowland areas became steadily more fully developed, the country came more and more to look to the Highland districts for its livestock.

In the Highlands the change was very marked. The growing wealth of the country put into circulation money for the improvement of estates. The enlightened policy of those responsible for the administration of the Forfeited Estates and the legislation which quickly followed showed the benefits of longer leases, and led to the establishment of a class of professional farmers with the knowledge and the desire to improve their farms and security of tenure to make this possible.[1] With the altered conditions had come too a change in the relationship of landlord and tenant. The end of the Rebellion and the abolition in 1748 of the old heritable jurisdictions of the chieftains and great landowners marked the close of a period when the existence of a multitude of small tenants was a desirable object. Amalgamation of holdings

[1] The Forfeited Estates Act of 1752 allowed leases up to twenty-one years to be granted and made provision for tenants receiving compensation for improvements, while the Montgomery Act of 1770 allowed heirs in possession of entailed estates to grant leases up to thirty-one years, the tenants being under obligation to keep the fences in order. Pennant in 1770 noted the effect of the 1752 Act in the increased amount of enclosing and planting. (Hume Brown, op. cit., III, 269. Pennant, *Tour in Scotland, 1772*, II, 92–3)

into larger units was seen to mean more economical working and easier administration, and this in turn led ultimately to the abolition of the tacksmen and the complex system of land tenure of which they formed an essential part. It was in these new conditions that sheep farming on a large scale came to the Highlands ; to a countryside where political and economic change had shaken loose the fetters which had bound it to an old way of life ; to hill grazings stored with the accumulated fertility of centuries of partial and inadequate use.[1]

In the middle of the eighteenth century, sheep farming on a considerable scale was already being carried on in the south of Scotland where, as has been seen, the hills of Tweeddale and the Southern Uplands had fed large flocks in the prosperous days of the monks. Though Scots sheep as a whole were not highly valued either as mutton or for their wool, the sheep of these southern areas, with richer grazing and more readily crossed with the improved breeds in England, were no doubt superior to the old inbred native sheep of the Highlands. A considerable trade already existed with England. By the year 1757 it was estimated that 150,000 sheep were sent each year across the Border,[2] and the demand for mutton in England is shown by the fact that as early as 1745 the number of sheep sold each year at Smithfield had already reached 600,000, though what proportion of these came from Scotland is uncertain.[3] By the middle of the century an increasing demand was arising for wool and mutton from the growing population of Central and Southern Scotland, from the expanding ports of the north-east coast of England and from the wool manufacturers of Yorkshire. Improved arable farming methods, and particularly the introduction of the turnip, greatly increased the possibility of fattening stock, while at the same time limiting the areas available for stock raising in the south of Scotland, and the sheep farmers of the South turned to the Highland hills and glens for new and extended breeding grounds. About 1759, farmers from the Annandale district of Dumfriesshire introduced, near Callander in Perthshire, south-

---

[1] The waste of hill grazing prior to the introduction of large-scale sheep farming had been accentuated by the absence of winter-feeding crops such as hay or turnips on the low ground and the almost complete lack of storage accommodation. This meant that the cattle must be brought down from the hills in time to join the droves to the low-country trysts—probably by the middle of September at latest.

[2] Postlethwaite, *Britain's Commercial Interest Explained and Improved*, 1757, I, 57

[3] *Report of Committee on Cultivation of Waste Lands, etc.*, 1795, Appendix A

country sheep of a kind known as the Linton breed which appear to have differed little in essentials from the black-faced breed of today.[1] From here the new vogue of sheep farming quickly spread, and by 1764 large tracts around the head of Loch Earn, in Glen Dochart, in Glen Falloch and in the Cowal district of Argyll had already been made over to sheep.[2] So quickly had the new system spread that Pennant, writing in 1772 of the growth of sheep farming in the Breadalbane country at the head of Loch Tay, complained : ' The livestock of cattle of this Kingdom decreases ; from whence will our Navy be victualled ? ' [3]

All through the second half of the eighteenth century, the spread of sheep continued through the Central and much of the West and North-west Highlands, and by the time the Statistical Account came to be compiled in the last years of the century a great change had come over the stock farming of Highland Scotland. In a large part of north and west Perthshire, in much of southern Argyllshire and in Morven, sheep were predominant. So, too, in the Lochaber district of Inverness-shire where James Hogg in 1803 found the whole of Glen Garry made over to sheep, while in the Kintail district Glenshiel had been let to a grazing tenant from Annandale and the houses of the old small tenants were in ruins.[4] Only in Skye, the Outer Islands and parts of Ross-shire and the far north and north-west were cattle still the main stock, though even here much of central Ross-shire was already under sheep. A description of Sutherland and Caithness in the 14th Report of the Commissioners for Highland Roads and Bridges speaks of an annual export of 80,000 fleeces and 20,000 sheep in 1828 as compared with an export in 1809 of a small number of cattle.[5] When in 1803 Telford planned his new road from Kyle Rhea to Killin to serve the droving traffic from Skye and the north-west to the markets of Central Scotland,

[1] Campbell, *Journey from Edinburgh through North Britain*, 1802, II, 375–6
[2] ibid.   [3] Pennant, op. cit., II, 17
[4] Hogg, *A Tour in the Highlands in 1803*, 53–4
How very local had been the spread of sheep farming at this time is shown by the fact that, in contrast to Glenshiel, James Hogg found the Dundonnell district ' so crammed full of stout able-bodied men and women that the estate under the present system must have enough to do maintaining them. The valleys are impoverished by perpetual cropping and saving for one farm in the north-east quarter . . . the extensive mountains are all waste ; for the small parcels of diminutive sheep which the natives have are all herded below nearest the dwellings and are housed every night ' (ibid. 92).
[5] *H.R. & B.*, 14th Report, Appendix D, No. 15, 61

he estimated that it would be used by 20,000 cattle and 80,000 sheep each year,[1] and in describing the road through Glencoe in his Survey and Report of 1803 he blamed the sheep, which had supplanted the cattle formerly pastured in the glen, for the frequent falls of stone from the hillside above.[2] 'The sheep farming system in Glencoe,' wrote a traveller in 1818, ' had done the work of extirpation of the inhabitants more effectively than the Massacre of 1692.' [3]

The introduction of the Linton breed of sheep had enormously increased the immediate productive capacity of the Highlands. The new sheep were larger than the old native breed. They were hardier too, while the new method of leaving them on the hills in the winter meant that the hill grazings were stocked throughout the year and not only in the short period when, under the old system, the cattle were herded from the shielings on the high pastures. But the fleece of the Linton breed, though heavier than that of the old sheep, was coarse, and with growing demand for wool as well as mutton, Scots graziers turned their attention to finding a breed which would combine in the fleece weight and quality. The mill owners of Halifax, Wakefield and other Yorkshire cloth-manufacturing towns required wool in increasing quantities and of the best quality, while between 1775 and 1797 the weight of wool made into cloth in the Galashiels district of Scotland had risen from 772 stones to 4,944 stones.[4] To meet this demand the Cheviot breed was, with the active support of Sir John Sinclair the compiler of the Statistical Account, introduced in the far North in the last years of the eighteenth century, and from this time onwards grew steadily in popularity. In his survey of the Northern Counties in 1795 Sir John made a strong plea for the introduction into Ross-shire, Sutherland and Caithness of sheep, and particularly those of the Cheviot breed. He produced detailed figures to show that under cattle the rent of the land was only about $2\frac{1}{2}$d per acre while under sheep it would be 2s per acre. The annual export from the Highlands would, he reckoned, be double the existing figure of £200,000 to £300,000 without taking into account the considerable value of the wool. His arguments had to overcome great opposition owing to

[1] See Appendix B (p. 227)
[2] Telford, *A Survey and Report of the Coasts and Central Highlands of Scotland*, 1803
[3] Larkin, *A Tour in the Highlands in 1818*, 221
[4] Hamilton, *The Industrial Revolution in Scotland*, 66

Plate 15   On the Corrieyairack Road
(Photo by Robert M. Adam)

prejudice and the deep-rooted belief that sheep must be housed in winter.[1] So rapidly, however, did the Cheviot breed grow in favour that the *Stirling Journal and Advertiser* for September 1827, describing the Falkirk Tryst of that year, reported : ' Till 20 years ago black-faced sheep was the favourite, but now Cheviots have been introduced all over the Highlands and are prospering. The black-faced breed—the hardy aboriginals—are now only seen on the rugged summits of bare mountains along with the blackcock, the ptarmigan and the eagle.' The arrangements for marketing the wool were also improved. Hitherto sheep and wool had been sold, with cattle, at the local trysts, the manufacturers of York-shire and the south of Scotland sending to the farthest parts of the Highlands to buy, but in 1817 a special market for sheep and wool was, with the support of the Yorkshire buyers, established at Inverness, where in the following year as much as 100,000 stones of wool were sold.[2] Writing of his work in the Highlands during the second quarter of the nineteenth century, Mr Joseph Mitchell, the road engineer, has so described the sheep and wool market of Inverness :

' Besides the local fairs throughout the country, there is a great sheep and wool market held annually in the month of July at Inverness. It was established in 1817, and has been for many years an important gathering. Chiefs and country gentle-men, great sheep farmers, factors, and mountain peasants, assemble at this market once a year to meet and transact business with south-country buyers.

' This meeting is unique. Here you see the portly figure of a wool stapler of Huddersfield and Leeds ; beside him the quick and intelligent Liverpool merchant, or the shrewd, broad-speaking woollen manufacturer of Aberdeen or Bannockburn. The burly south-country feeder stands at the street corner in deep conversation, and about to strike a bargain with that sharp, lynx-eyed, red-haired little man, who is the largest farmer in the North, and counts his flocks by 40,000 or 50,000. The greatest agriculturist in the North compares notes of his experience with the celebrated member of the Highland Society, who is also an extensive farmer in the Lothians. That stout man who is talking

---

[1] Sinclair, *General View of the Agriculture of the Northern Counties, etc.*, 1795, 182 and 184 et seq.
[2] Anderson, *The State of Society and Knowledge in the Highlands of Scotland*, 1827, 127-8

with the Highland drover came to the North some thirty-eight years ago a common shepherd. He is now a great farmer and owner of 12,000 or 15,000 sheep.

'You may notice also from their military air the retired colonel and captain, who in the Highland regiments bled on the fields of Spain and Waterloo, and who now as sheep farmers are passing the evening of their days in their native glens, and come here to dispose of their year's stock. That gentleman with sunburnt and weather-beaten visage, who for years cruised around the coasts in His Majesty's service, is now securely moored in a remote valley as the breeder of sheep. There is also the capitalist who has invested £10,000 or £15,000 in sheep and cattle, and who applies to this branch of husbandry all the knowledge and acquirements of agricultural science.

'Besides these there are small farmers, clad in homespun tweed of various colours, the real aborigines of the country, tall, stout, athletic fellows, some in kilts, with their plaids carelessly thrown over their shoulders. There also with their crooks are numerous common shepherds, in whose conversation you may overhear the deep guttural of the Highland brogue, and the broad Scotch of the border counties. The collie dogs must not be forgotten, the constant and vigilant attendants on their masters. Notwithstanding the kicks and ill-usage they encounter in the crowd, they cling to the shepherd's side, and look as if they had as great an interest in the market as the more intelligent bipeds.

'This market is perhaps the most singular in Great Britain. About 1,000 persons attend. No stock or samples are produced ; the buyers know the stock of each farm, and make their purchases without seeing either sheep or wool. They merely agree upon a price and exchange missives as to delivery and payment. Bargains are thus said to be made at the market to the amount some years of £400,000. A casual observer would stare at this motley crowd of well-dressed people on the street, lounging from morning till night for two successive days, without any apparent purpose.

.   .   .   .   .   .

'The market still holds, but alas ! the glory of it is gone. Almost all those fine fellows mentioned above, with warm hearts and generous sympathies, have gone to their rest. The frequent wool and sheep sales in the great towns in the South, and the rapidity with which the whole produce of the North is now transported to its destination by railway, have destroyed the interest that once belonged to this commercial and social gathering.'[1]

The revolution in the farming practice of the Highlands which took place in the second half of the eighteenth century and the early years of the nineteenth century was not carried through without great changes in the social system on which the old methods rested, and much distress among the people most closely affected. The new improved methods were directly opposed to the interests and the very existence of the small tenants cultivating their tiny strips of arable ground and exercising their limited rights of grazing in common on the hills. The introduction of artificial grasses brought with it the need for enclosing those arable parts of Highland farms where, up till then, the cattle of small tenants had grazed at large after the harvest. The demand for low-ground grazing and wintering for the stock of the new sheep farms was equally fatal to the old system, while the change in outlook which had come about as a result of the decay of the clan system removed the incentive to Highland landowners to maintain large populations in their glens.

' I have lived to woful days,' said an Argyllshire chieftain in 1788. ' When I was young the only question asked concerning a man's rank was how many men lived on his estate ; then it came to be how many black cattle it could keep ; but now they only ask how many sheep the lands will carry.'[2] The urge for high rents and the attraction of easier land-management and smaller obligations all tended in one direction, offering to Highland landowners the opportunity of compensating themselves for the loss of political power which they had suffered.

The outcome of the changes which were taking place was fully apparent to the men of the time, and the new trend was by no means universally welcomed, even by those to whose immediate advantage it seemed to be. The writer of the Statistical Account for the Parish of Glenshiel reported that a few years before, an offer of a threefold increase in rent from a sheep grazier had been refused by the proprietor on the ground that ' he would never prefer sheep to men,'[3] but James Hogg's description of the glen twenty years later shows that here, too, the pressure of economic change had proved irresistible.[4] James Anderson

---

[1] Mitchell, *Reminiscences of my Life in the Highlands*, I, 336 et seq.
[2] Scott, *The Highland Clans*, 36   [3] *O.S.A.*, Glenshiel, VII, 128
[4] Hogg, op. cit., 53–4, 56

writing in 1785 tells of the reluctance of landlords to disturb the sitting tenants, but foretells that ultimately their dispossession in favour of those offering more rent is inevitable.[1] Marshall ten years later predicted the depopulation of the Highlands,[2] and at the beginning of the nineteenth century Telford foresaw that the change-over to sheep would go too far, that a balance between sheep and cattle must be the ultimate object of Scottish stock-farming, but that before this came about a depopulation of the Highlands would take place which it might be hard to redress.[3]

The troubles which far-sighted men like Telford predicted did indeed come, and the end of the eighteenth and the beginning of the nineteenth centuries saw great distress in a large part of the Highlands. The period was one of rapid and wide-spread change, both economic and social. Growing industry meant a redistribution of population, while growing wealth, increasing knowledge and improved methods brought new ideas of land ownership and estate management. Prices were rising and rents with them, while improved medical knowledge and living conditions brought about a steady increase in population. In these circumstances it is hardly to be wondered at that the readjustment to a new way of life was not made without grave dislocation and great distress among that part of the rural population whose existence depended on the old conditions which were passing away.

From 1770 onwards a gradual exodus of population from the Highlands took place. Some drifted to the towns or the Lowlands, many emigrated to America, driven away by rising rents, by the enclosing of land for sheep farming or for the creation of larger and more economical farms. Some, like the small tenants of Glen Garry, went with the tacksmen whom the new conditions were driving from so many Highland estates and to whom they were bound by ties of sentiment, economic dependence or age-long custom.[4] By the end of the eighteenth century the depopulation of the Highlands had gone far to create the conditions which Telford had foreseen.

That the coming of sheep was partly to blame is certain. The sudden realisation of the possibilities of the new farming had induced a more commercial spirit in the outlook of the

---

[1] Anderson, *Account of the present state of the Hebrides*, 1785, 25-7
[2] Marshall, *General View of the Agriculture of the Central Highlands*, 1794, 52, 56
[3] Telford, op. cit.   [4] Hamilton, op. cit., 70

landlords towards their lands and their tenants. The urge was now to obtain with the minimum of trouble, obligation and capital outlay, the greatly increased rents which rising prices, due to the Continental Wars and the growth of commerce, enabled prospective tenants to offer. Economic pressure was great and in some cases eviction and emigration did without doubt follow directly as a result of the introduction of sheep ; but this was not the only cause. It is significant that the considerable emigration of 1770 took place before the growth of sheep farming had begun to have a wide-spread effect,[1] while even during the later period of emigration between 1783 and 1803 the Hebrides, which were little affected by the introduction of sheep, provided a large proportion of the emigrants, while Argyll which was much affected provided few.[2] The rise in population, the increased competition for farms and the gradual elimination of the tacksmen seem to have been more potent causes. Much has been written on the subject, and the determination of the part which sheep farming played has only incidental relevance to the present inquiry, but the evidence does appear to show that even if sheep farming had not come to the Highlands, emigration on a considerable scale would have taken place.

Despite the great development of sheep farming which took place at a time when the droving industry was at its height, the drove roads from the Highlands to the Lowlands remained for a great part of their existence primarily the routes of cattle. The earliest movement of stock in the Highlands was, as has been seen, largely the outcome of raiding expeditions, and sheep, as the old reivers knew, would not drive so easily, so quickly or so far as cattle. When more peaceful times came, cattle remained the chief droving stock, for the native sheep were little in demand for mutton, their chief value lying in their wool which, save perhaps in the case of the Aberdeenshire woollen trade, did little more than supply the needs of the local people, clad in the products of their own spinning-wheels and hand-looms. The demand for Scotland's livestock in the first half of the eighteenth century was largely a demand for meat to feed the growing towns of the South and to provision the trading and naval vessels of the English ports, and for this mutton was in less demand than beef. These were

[1] Adam, ' The Highland Emigration of 1770.' *Scot. Hist. Rev.*, Vol. XVI, 280
[2] Adam, ' The Causes of the Highland Emigration of 1783–1803.' *Scot. Hist. Rev.*, Vol. XVII, 73

conditions perhaps not unsuited to the character and inclination of the Highlander brought up in the tradition of his cattle-reiving ancestors. ' The Highlander, a child among flocks is a prince among herds,' wrote Scott of the eighteenth-century drover. ' His natural habits induce him to disdain the shepherd's slothful life so that he feels himself nowhere more at home than when following a gallant drove of his country's cattle in the character of their guardian.' [1] There was, too, another reason why up till the middle of the eighteenth century cattle took the road while sheep stayed at home. Before Wade built his roads, and indeed till well on in the second half of the eighteenth century, the roads of Scotland were primitive, and in much of the Highlands non-existent, and the rivers were almost all unbridged. While to the cattle drover these conditions presented little difficulty and were at times of positive advantage, it would have been very different for a drover of sheep. To drive a flock of sheep long distances day after day over rough, mountainous and open country would, in those circumstances, have been a slow and laborious task. Droving and shepherding the flocks by day and herding on the stance at night would alike present greater difficulty than in the case of cattle. The crossing of streams and rivers would have presented problems at times almost insoluble. Streams which even in moderate flood could be forded by cattle were for sheep formidable barriers, while rivers, narrow lochs and arms of the sea, which cattle could and did swim with ease, were for sheep impassable. In the last quarter of the eighteenth century when sheep traffic from the Highlands, stimulated by the growing demand for wool and mutton, was steadily increasing, considerable progress had already been made towards the improvement of the roads of the Highlands, and with the work of the Commissioners for Highland Roads and Bridges in the first part of last century, road and bridge construction in the Highlands made rapid strides. So the main growth of sheep farming came to Scotland at a time when conditions had made their droving possible.

The impression that sheep were unsuitable for droving appears to have persisted for some time after the improvement of Highland

[1] Scott, *The Two Drovers*, Chap. I

Scott was no doubt referring to shepherding in the Highlands at a time when the sheep population was still small in numbers, poor in quality and largely confined to the low-lying parts of the farms and the immediate neighbourhood of the farm buildings.

communications had begun. In 1794 Sir John Sinclair wrote of Lismore that cattle are the stock best suited to the island since 'they admit of being driven to distant markets,' while of the Island of Shuna he reports that 'the proprietor is thinking of abandoning sheep since they cannot be driven fat to market.' Another agricultural writer in the same year refers to the need of devising some method of getting sheep to market by water, dead or alive.[1] Sheep moreover could not be shod, and it may be that it was a general belief in the eighteenth century that their feet would not stand the long journey to the trysts. The history of the sheep trade in the nineteenth century shows, however, that none of these difficulties were in fact insurmountable, and it seems more probable that the explanation of the small part played by sheep in droving traffic during most of the eighteenth century is to be found in the small demand for mutton and the considerable local use of wool. A marked change took place towards the end of the century with the rapid growth of industrial population both in Scotland and England, and from that time on sheep formed an increasingly large part of the live-stock traffic to the trysts.

Throughout the first half of the nineteenth century the sheep traffic passing over the drove roads of Scotland showed a steady increase. Falkirk Tryst had displaced Crieff shortly after the introduction of large-scale sheep farming, and here the number of sheep brought to the Tryst as recorded in the local press of the day, shows clearly the rapid rise of the new stock farming. An agricultural report of 1812 estimated the number of sheep sold at Falkirk that year at 40,000,[2] and 150,000 sheep were reported to have been sold in 1818 at the newly established market at Inverness.[3] At the Falkirk Tryst of October 1836 the number sold there had grown to 75,000,[4] and before the middle of the century when the numbers at the September and October markets had almost reached 200,000, the trade in sheep is reported to have surpassed the trade in cattle.[5] From then onwards, though the increase in Highland sheep farming was to continue for another twenty-five years, the growth of the railways caused a gradual decline in the traffic on the drove roads.

[1] Robson, *General View of the Agriculture of Argyll and West Inverness-shire*, 1794, 20–1, 34
[2] Graham, *General View of the Agriculture of Stirlingshire*, 1812, 334
[3] Anderson, *State of Society and Knowledge in the Highlands of Scotland*, 1827, 127–8
[4] *Stirling Journal*, October 1836   [5] *Stirling Journal*, 1840–50, *passim*

But it was not for the trysts alone that sheep traffic passed along the old routes, and when in the second half of the nineteenth century a stricter view of land ownership and the growing importance of sporting rights gave rise to litigation, the testimony of the older witnesses in support of the traditional routes disclosed the existence of a widespread and cross-country traffic in sheep. Many indeed spoke of droving traffic to the trysts, but others told of sheep traffic caused by the movement of young stock between grazings widely separated or to the low ground and coastal farms for fattening or for wintering. Throughout the whole period of rather over a hundred years which elapsed between the beginning of large-scale sheep farming in the Highlands and the final decay of the droving industry in the seventies and eighties of last century, the routes used by the sheep traffic seem have differed little if at all from those used by the cattle droves. The evidence of contemporary writers and Court witnesses and the recollection of the few shepherds and drovers who still recall those days, is of sheep on all the old established drove routes. On the road from Ullapool and Wester Ross to Muir of Ord and through Strath Glass to Fort Augustus ; on the Corrieyairack Pass and on the road by Kingshouse and the Black Mount to Tyndrum ; on the hill tracks from Upper Donside to the Dee and in the passes leading to the Angus glens, sheep were on the move following the old routes marked out by the feet of the cattle whose place they had so largely taken.[1]

The growth and spread of sheep farming in Scotland continued throughout the greater part of the nineteenth century, reaching its peak about 1870. Then, from a variety of causes, a gradual decline in its prosperity set in, a decline which, with some fluctuations, has continued till very recent years. Many of the causes had been foreseen when sheep farming on a large scale first came to the Highlands. The enthusiasm with which the new farming was welcomed had induced many to stock their farms entirely with sheep, encouraged by their initial success on hill pasture enriched by the old system of cattle grazing. Little

[1] *McGregor & Others* v. *Breadalbane*, 1846, Court of Session Cases, 9 Dunlop's Reports, 210 ; 7 Bell's Appeal Cases, 43.

Mackenzie v. *Bankes*, 1868, Court of Session Cases, 6 Macpherson's Reports, 936

Scottish Rights of Way Society v. *Macpherson*, 1887, Court of Session Cases, 14 Rettie's Reports, 875

Winans and Chisholm v. *Tweedmouth*, 1888, Court of Session Cases, 15 Rettie's Reports, 540

thought was given to whether the hills so made over to sheep were indeed suited to them, or whether a mixture of sheep and cattle would, as more prudent men believed, be better. Heavy stocks of sheep, grazing the hills more constantly than cattle had done under the old system, ate steadily into the stored fertility of ground which received little or nothing in return, and it was not till about 1884 that serious attention was given to the advantages of a mixed stock, in which the less-searching grazing habits of the cattle would be complementary to the ' close inquisitive bite ' of the sheep.[1] By that time other factors had appeared which were to bring ruin to many of the sheep farmers. The demand for sheep to stock the new ground was dwindling and the low-ground farms were in active competition for the trade, while with foreign supplies the prices for wool and mutton were also declining.[2] The coming of sheep farming on a large scale had brought another change to the Highlands. Under the old system of cattle grazing on the hills, bracken appears not to have been a serious menace. The cattle on the hills no doubt trampled it down and kept it in check. The larger population of the Highlands at that time meant cultivation of much of the more fertile parts of the lower hill ground where the bracken thrives, and the cutting of such bracken as did grow to supply the cheapest and commonest form of thatch and bedding then available.[3] With the coming of sheep and the fall in population the bracken spread largely unchecked, to add one more to the list of problems of Highland resettlement, many of which date from the start of Scotland's eighteenth-century agricultural revolution, and some of which are still unsolved.

[1] *Napier Report* (Crofters' Commission) 1884, V, 45
[2] *Report of Committee on Hill Sheep Farming in Scotland,* 1943, 8
[3] While there appears to be general agreement that the spread of bracken on hill grazings was encouraged by the reduction in the number of cattle on the hills and the increase of sheep, the presence of bracken in seemingly large quantities is noted at least as early as 1808 when the growth of sheep farming was still in its early stages. Walker in 1808 refers to it as being particularly hurtful in sheep walks, and blames it for braxy among sheep. He classes it, however, as a valuable manure and considers that its destruction can best be achieved by cutting for use as manure or as thatch, or by burning. After three years cutting, he writes, it is reduced to negligible proportions. (Walker, *Economical History of the Hebrides and Highlands,* 1808, I, 158–60)

12

THE DECLINE OF THE DROVE ROADS

WERE the progress of the Scots droving trade after the Union of 1707 to be illustrated by means of a graph, it would be seen that the index line, after a relatively slow ascent in the first half of the eighteenth century, rose from the middle of the century with increasing steepness to reach its peak about 1835, and that its descent was short, sudden and complete. At the close of the eighteenth century the number of beasts—cattle and sheep—driven south from the Highlands and the grazing areas of south-western Scotland was increasing year by year. The growing industrial towns of North England and the Midlands meant a rising meat consumption; the demand from London continued to expand, while the French War kept the needs of the Navy at a high level. In Scotland itself the demand for beef and mutton, though still relatively small, was steadily growing to meet the increasing needs of the towns of the Lowlands, where Glasgow's population alone had risen from 12,000 to 84,000 in the course of the century.[1] 'If a dry season lessen the demand from England,' says the Statistical Account of Crieff, 'the extensive pastures and vast consumpt in the south of Scotland suffers not the drovers to be disappointed of a sale.'[2]

Until the last years of the eighteenth century little in the shape of a comprehensive survey of Scotland's livestock had been attempted, and estimates based on the numbers sold at the various trysts are misleading, for the same animals might change hands at successive markets on the way, giving the impression

[1] As late as 1816 there were no butcher's shops even in Edinburgh, and in the rural districts meat was seldom seen unless a beast died or a 'mart' was killed for salting in the autumn. In the northern counties, reported Sir John Sinclair in 1795, not five pounds of meat was consumed on a farm in a whole year and an egg was a luxury. 'We have seen in the summer season a haddock occasionally as a wonderful regalement.' Somerville reports that beef was seldom to be had except at fairs or on special occasions such as the land-setting at Hawick, when the beast was garlanded and led through the town by the town piper. George Robertson writing of Kincardine-shire in 1829 reported: 'Cheap as fish is here, there is but little of it used by the farm servants and still less of butcher meat.' (Croal, *Living Memories of an Octogenarian,* 16. Sinclair, *Agricultural Survey, Northern Counties* etc., 1795, 82. Somerville, *My Life and Times,* 1741–1814, 332–3. Robertson, *Rural Recollections,* 1829, 422–3)
[2] *O.S.A.,* Crieff, IX, 597

of a larger trade than in fact existed. The figures for the various parishes contained in the Statistical Account now for the first time gave some indication of the total cattle population in Scotland, and these figures, together with the County Agricultural Surveys, both of which we owe largely to the energy and initiative of Sir John Sinclair, make it possible to assess with some accuracy the volume of the droving traffic at the close of the eighteenth century. Writing in 1795, Sir John estimated the annual value of cattle sold from the Highlands at £200,000 to £300,000.[1] Taking the value per head at £4, which was the average price realised at Falkirk Tryst in 1794,[2] this would appear to represent a total of over 60,000 cattle, a figure which corresponds closely with contemporary estimates of the number sold at Falkirk. The droving trade from the south-western counties augmented by imports from Ireland had also reached large dimensions. Estimates in the last year of the eighteenth century of the number of cattle paying toll at the crossing of the Nith on the road to England place the total at over 20,000 per annum, and by the close of the century the total number of cattle driven from Scotland to England each year is believed to have reached 100,000.[3]

While the total volume of droving traffic was thus steadily rising towards its peak, a marked change had taken place in the sources from which it came. From Skye and the Hebrides came still a steady flow of beasts treading the well-worn paths from Lochaber, Rannoch and the Argyllshire coast. Writing in 1811, James Macdonald in his *General View of the Agriculture of the Hebrides*, estimated the total cattle population of the islands at 110,000, of which one-fifth were sold to the mainland each year, an estimate which accords well with Telford's estimate that 20,000 cattle each year would use the new drove road which he planned from Kyle Rhea by Rannoch to Killin and the South ;[4] but these numbers showed no increase in any way proportionate to the increase which was taking place in the total volume of droving traffic to the South. The numbers reported in the Statistical Account as crossing Kyle Rhea from Skye in 1794[5] were in fact

---

[1] Sinclair, op. cit., 185   [2] *O.S.A.*, Falkirk, XIX, 83

[3] It may be noted, however, that even in 1813 a writer on the Agriculture of Inverness-shire refers to the difficulty in estimating, the size of the cattle trade being so great that no two people can be found to agree on the numbers brought from the Highlands each year. (Robertson, *General View of the Agriculture of Inverness-shire*, 1812, 303)

[4] See Appendix B (p. 227)   [5] *O.S.A.*, Glenelg, XVI, 270

considerably less than those noted by Pennant twenty years earlier, nor is any increase apparent in the numbers ferried from Mull or Jura.

The development in Scottish agriculture and the growing demands from the South had indeed affected very little the volume of the cattle traffic from the Islands and the west coast. Here from an early date the division of the land among many small tenants, each with his rights in a common grazing area, had already raised the numbers of stock up to, if not beyond, the capacity of the land. Disregard of the Winter Herding Act and the almost total absence of storage accommodation deterred tenants and sub-tenants from growing hay or turnips for winter food. The system of tenure and the temperament of the tenants were alike unfavourable to the adoption of the new methods which were fast transforming the stock farming of north-east Scotland, and it is in these north-eastern districts that the reasons must be sought for the expansion of droving traffic to its highest point in the second quarter of last century.

The rapid improvement in Scottish agriculture after 1760 resulted, as has been seen, in the restriction of the area given over to cattle grazing, and pushed that industry farther and farther north. The greatest effect of the change was felt in the north-eastern counties where a new mode of farming based on stock raising was tending to displace the traditional and cumbrous system of arable cultivation. All through the latter part of the eighteenth century the cattle trade of these north-eastern counties grew steadily. The demand from the South was growing for the better quality of cattle which the new farming was producing. By the end of the century the beasts driven south from Aikey Fair alone were in one year estimated at 6,000,[1] and the annual sales of one Aberdeenshire drover—Williamson of Fyvie—had reached 8,000.[2] From Morayshire too went a steady flow, while Kincardineshire and Angus added their quota, and each successive year saw more and still more beasts from the north-east bought at Falkirk for the grazings of Cumberland, Yorkshire and Norfolk.

Prices followed the rising demand. By 1811 the value of cattle sent southward each year from Aberdeenshire was estimated at £150,000.[3] Long before the French War ended, cattle were

---

[1] Alexander, *Northern Rural Life in the 18th Century*, 81
[2] Keith, *General View of the Agriculture of Aberdeenshire*, 1811, 466
[3] ibid.

being sold at Falkirk for as much as £25 a head,[1] while evidence given in the course of litigation in the Court of Session in 1800 disclosed dealings between one cattle dealer and an Angus farmer to the extent of £30,000 per annum.[2] Most of the cattle sold from the north-east counties were beasts locally bred, but some were brought to the richer grass from the Highlands, and the description of an Aberdeenshire cattle dealer's life in the early years of the century shows him buying as far afield as Caithness, Sutherland, Skye and the Western Isles.[3]

The peak of prosperity to which droving rose in the second quarter of last century was the Indian summer of the trade. Already certain adverse factors were at work, while others, more deadly still, were soon to emerge. From first to last the prosperity, the very existence, of the trade depended above all else on freedom of passage, freedom of wayside grazing and freedom of nightly stances. Each was essential, and the absence or severe restriction of any one would be fatal to the whole enterprise. As the years went on, increasing population, rising standards of knowledge and growing skill in the management and cultivation of land, encroached more and more on these essential freedoms, and by the end of the eighteenth century, despite the growing volume and value of the trade, it must have been increasingly clear to the more far-sighted among the drovers that the time was not far off when their trade must fight for its life. The first sign of changing times had indeed become apparent soon after the middle of the century when Crieff Tryst, hitherto the centre of the cattle trade in the Highlands, gave way before the growing importance of the Tryst at Falkirk. Falkirk was more accessible for buyers from the South, but the chief reason for the change, as reported by contemporary writers, lay in the importance to drovers of reaching the market from the North by the easiest and quickest routes. 'For a considerable time after the beginning of the century,' reported the writer of the Statistical Account for Crieff in 1794, 'the drovers from Argyll, Inverness, Ross-shire, etc., paid nothing for the pasturing of their cattle on the way to market ; but in the improved state of the country grass became more valuable, the roads more confined and the drovers were forced to enquire after the most convenient and cheap roads from

---

[1] Belsches, *General View of the Agriculture of Stirlingshire*, 1796, **45**
[2] *Old Session Papers*, Signet Library, 1800, I, 410
[3] McCombie, *Cattle and Cattle Breeders*, 99

their several homes to the principal market place now at Falkirk, where the roads leading by the shortest course from every quarter of the Highlands towards England naturally unite ; and where the whole of the Argyll and near half of the Inverness-shire cattle can arrive some days' journey earlier than if they came by Crieff. Additional travel was no loss while the pasture cost nothing, but would now considerably affect their profits.' [1]

The reasons for the decline of Crieff Tryst were symptomatic of a widespread and permanent change which had set in affecting by degrees the whole of the country cultivated or capable of cultivation. In some parts this took the form of the enclosing of pasture and arable fields by the dry-stone dykes which had already caused serious rioting in Galloway as early as the beginning of the eighteenth century. In others the drovers' routes were themselves enclosed by dykes or turf walls to protect the arable ground through which they passed. Everywhere the drovers were coming to be more narrowly hedged in and deprived increasingly of the wayside grazing which had hitherto been their traditional and unchallenged right.

The early years of the nineteenth century brought more trouble to the drovers. When Wade built the first properly constructed roads in the Highlands, the routes he chose were selected with a view to military rather than civilian or commercial use. Some of these, like the route over the Pass of Corrieyairack, through Drumochter Pass and by Dalnacardoch to Crieff, were in fact routes long in use by the drovers, and one of the arguments used by those who resented Wade's work was that the new roads would wear the feet of the beasts. The argument had little substance, for at that time the droves were still free to wander almost at will on or off the road and, as has been seen, there is reason to think that where the roads were used by droving traffic, the resulting damage was to the roads and not to the beasts. The extension of the military road system which took place after Wade's time was for similar reasons probably not a serious matter for the drovers, but when early in the nineteenth century the Commissioners for Highland Roads and Bridges took over the old military roads and embarked on the work of road-building which the Scottish Highlands owe largely to Telford, a new situation arose. By now the new agriculture and the new outlook on land ownership had become a major factor. Many byways and

[1] *O.S.A.*, Crieff, IX, 596

cross-country routes were still open to the drovers, but more and more as time went on did they find themselves forced on to the made roads. Now, the grievances previously urged by Wade's opponents became more real, and from this time onwards the shoeing of cattle at intervals on certain parts of their journey to the South was a necessary part of the drover's work.[1] The new roads had for the drovers a further drawback. The old roads had followed closely the contours of the ground uphill and down dale, but as the technique of road-making improved, cuttings and embankments came into use, still further restricting the wayside grazing of the travelling beasts.[2]

Wade's roads and the system of military roads constructed after his time were made and kept up entirely by military labour, and up to the middle of the eighteenth century other roads in so far as they existed at all were in theory maintained by statute labour—a system by which proprietors and occupiers through whose land a road ran, were obliged either to pay a small sum based on the rental of their land or to give a certain number of days' work on the roads. The system proved highly unsatisfactory, but about 1750 increasing use began to be made of the system of turnpikes, and between 1750 and 1844 upwards of 350 Turnpike Road and Bridge Acts appear to have been passed in Scotland, setting up Turnpike Trusts empowered to levy tolls on traffic using bridges or sections of the road under their care.[3] Tolls on bridges at certain points had long been common in Scotland, but for the most part the drovers of these days could and did avoid the crossing of bridges, preferring to ford, ferry or swim the rivers. Scope for this was now becoming restricted, and tolls on roads and bridges became a material and growing item in the drovers' budget.[4]

[1] It must be admitted that it is not easy to reconcile this entirely with Telford's plan to construct a road specifically for drovers from Kintail to Killin. He clearly cannot have regarded a constructed road of this sort as unsuitable for droving traffic, nor does it appear that the opposition which led to the abandonment of the plan came from drovers who feared its effect on the feet of the stock using the road.

[2] The trend of subsequent legislation affecting the use of highways for the driving of stock may be judged by the inclusion in a recent Order of the following clause :

' The owner of any cattle or horses or any person for the time being in charge thereof who wilfully and habitually creates an avoidable nuisance by permitting the same to use any footway on the side of a public highway so that the said footway is damaged or littered with excremental matter shall be guilty of an offence and shall be liable on summary conviction to a penalty not exceeding Twenty Pounds.' (*Fife County Council Order Confirmation Act*, 1949, ch. lvii)

[3] *Report by Commissioners for Enquiring into matters relating to Public Roads in Scotland*, 1859, xvi   [4] See Appendix G (p. 242)

Freedom of passage had been challenged and freedom of wayside grazing restricted. Freedom of nightly resting-places for the droves was now to be attacked. When cross-country droving in Scotland on an appreciable scale first began, and for many a year thereafter, a great part of the Highland and upland areas of the country was common land, or at the least land which, while nominally owned by the local chieftain, was in fact unused and uncared for. In the earliest rentals for Islay and Kintyre, for example, the figures representing the total of the ' merk lands ' held by the tacksmen from the local chieftains do not amount to more than about one-third of the total extent of these areas as shown on modern maps. The rest was wasteland which was gradually merged into the tacksmen's holdings with the progress of agriculture.[1] The process by which this great unused area was absorbed into the holdings of the tacksmen or their sub-tenants was a gradual one, and not until sheep farming on a large scale became common in the Highlands were these upland areas put to fuller use than for the grazing of cattle from the sheilings in summer and early autumn. On the lower ground the position was more difficult for the drovers, and after the middle of the eighteenth century they found their old privileges of grazing their beasts at night increasingly challenged. The steady increase in droving traffic from now onwards aroused tenants and proprietors, particularly on the approaches to the trysts, to the opportunities of profiting by the demand which now existed for grazing on a scale which constituted a substantial burden on land, the increasing value of which had come to be recognised. So the old days of free grazing gave way to a new era in which stance rights had to be paid for on a scale which gradually increased from a nominal sum to the substantial payments which had become common before the droving industry came to an end. To avoid this burden some of the larger drovers started to rent grazings of their own at strategic points on the main routes to the trysts, and Cameron of Corriechoillie is said to have been able to pasture his beasts on grazing of his own all the way from Lochaber to Falkirk ; but operations on such a scale were possible only to a very few, and to the great mass of the drovers the increasing cost and difficulty of stance rights was a growing menace.

Despite the growing practice of demanding payments for

[1] McKerral, ' The Tacksman and his Holding in the South-West Highlands.' *Scottish Historical Review*, Vol. XXVI, 10–25

Plate 16 The Kyle Rhea Crossing in Modern Times
(Photo by Robert M. Adam)

nightly grazing there still remained many areas of common land where the night's grazing of a passing drove was unchallenged, and probably in many cases free, but as time passed this privilege too was attacked. In 1695 an Act of the Scots Parliament had provided for the division of common lands with a view to avoiding the disputes to which common ownership so often gave rise.[1] For many years little use was made of the new legislation, but in the second half of the eighteenth century the division of common land became increasingly frequent. The procedure before the Sheriff or the Court of Session was complex and often long-drawn out, but some idea of the extent to which common lands were divided may be obtained from the fact that between 1750 and 1890 the number of Processes of Division of Commonty before the Court of Session alone, as recorded in H.M. Register House, Edinburgh, is over 450.[2] These included Hawick [3] and Gretna,[4] important stages on the drove route to England ; Sheriffmuir,[5] the last and most important resting-place for cattle from the Highlands bound for Falkirk, and the common land near Falkirk itself which was the original site of the Falkirk Tryst.[6]

While the rights of stance were thus becoming increasingly costly and circumscribed in the more cultivated districts and on the approaches to the trysts, they remained in the Highland districts for the most part unchallenged, and it was not until the middle of last century that the droving industry, already on the decline, was called on to meet an attack on rights vital to its continuance. It will be recalled that one of the main drove routes from Skye and Lochaber to the South ran from Fort William by Kinlochleven and the Devil's Staircase to the head of Glencoe, and so skirting the western edge of the Moor of Rannoch, by Inveroran, Bridge of Orchy and Tyndrum to Crieff and Falkirk. On this route, at intervals of approximately ten miles, were stances for the night—at Altnafeadh near Kingshouse, at Inveroran, at Tyndrum, at Luib in Glendochart and at Balquhidder. In 1844 Lord Breadalbane proposed to close the

---

[1] *A.P.S.*, IX, 462

[2] See Index to Processes of Division of Commonty, 1661/1890, H.M. Register House

[3] Hawick. *Currie Office* (Dalrymple), H. Bundle 4, 1768, H.M. Register House

[4] Gretna, *Mackenzie Decreets*, 9/8/1770, H.M. Register House

[5] Sheriffmuir, *Durie Decreets*, 2/12/1772, H.M. Register House

[6] Falkirk, *Durie Decreets*, 19/12/1807, H.M. Register House

stance ground at Inveroran, offering in its place another site at Clifton near Tyndrum. The new site was seventeen miles from Kingshouse and fourteen miles from the stance at Luib, distances too great for a drove of sheep or cattle to cover in a day, while it would make useless the existing site at Tyndrum. Faced with a change which threatened to make impossible for a drove the crossing of the Moor of Rannoch, the drovers were forced into a litigation [1] on the result of which depended the legal basis of stance rights enjoyed for generations.[2] The action was defended on behalf of drovers from Skye and the Outer Isles, from Knoydart and Lochaber, from Ardnamurchan, Morven and Ardgour, from Wester Ross, Sutherland and Inverness-shire and from south of the Border. The Court of Session favoured the claims of the drovers,[3] accepting their contention that, though in this case paid for, the right of stance was an essential part of the right of passage for livestock, which latter right was not then in dispute. The House of Lords thought otherwise, and on an appeal by Lord Breadalbane held that the drovers had failed to make out a relevant case and that the stance rights claimed had no legal foundation.[4] Consideration of the grounds on which the decision was based are beyond the scope of the present work, but it seems at least probable that a court of law today would endorse the view taken by the House of Lords in 1848 that the extensive but undefined stance and pasture rights then claimed, though based on the custom and unchallenged usage of centuries, constituted a

---

[1] *MacGregor and Others* v. *Breadalbane*, Court of Session Cases, 1846, 9 Dunlop's Reports, 210

[2] The importance of the route for these drovers is clear from a report of a committee appointed by them to inquire into the position, which showed that the route was used by 70,000 sheep and 8,000 to 10,000 cattle each year. (*Breadalbane Papers*, (*Roads*), Box 4, H.M. Register House)

[3] So did a portion of the contemporary press. After noting with approval John Stuart Mill's view that uncultivated land should be looked on as held in trust for the community, the *London Daily News* of 30 August 1848 commented thus on the position : ' Rights of road, especially footpaths and drift ways over enclosed land have been almost annihilated in England, and the Highland proprietors of Scotland seem to be rapidly effecting the same thing in the North. . . . There is too much reason to fear that the encroaching proprietor with an ultimate right of appeal to a Tribunal of his own class will be more than a match for the public. . . . Now this right [of stance] which has existed for centuries is not displaced to make way for cultivation or improvement of any kind but to foster the barbarous and puerile passion for artificial wild sports : and the feudal spirit of the House of Lords assists the purblind owners of Highland estates to push their proprietary right to this mischievous extreme.'

[4] *MacGregor and Others* v. *Breadalbane*. Court of Session Cases, 1848, H. L. 7 Bell's Appeals, 43

limitation on the ownership of land unknown to the law of Scotland.[1]

It might have been expected that the result of the Breadalbane litigation would have been a widespread closing of stances and so, in effect, of drove roads throughout the Highlands. There is little evidence that this took place on any large scale. The inevitable outcome of the House of Lords decision had it been fully and widely applied would have been the end of all droving, and it is doubtful whether public opinion would have supported a widespread attack on an ancient traffic the value of which was still considerable. The latter half of the nineteenth century did, however, see an increasing movement among the proprietors of Highland estates towards the closing of drove roads, the regular use of which was then fast diminishing. To combat this the drovers varied their routes where possible in an attempt to keep open to their traffic ways which otherwise would have been lost by disuse and lapse of time. Despite this device very many drove roads must have fallen into disuse, and, while it would be neither possible nor profitable to determine the routes so closed, it is beyond any doubt that those which still preserve the character of rights of way are but a remnant of the network which at one time covered the country.

Litigation of a major character took place on at least three occasions in the second half of the century, but in each case it was the right of way rather than the right of stance that was attacked. In 1868 the road up the Gruinard River used by the Lewis drovers from Aultbea and Gruinard in Wester Ross-shire was in dispute.[2] In 1887 an attempt was made to close the road through Glen Callater and Glen Doll to Kirriemuir,[3] while in the following year that from Strath Glass by Guisachan to Glen Moriston came under challenge.[4] In each case the right of way was upheld, the testimony of witnesses providing a wealth of

---

[1] The final outcome of the Inveroran litigation was that an alternative stance was provided at Bridge of Orchy, a mile farther south. Here the tenant of the farm of Achallader, on whose land the new stance was situated, is still bound by his lease to keep open the stance ground, ' having in return the right to levy the dues and charges which according to custom are now levied.'

[2] *Mackenzie* v. *Bankes*, Court of Session Cases, 1868, 6 Macpherson's Reports, 936. Notes of Evidence, *Session Papers*, Signet Library.

[3] *Scottish Rights of Way Society* v. *Macpherson*, Court of Session Cases, 1887, 14 Rettie's Reports, 875.

[4] *Winans and Chisholm* v. *Tweedmouth*, Court of Session Cases, 1888, 15 Rettie's Reports, 540

evidence as to the droving traffic of the districts concerned, stretching back to the early years of the century.

The increasing tendency to close to the drovers these cross-country routes was the outcome of a strict view of land ownership at odds with a trend to more liberal thought, a conflict which characterised the latter part of the nineteenth century. A new factor too in the shape of sporting interests was now emerging which added emphasis to the desire for the preservation of land. How early sporting rights became of material interest to Highland proprietors, either for their own use or as a source of profit, seems rather uncertain. Burt appears to have engaged in both shooting and fishing, if one can judge by the mention in his *Letters from the North of Scotland* that he did not shoot plover ' except to busk his flies for fishing.' Half a century later Colonel Thornton had great sport both shooting and fishing in Badenoch.[1] Grouse were being regularly shot there and in Ross-shire before 1815. The Marquis of Huntly's party killed ' 553 brace of muirfowl ' in the first week's shooting of 1816,[2] and a traveller of 1818 refers to the inn at Kirkmichael being much frequented during the grouse-shooting season.[3] Anderson's *Guide to Scotland* in 1834 states : ' it has now become a common practice for Highland proprietors to let the right of shooting over their grounds. Moors may be had at all prices from £50 to £500 for the season with accommodation varying according to circumstances.' [4] Of the year 1833 the Earl of Malmesbury wrote in his Memoirs : ' This was the first year that the Highlands became the rage and that deer forests were made and rented, but for prices not exceeding £300 a year. . . . I went later (1833) to the Isle of Skye and to Harris. I was harboured at the latter by Mr Stewart a gentleman farmer and breeder of cattle, and had the run of the Island which belonged then to Macleod, and the grouse, deer forest and fishing, all of which were first rate, were offered to me at £25 a year.' [5] From now on the possibilities of the Highlands to the sportsman became increasingly recognised. Deer stalking grew steadily in popularity all through the nineteenth century, and the conflict of interest between the proprietor of a Highland deer forest and a drover who sought to cross the hills with his beasts, and in the

[1] Thornton, *Sporting Tour*, 1804, Chap. 5
[2] *Inverness Courier*, 25 August 1816
[3] Larkin, *A Tour in the Highlands in 1818*, 36
[4] Barron, *The Northern Highlands in the 19th Century*, II, xxxvi
[5] Quoted by Barron op. cit., xxxvi–xxxvii

crossing to graze the corries at any time from June to October, needs little emphasis.

The great advance in agricultural knowledge which spread over Scotland after 1750 had, by the end of the century, gone far to transform Scottish farming methods, particularly in the east and north-eastern districts. At first the effects of the changes were almost wholly favourable to the droving industry. As late as 1779, Mr Andrew Wright, surveyor on the Annexed Estates, travelling through Aberdeenshire, had reported that ' he could observe no grass until he alighted and put on his spectacles ' ; but the practice of sowing artificial grass seeds and enclosing young grass and hay which became common in Aberdeenshire in the last quarter of the century, brought a steady improvement in the quality of the grazings. Stock breeding was still commoner than stock fattening, and the better grass in conjunction with steady demands from the South meant more and better cattle driven to the trysts, where prices rose to their peak as the French War approached its climax. But the new agriculture was based largely on a system of crop rotation made possible by the introduction of the turnip, and with its increasing cultivation came a fundamental change which was to prove in the end fatal to the drovers.

Turnips had been introduced into East Lothian shortly after the middle of the eighteenth century, but it is reported that as late as 1773 they were still regarded as such a rarity as to be served as a dessert on Edinburgh dinner tables.[1] A report of the Highland Society in 1812 mentions them as being tried by some tenants but not widely grown, and in the previous year a prize offered for the best acreage under the new crop was not awarded, no competitor of sufficient merit having come forward.[2] In Aberdeenshire itself where the new crop was to spread so rapidly, it is reported that until about 1820 few turnips were grown.[3] The next few years saw a rapid change, and by the date of the preparation of the New Statistical Account turnip growing in the main cattle-breeding districts of Scotland had become general. From parish after parish of Aberdeenshire came reports

[1] Topham, *Letters from Edinburgh*, 1776, 229
[2] *Transactions of Highland Society*, IV, 505, note
[3] McCombie, op. cit., 55
The value of turnips seems, however, to have been recognised before this date by some Aberdeenshire farmers. A description of the agriculture of the County in 1811 refers to the brothers Williamson of St John's Wells, near Fyvie having 200 acres of turnips. (Keith, *Agricultural Survey of Aberdeenshire*, 1811, 466)

of the great changes which it was bringing about. ' Nothing for many years back,' wrote the minister of the parish of Old Deer in Buchan, ' has contributed more to improve the farming interest in this part of the world than the discovery and general use of bone manure for the raising of turnips.' [1] His report was typical of many. From the parishes of Alford, Garioch and Ellon came similar reports,[2] while from Wigtownshire, Kirkcudbrightshire and Dumfriesshire the tale was the same.[3] The growing knowledge and new farming methods had moreover come at a time when the farmers of Scotland were at length in a position to take advantage of them. ' The improvements introduced by the landowners towards the conclusion of the last century,' wrote the minister of the Aberdeenshire parish of Tarves in 1840, ' were at first but slowly adopted by the tenantry. Depressed by bad seasons and deficient in capital, they had neither the courage nor the means to attempt expensive innovations. The rise however in the price of agricultural produce which succeeded the breaking-out of war between this country and revolutionary France, by increasing the capital of the farmers, enabled them to take advantage of the more decided and valuable improvements . . . and from this period the progress of improvements was extremely rapid.' [4] With turnip growing and the improvement of pasture came a change from stock breeding to stock fattening, and the same districts which reported the growing of the new crop reported also the keeping and feeding of cattle during the winter, now at last made possible.[5]

Had the changes in farming methods been unaccompanied by other great developments, the effect on the droving industry might have been little more than the increase in numbers, quality and price which was noticeable at the great trysts in the early part of last century. But now for the first time serious competitors to the drovers were entering the field. As the light failed on an October evening of 1786, a Highland drover resting

---

[1] *N.S.A.*, Old Deer, I, 154
[2] *N.S.A.*, Garioch and Ellon, XII, 575, 911–2
[3] *N.S.A.*, IV, Whithorn, Wigtown, Kirkcudbright, Kirkpatrick-Irongray, Sorbie, Crossmichael and Tongland.
[4] *N.S.A.*, XII. Tarves, 671
[5] The number of cattle which passed through the village of Tarves on their way south after Aikey Fair in 1836 was 2,200—little more than one-third of the number counted on the corresponding day about the beginning of the century. By 1876 the number sold at the fair was reported to be not more than 250. (Alexander, op. cit., 81)

beside the cattle which he had brought to the Falkirk Tryst, on its new site at Stenhousemuir, might have seen to the eastward a glow in the sky, brightening as the twilight deepened. A quarter of a century earlier the first of the new furnaces had been blown in at Carron, a site chosen by Dr Roebuck and his colleagues for its central position and its proximity to iron-stone and coal supplies, to replace the old fashioned 'bloomeries' in the West and North-west Highlands soon to decline with the exhaustion of the natural forests which had hitherto fed them.[1]

If the reflection of the Carron furnaces meant little to the Highland drover it was in fact full of significance for the future of his calling. The enterprise at Carron had been successful, and the furnaces now hard at work smelting iron for 'carronades' and shot for the British Navy and Army were soon to be yet busier helping to arm half the nations of a continent at war ; but Carron was the birthplace of other developments heralding a new age in which droving would have no place. Here, a few years before, had been constructed the first steam engine for winding coal and within the next few years Carron was to see the birth of the steamship. The first commercial steamship with engines made in the Carron works was launched on the Carron River in 1789, and soon ships of the Carron Company were regularly carrying goods and passengers between Carron and London.[2] The full effect of the new method of transport was not felt for another quarter of a century, but between 1820 and 1836 a marked change took place in the transport of cattle from the north-eastern districts. The new farming methods were now producing fat beasts not suited for droving, and farmers and buyers alike were becoming increasingly aware of the loss of weight and condition which the journeys by road entailed.[3]

[1] From the correspondence which passed between the promoters before the site at Carron was finally chosen, it appears that the availability of charcoal supplies was also taken into account. Indeed the Carron furnaces in their early years were operated entirely with charcoal, and at one time the Company purchased wood on the Glenmoriston Estate for this purpose at a cost of £900. The prospect of planting woods near Carron was also considered, but coal soon became the chief fuel used there. (Cadell, *The Story of the Forth*, 151, 152. Macadam, *Notes on the Ancient Iron Industry of Scotland*. Proc. Soc. Ant. Scot., 1886–87, IX, new series, 90)

[2] Cadell, op. cit., 184

[3] Arthur Young, discussing the loss of weight of the cattle on the road, quotes an instance of six bullocks of 50 stone each which, on a journey of 70 miles to Smithfield, lost 14 lb. each. Another writer of last century quotes an estimate that during the journey of a fortnight from Holkham in Norfolk to London the beasts dropped in value by as much as three guineas a head. (Unpublished MS. *The Elements and Practice of Agriculture*, Vol. 28, British Museum)

Already a small demand existed for transport of cattle from Aberdeen to Leith and London by sailing boat at a cost of £1 10s a head, and as the size and value of the beasts increased, graziers and dealers in Aberdeen, Banff and Wick took increasing advantage of the new steamship transport now becoming available, judging the chance of quicker passage to the South worth the risk to the beasts at sea and the freight charges of £2 10s to £3 a head.[1] 'The introduction of bone manure and the short-horned breed of cattle and the contemporaneous opening of the English markets for fat cattle by steamer,' wrote the minister of the Parish of Logie Buchan in 1840, 'have been productive of the greatest benefit to the agricultural interest,' a view which finds expression in page after page of the New Statistical Account of the parishes of north-east Scotland.

An account of the early development of cattle shipping from Aberdeen written by one who remembered it, makes it clear that the risks to the shippers and to the beasts were by no means small :

'Sometimes they made quick passage,' he writes, 'but this was uncertain and I have known them a month at sea. I have seen the same cargo of cattle driven back to Aberdeen two or three times. . . . Although the loss by deterioration in condition must have been great, it was astonishing how few deaths occurred in the sailing ships ; the proportion was greater in the steamers. A year seldom passes without the shippers having heavy losses. I was owner of a part of the cattle when every beast aboard the *Duke of Wellington* except three were either thrown overboard or smothered in the hold. . . . I have made enquiries of a cattleman as to the scene in the hold of a ship in a storm among the cattle. He says " I went once down to the hold among them but I was glad to get back with my life, and although you had given me the ship and all aboard her, I would not have gone back ".'[2]

In the cattle-breeding districts of the south-west the new sea transport was making similar inroads on the drovers' trade. By 1835 cattle were being transported regularly by steamship from Kirkcudbright to Liverpool, and others from Dumfries and Annan, while the running of steamers from Ireland to Liverpool

---

[1] McCombie, op. cit., 102   [2] McCombie, op. cit., 104

and Glasgow had so cut into the Irish cattle trade to Portpatrick that the traffic to the Wigtownshire coast, which in 1812 had reached the figure of 20,000 per annum, had fallen by 1837 to only 1,080. The writer of the New Statistical Account for the parish of Kirkpatrick-Irongray in Wigtownshire reported in 1842 that 'many of the farmers are beginning to adopt a different system, viz. to fatten their cattle at home and then send them south by steam to the market. This system, if fully acted upon, will put an end to droving which has proved of late years ruinous to all concerned.'

In the Hebrides the effect of the new methods of transport made itself felt more slowly, and until well on in the second half of last century the old sailing smacks remained in use for bringing cattle from the Outer Islands to the mainland. Shortly after the turn of the century, however, the newly formed shipping companies to the Islands began to introduce special facilities for loading cattle on to their steamers, and by about 1880 transport of cattle by steamer to the rail heads at Strome Ferry, Mallaig and Oban had almost entirely superseded the old methods.

The development of railways in Scotland was not at first unfavourable to the droving trade. The first railways to be built were largely for the transport of coal and iron. For many years the lines constructed were purely local with no kind of through connection, and not until 1848 did the Scottish Central Railway open a line giving access from the south of Scotland to Perth, the same year in which the North Eastern Railway Company completed a line to Aberdeen.[1] For some years after this the effect of the railways on the droving traffic as reflected in the numbers of beasts sold at Falkirk Tryst was negligible. Falkirk was now more accessible to buyers coming from the South, but the animal traffic by road from the Highlands suffered little reduction. As late as 1860 the local press commenting on the progress of Falkirk Tryst reported : ' It had been expected that after the introduction of railways the trysts would decline owing to facilities for buyers to go further north to buy, but this has not been the case. On the contrary, Falkirk tryst has continued to be the rallying point as being central.' [2] Shortly after this date, however, a rapid change set in. Buyers from the South started to go to the Highlands to buy direct from the graziers, and with the growing

---

[1] Hamilton, *The Industrial Revolution in Scotland*, 250
[2] *Stirling Journal*, 9 October 1860

practice of sending beasts south by rail from the Highlands and the grazing areas of the north-east, the railways came in the last quarter of the nineteenth century to constitute a major factor in the decline of the droving trade. In December 1888 the North British Railway carried 1,016 fat cattle from Aberdeen to London for the Christmas market, and in the same month of the following year the Caledonian Railway carried 1,048. During the year 1889 the Highland Railway transported 250,000 sheep to the South.[1]

Despite the growing use made of sea transport from 1820 onwards, Falkirk Tryst remained until past the middle of the century the centre of a great trade, and reports of the numbers of beasts sold there year by year as appearing in the local press of the time are a fair index of the fortunes of the industry. Here are recorded the total numbers of beasts at the trysts, the districts from which they came, and the prices realised with many a colourful description of the scenes on the tryst ground. By the closing years of the Napoleonic wars the numbers of stock sold each autumn at Falkirk had risen to about 50,000 cattle and nearly as many sheep, while the demand from the South had raised prices to such an extent that the total value of the stock sold in 1812 was estimated at nearly half a million pounds.[2] The end of the war though it ruined many an individual drover did not halt the upward trend in the total numbers of beasts sold, and contemporary reports show that at the two Falkirk Markets in September and October 1827 a total of 130,000 cattle and close on 200,000 sheep changed hands.[3] The extent of the cattle trade to England about this time may be gauged by the fact that in 1825 as much as £80,000 to £90,000 in Scots notes are believed to have been put into circulation at Carlisle each week during the main droving season.[4] The Aberdeenshire cattle breeder, William McCombie, writing of his experiences during the first half of the nineteenth century, has recorded having seen 1,500 cattle belonging to one breeder passing through Carlisle in a single drove bound for Norfolk,[5] and in 1844 the local press reported that at a recent Falkirk Tryst one bank alone had honoured bills to the extent of £150,000.[6]

[1] Acworth, *The Railways of Scotland*, 141 and 142
[2] Graham, *General View of the Agriculture of Stirlingshire*, 1812, 334
[3] *Stirling Journal*, 13 September and 11 October 1827
[4] Hamilton, op. cit.   [5] McCombie, op. cit., 71
[6] *Stirling Journal*, 27 September 1844

Though there were few indications that the Tryst was nearing its end, shortly after the turn of the century references to cattle salesmen, the forerunners of the auctioneers, began to appear.[1] At first the salesmen did their business at the trysts, but later they conducted their own sales in Edinburgh and Glasgow, and with the spread of railways to the North regular auctioneering businesses established themselves at Perth, Oban and Inverness. The sales at Falkirk in 1870 were said to be the smallest then on record, and five years later only 2,000 sheep appeared at the September Market.[2] The reason given was that buyers had gone north and were adopting the practice of buying year after year the stock of particular grazings over which they had obtained a right of pre-emption. As late as 1880, 15,000 cattle and 20,000 sheep were at the October Tryst,[3] but this seems to have been the last flicker of a dying flame. In the late eighties a few thousand cattle were still being driven each autumn from Oban and the West Highlands, but year by year the numbers dwindled, and before the century ended Falkirk Tryst had virtually passed from active life into the annals of Scottish Agriculture.

The closing years of the nineteenth century saw the last of the cattle and sheep droves passing over Wade's old road by the Corrieyairack Pass,[4] and about 1906 the last of the Skye droves crossed Kyle Rhea to the Glenelg shore where they were exposed for sale on the market stance near the ferry on the south side. Later they passed by Glenshiel into Glen Garry, taking for the last time Telford's route by Glen Ci-aig to Loch Arkaig and the crossing of the Spean.

The threads of living recollection which still link us with the droving days are slender, and each year sees the breaking one by one of the few that remain. There are still (1952) men living who have seen the cattle boats sailing into Loch Dunvegan with the Uist droves, or the ferry boats from Lagg bringing the Islay cattle across the Sound of Jura. Others tell how they helped in their youth to bring droves from Kintyre and Knapdale by Inveraray and Loch Lomond to Falkirk, or from Don-side across

---

[1] The risk of cattle disease or 'murrain' appears to have been an additional factor in the decline of the cattle trade, particularly to England. The local press for 1850 and 1865 reports that the September and October markets at Falkirk were largely spoiled by outbreaks of the disease. (*Stirling Journal*, 11 October 1850 and 9 October 1865)

[2] *Stirling Journal*, 17 September 1875

[3] *Stirling Journal*, 15 October 1880

[4] J. B. Salmond, *Wade in Scotland*, 250

the Dee to the Angus glens on the road to Perth. Their part in the last of the droving days is recalled with pride in an old and honourable trade ; with regret too for the passing of the peace of mind and the contemplative outlook of those less hurried days.

The brown sails of the cattle boats have gone from the Minch. On slipways and jetties from Skye to Kintyre thrift grows undisturbed in the crannies of stones once smooth and polished with the tread of hooves. The hills round Loch Ainort look down on lonely saltings where the Uist droves once grazed, while throughout the Highlands, in hill pass, moorland and upland valley, as in the minds of men, the passing years increasingly dim and obscure the mark and the memory of the men and the beasts that once travelled the drove roads of Scotland.

THE END

APPENDICES

APPENDIX A

(*page 57*)

THE SALTING OF BEEF IN SCOTLAND

SOME export of salted beef from Scotland, particularly to Flanders, appears to have existed in the sixteenth century while at the beginning of the eighteenth century Caithness, Orkney and Shetland were carrying on a similar trade with Leith ; but the quality of home produced Scots beef was not in general suitable for salting. William Mackintosh of Borlum, the great advocate of the enclosing of agricultural land, writing in 1729 forecast the improvement in the quality of stock which would result from enclosing. ' Our over-seas trading Merchants,' he wrote, ' who have occasion to send their ships far voyages will find in their own Mercats beef that will bear salt which our own half-fed beef heretofore would not do, and the ships were forced to call at some town in England or Ireland to have beef or pork to make a Mediterranean or American voyage or endanger the lives of their crew with the thin, lean, hard beef their own Mercats could afford.' (Mackintosh, *Essay on Enclosing*, 1729.)

A further reason for the lack of a successful salting industry in Scotland was the absence of suitable salt in Scotland for the purpose. The salt-pans on the Forth produced considerable quantities, and salt is mentioned by Fynes Moryson in 1598 as one of the exports of Scotland ; but though some was exported, the *import* of salt was being encouraged as early as 1535. The reason appears to have been that the home produced salt was not suitable for curing, and there are frequent references to the ill-effect of trying to cure with salt obtained from salt water. The development of the Scottish fishing industry made it necessary to import finer salt for curing and the recital to an Act of 1587 narrates that ' refynit salt utherwayes callit salt upone salt is verie necessar and proffittable for salting salmound, keilling, ling and utheris grite fisches, quhilk . . . now is accustumat to be maid and hes bene maid befoir within this realme.' This ' salt upone salt ' appears to have been obtained mainly from Spain or Brittany. Though the chief mention in contemporary records is of difficulty in salting fish, it seems probable that the difficulties in salting beef must have been at least as great (*A.P.S.* III, 494).

It appears that there are two chemical reasons why salt obtained from salt water is not suitable for curing. In the first place, the total saline matter in salt water—approximately 3·6 per cent—consists partly of magnesium sulphate and calcium sulphate. These give an unpleasant flavour which would be imparted to meat cured in this way. Further, these two chemicals produce in contact with the muscular tissues of the meat, hard and most unpalatable products, a result which would be particularly apparent in the case of lean meat

225

as Mackintosh of Borlum no doubt realised. For these reasons a high standard of purity in the salt used is required in the curing of meat today.

The establishment of a successful salting industry in Scotland up till the end of the eighteenth century was made still more difficult by the extremely complex Salt Laws regulating the use of imported salt. The writer of the *Statistical Account* for the Parish of Sorbie reported that, but for the Salt Laws, Scots cattle might be fattened, killed and salted at home for the use of the navy. (*O.S.A.*, Sorbie, I, 248.) Restrictions on the supply of salt appear to have had a further effect on the cattle trade. From the want of this article the farmers ' cannot even supply themselves in the proper season with butter and cheese and are therefore obliged very frequently to bring up more young cattle by means of the milk in summer than they can support in winter.' (Knox, *Tour through the Highlands*, cxlix.) These Salt Laws bore particularly hardly on the fishermen, and throughout the greater part of the eighteenth century bitter complaints of their adverse effects on the fishing industry came from Gigha, Lochalsh, Rum and many other parts of the west coast. ' With a view to secure this revenue ' (from salt) wrote Knox, ' the fisheries have been laid under such restraints and subjected to such intricacies of the Custom-Houses that numbers abandoned the business and others were preparing to go to Ireland with their capitals, their vessels, and their experience where few or no impediments to fisheries exist.' (Knox, *op. cit.*, cxlvii.)

Attempts appear to have been made at various times to produce in Scotland a finer kind of salt more suitable for curing, and in 1696 the Scots Parliament had before it an Act in favour of Sir John Shaw of Greenock, John Haldan, Laird of Glenegies and others for making salt by a new process. The narrative of the Act, which was passed despite the opposition of the salt-masters, shows that Shaw and Haldan intended to set up a fishery and for that purpose ' project to make salt after a new fashion not formerly practiced within this Nation fit for curing of fishes without the help of any forraigne salt.' Their plans apparently included the purchase of land on the foreshore of the north side of the Forth ' betwixt the Toun Alloway and Crown Point below Culross . . .' (*A.P.S.*, X, 67 and 80.)

Report and Estimates by Thomas Telford relative to the
Rannoch Road, included in the *Fifth report of the Commissioners for Highland Roads and Bridges—1811*

IN improving the Highlands of Scotland, by means of Roads, Bridges,
and Ferries, particular attention has been given :

1   To open communications between the hitherto remote and
almost inaccessible Districts on the main land and Western
Islands, and the more cultivated part of the Country, the
principal Towns, Markets and Fairs :

2   To explore and establish general Lines of practicable communication, which as Drove Roads, might best accommodate
those extensive tracts from whence Black Cattle and Sheep
are sent to the markets in the southern parts of Scotland.

With a view to the immediate convenience of the Highland Proprietors, and all persons having occasion to travel in that country, the
formation of those Roads which fall under the first description has
naturally attracted the earliest attention.

Communications of the second description passing through the
Estates of many different Proprietors, very remote from each other,
though of material importance to the interest of every individual, are
scarcely known to them as objects worthy of a combined effort. From
this cause, the subject has hitherto undergone less investigation than
it merits ; for it is of importance, even to the Public, that the most
direct and commodious communications with the extensive Cattle-
rearing Countries should be established.

It is well known that the produce of the whole of the Western
parts of Scotland, northwest of the great Glen of The Caledonian
Canal, and including the Isle of Skye, consists chiefly of Black Cattle
and Sheep, and that they are sent to the markets in the south of Scotland
held at Crieff, Callander, Falkirk, and Dumbarton, from whence
they are driven into England. The Districts towards the Eastern side
of Scotland being more arable than pasturage, do not furnish any
great proportion of lean stock.

The chain of Lakes and Rivers which occupy the great Glen, and
the unbroken mass of lofty mountains which extends along the Southern
side of that valley between Inverness on the East and High-Bridge near
Fort William on the West, have hitherto compelled the Drovers to
take such directions as enable them to pass either by the Eastern or
Western extremities of the great Glen, and of the ridge of mountains
parallel to it.

The principal communication has hitherto been by the Western extremity, near Fort William, but previous to arriving at this point, the Highland drovers have hitherto passed through circuitous valleys, over rugged ridges of mountains, and dangerous and inconvenient ferries ; the delays, loss of Cattle, and general embarrassment thus arising from the want of convenient communication, are strongly felt by the Northern Sheep Farmers and the Cattle Dealers from the South who make purchases of them ; and although the personal inconvenience and toil are more immediately felt by these two classes of men, it is obvious that the pecuniary loss falls upon the Land Owners, and that the Public Markets are the less abundantly supplied.

Immediately to the South of Fort William the communication is difficult and circuitous ; for it is either by crossing steep ridges on the old Military Road by the top of Loch Leven and over the Devil's Staircase, or more to the Westward by crossing the Ferry of Ballachulish and proceeding up the rugged Pass of Glencoe to the King's House at the West side of the Moor of Rannoch.

From thence the communication continues, across the Black Mount to Tyndrum, and afterwards eastward down Glendochart toward Killin, at the head of Loch-Tay, three miles short of which it turns Southward to Callander and Crieff. Near Tyndrum, at Fillan, a Branch passes southward down the west side of Loch Lomond to Dumbarton.

The Northwest part of Scotland comprising the principal rearing Districts, Inverness is much too far eastward to answer for a general Drove Road, except for Sutherland and the eastern parts of Rossshire ; it is therefore to the Western extremity of the great Glen we must look for establishing a better communication between the rearing Countries in the Highlands and the Cattle Markets in the south.

It results from the general conformation of the Country, that the most important points upon this Line of Communications are High-Bridge near the Southwest end of Loch-Lochy, and Killin at the west end of Loch Tay. This is well known to all persons concerned in sending Sheep and Black Cattle in this direction to the Southward, and will appear evident from considering : 1. The nature and extent of the Communications from the N.W. Districts which may be concentrated at or near to High-Bridge ; 2. The comparative facility of proceeding from High-Bridge to Killin ; and 3. The nature of the Communications from thence to the Southern Cattle Markets.

---

1 Of the nature and extent of the Communications from the N.W. Districts which may be concentrated at High-Bridge : The great extent of the Isle of Skye will always render it an object well deserving attention. Although it appears probable that when the Loch Carron Road and the Ferries connected with it are completed, the intercourse between Skye and the East coast of Ross and Inverness will be carried on in that direction ; yet Kyle-Rhea, on account of the narrowness of

the Channel, will always remain the usual Ferry for the Black Cattle of Skye ; and this consideration, together with the importance of making a convenient outlet for the produce of the adjacent country of Glen-Elg, and accommodating at the same time the Districts of Loch-Alsh and Kintail, will necessarily require a good Road to be made from Kyle Rhea to the Southward.

This communication must either be through Glen-Elg by Loch Hourn-Head and part of the Glengarry Road, or by Glensheil and the Rhiebuie Road to a point on the Glengarry Road called Inch-Laggan ; the reason of uniting them at this point is, that from thence a direct and easy line may be carried Southward by the east end of Glen-Arkeg and the West end of Loch-Lochy to High-Bridge.

Glen-Elg consists chiefly of two valleys, the general direction of both running nearly between Kyle-Rhea and Loch Hourn-Head ; those valleys are included, excepting on the sea-side, by ridges of mountains, through which there is no Pass lower than that over Marn-Raatachan. At the south end of the two before-mentioned valleys there are Passes apparently of the same level as Raatachan, and about fourteen hundred feet perpendicular above the level of the sea. Of these two valleys which have been diligently explored, the Eastern one is most convenient for a Road, which would pass through the finest part of Glen-Elg with a uniform ascent for about twelve miles from Kyle-Rhea. Near the upper end of the valley the hills are steep, and much side-cutting would be required. From this summit to the head of Loch-Hourn, the country is rough and rocky and near to the Loch very precipitious. By preserving a uniform declivity from the summit to the termination at Loch-Hourn-Head, a distance of six miles, a commodious Road may be formed, but this would be accomplished at too great an expense as the rock-cutting, breast-works and parapets, would in many instances be an arduous task. The annexed Map shews, by single lines, in what direction these Glen-Elg Roads must pass, if ever attempted to be made. From Loch-Hourn-Head there is for about three miles a steep ascent on the Western part of the Glengarry Road ; afterwards that excellent Road may be considered as level.

But the most commodious line of Road from the Isle of Skye and Kyle-Rhea must pass through the northern part of Glen-Elg, and over Marn-Raatachan to Sheil-House (a distance of about twelve miles) by commencing the acclivity at a sufficient distance on each side of that pass, and this may be done at a comparatively moderate expense. From Sheil-House by the summit of Glen-Sheil to Rhiebuie the country is rugged, but not nearly so impracticable as the last six miles in Glen-Elg, towards Loch-Hourn-Head. From Rhiebuie to the Southward across Glen-Lyne to near Inch-Laggan (a distance of ten miles) a line sufficiently level may be formed.

By any Road through Glen-Elg to Loch-Hourn-Head, the Skye and Glen-Elg communications to the southward would be direct, but

Loch-Alsh and Kintail would be excluded from benefit, unless a Road was also made over Marn-Raatachan, and even then their journey would be circuitous ; but what is of still greater importance, the extensive tracts comprising the upper parts of Glenmorrison, Strath-Glass and of Loch-Carron, would remain without accommodation unless the Road between Rhiebuie and Inch-Laggan was made.

By Glen Sheil and Rhiebuie to Inch-Laggan, the summits to be passed over and the distance to be travelled even by the Skye and the Glen-Elg Cattle, would be more favourable than through Glen-Elg and by making a few miles of road between Sheil-House and Toteig-Ferry, the accommodation to all the other beforementioned Districts would be as perfect as the nature of the country admits.

The comparative distances are as follows :

By Loch-Hourn-Head

	Miles	Yards
From Kyle-Rhea to Loch-Hourn-Head	18	100
From Loch-Hourn-Head, by the Glengarry Road, to Inch-Laggan	17	1500
	35	1600

By Marn-Raatachan and Rhiebuie

	Miles	Yards
From Kyle-Rhea to Sheil-House	11	840
From Sheil-House to Rhiebuie	11	1566
From Rhiebuie to Inch-Laggan	10	593
	33	1239
Difference in favour of the latter road	2	361

By these statements it is evident that for the general accommodation of the beforementioned extensive tracts of country, and still much farther along the Northwest coast, that a Road from Kyle-Rhea by Marn-Raatachan and Rhiebuie to Inch-Laggan in Glengarry, is unquestionably the most eligible.

To complete the communication on the north side of the great Glen, instead of passing from Inch-Laggan, ten miles along the Glengarry Road to Invergarry, and thence by the side of Loch-Oich and Loch-Lochy to High-Bridge (a further distance of about eighteen miles) making together twenty eight miles, a Road may be carried through a Pass of the Mountains immediately South from Inch-Laggan, which would cross the river Arkeg near its mouth, and passing by the Western end of Loch Lochy, would arrive at High-Bridge by a route about ten miles shorter than the former, and without crossing a single Ferry. The comparative distances are as follows :

	Miles
From Inch-Laggan to Invergarry	10
From Invergarry to High-Bridge	18
	28

	Miles	Yards	Miles	Yards
From Inch-Laggan to the foot of Loch Arkeg	10	950		
From the foot of Loch Arkeg to the Burn of Culross	4	—		
From the Burn of Culross to High-Bridge	3	224	17	1174
Difference in favour of the latter Road			10	586

This is nearly equal to a day's journey for a drove of Cattle or Sheep.

The Branch Road between Sheil House and Toteig Ferry mentioned in the preceding page as a useful auxiliary to the Main Road from Skye, has been estimated at £1,943. It is almost five miles in length, and is wholly in Rossshire.

The Expense of making a Road from Rhiebuie to the Upper Bridge of Morrison (to which the Glenmorrison Road, now under contract, extends) would be £3,210. Of this estimate £1,563 must be expended in Rossshire, and this has hitherto operated as an obstruction to the undertaking, the Road promising little benefit to that County.

In addition to the Districts which have here been already considered, the countries of Glen-Arkeg, Morer and Arassaig, will conveniently centre their communications at High-Bridge by means of the Loch-na-Gaul and Lochyside Roads and the Bridge which the Caledonian Canal Commissioners will construct upon the new River course intended at Mucomer, or otherwise by the Ferry of Lochy.

---

2 Of the Line from High Bridge to Killin.

Having stated the manner in which improved Drove Roads may be made to centre at High-Bridge, it is equally important to consider in what manner the communication can be rendered most perfect between that place and Killin, at the Western end of Loch Tay.

At present the Drovers travel Southward sometimes along the old Military Road from High-Bridge, by Fort William to the head of Loch-Leven, beyond which, from crossing sundry rugged and steep ridges, it is named the Devil's Staircase ; or in order to avoid this tedious and almost impassable piece of Road, pass from Fort Willlam down the side of Loch-eil and crossing Loch-Leven at Ballachulish Ferry, turn Eastward up Glencoe.

The Road up Glencoe, though preferable to the Devil's Staircase, is one of the most rugged in the Highlands ; the mountains on each side are extremely steep, and from the action of the frost and rain, sheets of rocky fragments are formed, which are successively precipitated to the bottom of the valley. In this direction it is impossible to avoid this dreadful Pass, because the country to the Southward is equally rugged, composed of similar materials and intersected by lakes which penetrate far inland.

From the junction of these two bad Roads at the top of Glencoe, Cattle pass on to The King's House, Eastward of which is an extensive open District, which in such a rugged country may be comparatively called a plain ; it is named the Moor of Rannoch. The Military Road passes by the Western extremity of this plain across the sloping skirt of a hill well known by the name of the Black Mount, at a height found by Mr. Nimmo to be six hundred feet above the level of the King's House, and thirteen or fourteen hundred above the level of the sea. From the Black Mount the Military Road goes to Tyndrum, and thence Eastward down Glen-Dochart, till it approaches Killin.

The objections to this Road are, its circuitous course, the danger and delay of the Ferry of Ballachulish, the difficult Pass of Glencoe and of the Black Mount, and subsequently the delay caused by passing Eastward from Tyndrum down Glen-Dochart to near Killin.

To remedy these very imperfect communications, a Line has been suggested to the Commissioners for Highland Roads and Bridges, and by their direction has been carefully examined and reported as not only practical but advisable. It commences near High-Bridge, and passes considerably to the East of Ben-Nevis by the side of Loch-Treag, and across the Moor of Rannoch direct to Killin. This line is not only very direct but from the following description it will appear to be particularly level and easy, considering the rugged character of the country.

From near High-Bridge, the Road would pass nearly on a level about seven miles along the Loch-Laggan Road to Tulloch, where it would cross the river Spean and ascend in an easy manner to the foot of Loch-Traig (sic), which is about seven hundred feet above the sea ; the Road should pass along the Eastern side of the Loch, from which, with few exceptions, the mountains rise with a regular slope, not much cut by torrents and protected by natural birch wood. The ascent to the summit, at the head of the lake, may be rendered one in fifty, this summit continues about eight miles nearly on the same level, and is about 1128 feet above the sea ; from hence the descent to the plain of the Moor of Rannoch is no more than a hundred feet.

Entering the Moor of Rannoch, the Line must pass near the East end of Loch-Lydoch and over a flat morassy tract, in nearly a straight direction, to the pass of Gual-Vearan, the head of which is the summit of this part of the country, from whence the water runs both to the

Eastward and Westward ; it is fourteen hundred feet above the level of the sea and is gained by an ascent of about one in a hundred. From thence to the head of Glen-Lyon the rate of descent may be about one in fifty, and a moderate rise carries the Line to the Pass called Larig-na-Loone, at the head of Glen-Lochy, down the north side of which the road may be carried along comparatively favourable ground and at a descent not exceeding one in thirty to Killin.

From High Bridge to Killin, along the present Road by Fort William, Ballachulish and Tyndrum, the distance is	68 miles
From High-Bridge to Killin, by the Rannoch Road .	53
Difference in favour of the new line	15 miles

Thus it appears that the saving of distance in this District would be fifteen miles ; the ascents and descents much easier and no Ferry to be crossed. These advantages may be reckoned equal to two or perhaps three days journey for a drove of Cattle or Sheep.

3 From Killin to the Southern Cattle Markets.

From Killin, the communications after crossing by the Pass of Larig-Eilie and down Glen Ogle to the head of Loch-Earn, pass Eastward in a direct line by the north side of this Loch to Comrie and Crieff, or by a shorter route from Killin along the south side of Loch Tay for about six miles and by the new Road through Glen Lednaig to Comrie and from thence either Eastward to Crieff or Southward to Dunblain, Stirling and Falkirk. Southward from Loch-Earn-Head a Road passes down the east side of Loch-Lubnaig to Callander, Doune, Stirling and Falkirk, or from Callander to Dumbarton and Glasgow. From Killin, therefore, to the Southward, the communications are commodious and direct.

In addition to this direct communication between the northwest rearing Districts and the Southern Cattle Markets, this Road, by passing from High-Bridge through the interior of the country to Killin, affords many opportunities for collateral connexion ; part of Strathspey might be connected by means of the Loch-Laggan Road, and in another way by Loch Ericht. From the south side of the Moor of Rannoch a branch might conveniently unite with the present Military Road and pass by Tyndrum and Loch Lomond to Dumbarton and Glasgow, while another might be carried Eastward along Loch Rannoch and Loch Tummel to Dunkeld, Perth and Dundee.

Besides the Line from High-Bridge to Killin, which it has been considered most advisable to recommend, all the other Passes of the adjacent country have been examined ; but as they have been found more or less objectionable, it is unnecessary to incumber this Report with any account of them.

The advantages to be derived from thus lessening the distance, avoiding Ferries and acquiring regular and easy acclivities throughout this extensive Drove Road, are alone sufficient to demand the most serious attention of all the Landowners in the Northwest and interior parts of the Highlands of Scotland ; but besides this first and most important object, the proposed Line would also be the most direct and commodious communication for Travellers of all descriptions from the Southern parts of Scotland to the aforesaid extensive Districts.

The practicability of this important Line of Road having been ascertained, and its direction described as illustrated by the annexed Map, the following is an Estimate of the Expense at which the different portions of it may be completed :

ESTIMATES

of the expense of completing a Road from Kyle-Rhea in Invernessshire to Killin in Perthshire.

	Miles	Yards	£	s.	d.
From Kyle-Rhea to Shiel-House					
(Inverness £2056 8 0 ; Ross £2502 15 0)	11	840	4559	3	–
From Shiel-House to Rhiebuie					
(Ross £4802)	11	1566	4802	–	–
From Rhiebuie to Inch Laggan					
(Inverness £1102 10 ; Ross £2598 16 0)	10	593	3701	6	–
From Inch-Laggan to near Auchnacarrie					
(Inverness £5343 19 0)	10	950	5343	19	–
From near Auchnacarrie to High-Bridge					
(Of which remains to be done 2½ miles					
in Inverness £800)	7	224	800	–	–
From High-Bridge to Killin					
(Inverness £5760 ; Perth £9600)	53	—	15360	–	–
	104	653	£34566	8	–

A Moiety of the estimated Expense is £17283 4 –

The immediate advantage to be derived from this expenditure
will result to the Breeders of Sheep and Black Cattle ; and
has been estimated by Mr. Nimmo of Inverness on the sup-
position that 80,000 Sheep are annually driven in the direction of the proposed Road and that a saving of three or four
days in Droving expenses, and the better condition of the
animål at market, is equal at least to one shilling each, or   £4000

And that a similar saving and augmentation of value will take
place on 20,000 Black Cattle at eight shillings each to the
amount to   8000

Estimated annual advantage   Total   £12000

(*Signed*) THOMAS TELFORD
May 1810.

234

CONTEMPORARY DESCRIPTIONS OF THE CATTLE OF THE HIGHLANDS

NUMEROUS descriptions of the cattle of the Scottish Highlands can be found in the writings of those who wrote of Scottish agriculture at the end of the eighteenth and in the early years of the nineteenth centuries, but the following description taken from James Macdonald's *General View of the Agriculture of the Hebrides*, 1811 (425 *et seq.*) is probably the most comprehensive :

A bull of the Kyloe breed should be of a middle size, capable of being fattened to fifty stone avoirdupois. His colour should be black (that being reckoned the hardiest and most durable species), or dark brown, or reddish brown, without any white or yellow spots. His head should be rather small, his muzzle fine, his eyes lively and prominent, his horns equable, not very thick, of a clear, green, and waxy tinge ; his neck should rise with a gentle curve from the shoulders, and should be small and fine where it joins the head ; his shoulders moderately broad at the top, joining full to his chine and chest backwards, and to the vane of his neck forwards. His bosom should be open, his breast broad, and projecting well before his legs ; his arms, or fore thighs, muscular, and tapering to his knee ; his legs straight, well covered with hair, and strong boned. His chine or chest should be so full as to leave no hollows behind his shoulders ; the plates strong, to keep his belly from sinking below the level of his breast. His back or loin should be broad, straight, and flat ; his ribs rising above one another in such a manner that the last rib should be rather the highest, leaving only a small space to the hips or hooks ; the whole forming a roundish, barrel-like carcase. His hips should be wide placed, rounded or globular, and a very little higher than the back. His quarters (from the hip to the rump) should be long and tapering gradually from the hips backwards, and the turls, or pot-bones, not in the least protuberant ; his rumps close to the tail ; his tail itself should be thick, bushy, well haired, long, and set on so high as to be in the same horizontal line with his back. His general appearance should combine agility, vivacity, and strength ; and his hair should be glossy, thick, and vigorous, indicating a sound constitution and perfect health.

For a bull of this description Mr Macneill of Collonsay lately refused 200 guineas ; and for one of an inferior sort he actually received L.170 Sterling. Mr Macdonald of Staffa bought one, nine years old, at 100 guineas.

It is unnecessary to enter in detail upon a description of a Kyloe, or West Highland, or Hebridian heifer, as the above, with some very obvious modifications, answers for animals of both sexes. Strangers, on visiting the Western Isles, cry out against the folly of the people in keeping cattle of a small breed ; when by changing it for the Irish, or the Lowland Scotch, they might greatly enlarge the carcases of their stock. But this is often a rash opinion. The great question in Hebridian grazing and rearing is, what breed will best answer the land and climate, and what size can be most easily and securely raised at the smallest expense ? Heavy cattle cannot seek their food in bogs and marshes, leap over ravines, rivers, and ditches, or scramble through rocks, and in the faces of cliffs and precipices, like the present breed, which is almost as active and nimble as a Chamois goat ; nor can the poor Hebridian tenant afford to breed any stock which is not proof against the inclemency of his rains and storms all the year round. It is infinitely safer for him, therefore, in the present imperfect state of his agriculture, and perhaps even at all times, and in all circum- stances of his country to rear too small, than too large a breed of cattle ; and to improve his indigenous, hardy, excellent species, than to import from other districts such breeds as may be indeed profitable for their circumstances and climate, but, which would probably perish in the Hebrides, without more attention being paid to them than, in his situation, he can conveniently afford. A moderate size is accordingly preferred by all skilful graziers, i.e. bullocks or stots, which, fattened at the age of five, weigh 30–36 stone avoirdupois, and heifers which weigh, at the same age, 24–30 stone. This rule, no doubt, admits of considerable latitude of application ; and while the weight or size now specified answers extremely well for the common average of the best breeds used by gentlemen farmers in Islay, Mull, Coll, Tyree, and Skye, it may be deemed an under size on the lands occupied by the proprietors of Islay and Collonsay, and by some of their people, who have lately introduced green crops, and, by a skilful mode of managing their lands, can afford food and shelter for their cattle in abundance during the whole year. Those gentlemen may raise the native breed (still, however, preserving the same identical genus and species of cattle) to the weight, when fattened, of from 34 to 42 stone for their bullocks and heifers . . .

The following description of the cattle of Argyll is taken from John Smith's *General View of the Agriculture of the County of Argyll*, 1798 (235 et seq.) :

' The most profitable breed of cattle, and that which is found to be best suited for Argyllshire is the true West Highland breed. It was for some time considered as an improvement upon this breed to cross it with cattle brought from Sky. But from superior breeding, and greater attention in rearing, the native breed of Argyllshire is now of much greater size than that of Sky.

The form most wished for is, to get them short in the legs, round in the body, straight in the back, and long in the snout. They are of various colours, black, dun, branded and brown ; but the black is the most common, and the most run upon.

When in good condition, and from three to four years old, when they are commonly sold off, the carcase may weigh from 360 to 400 lb. avoirdupois. But such as are brought to better pasture as in England, may be brought to weigh 560 lb. or more. The price is generally according to the size and shape, but occasionally varies according to the demand.

They are not wrought, nor supposed to be well calculated for working, as they are too light for that purpose. . . .'

APPENDIX D
(*page 89*)

ROY'S SURVEY OF SCOTLAND, 1747–55

AFTER the Rebellion of 1745, those responsible for the patrolling of the Highlands found themselves greatly handicapped by the absence of a reliable survey of the country. In 1747 Colonel Watson, who was stationed at Fort Augustus, proposed to the Duke of Cumberland that a survey of the Highlands should be made, and through the Dukes' influence sufficient additional men were added to the small staff of surveyors then available to make the work possible. Among those added to the survey staff was William Roy, who is believed to have been previously employed in the post office in Edinburgh. Roy's subsequent part in the work became so important that the survey which resulted is commonly known as General Roy's Survey, though, at the time of the work, he held only a very junior rank at a pay of 3s a day. The Survey, which was latterly extended to cover the Lowlands, appears to have been completed in 1754. It was never engraved and though a copy on a reduced scale of $2\frac{1}{2}$ miles to an inch was made, and apparently used, Roy's original survey itself remained practically unknown till the beginning of the nineteenth century. It may be that the outbreak of the Continental Wars in 1756 and the progressive settlement of the Highlands detracted from the interest in the work, besides removing some of those, including Colonel Watson, who were engaged on it.

In 1805 Arrowsmith undertook the construction of a map of Scotland which was published in June 1807. In the course of the work he obtained access to Roy's Survey which had hitherto remained practically unknown, in the King's Library where it had been deposited after Roy's death. In a Memoir, published in 1809, a copy of which is printed with the Reports of the Commissioners for Highland Roads and Bridges, Arrowsmith has described the discovery of the Survey and has given some detail about its construction, obtained from Sir David Dundas, who had himself been employed on part of the survey, and who was mainly responsible for making it available to Arrowsmith.

It appears from Arrowsmith's account that Colonel Watson had five junior surveyors under him, each of whom surveyed an allotted district, Roy being the principal organiser of the whole of the surveyors' work. Each of the surveyors was assisted by one N.C.O. and six men. One carried the theodolite, two measured with the chain, two marked the fore and back stations, and one acted as batman. The instruments used were plain theodolites of 7 in. diameter or $3\frac{1}{2}$ in. radius with common sights unfurnished with telescopes. The instruments were made by Cole of London, as were also the chains of 45–50 ft. As the party slept under canvas they were able to penetrate into the farthest parts of the Highlands. The summer months were spent in the field and the winter months at work on the survey in Edinburgh, the finished work being taken every year by Colonel Watson to London for inspection. The courses of all the rivers and streams were followed to their source and measured, while all the roads and the fresh and salt water lochs were surveyed. Each surveyor kept a field book and a sketch book in the latter of which he delineated the various stations and the face of the country which, says Arrowsmith, ' was then much less inclosed and woody than at present and favourably featured for a military sketch.'

The original survey is contained in 38 sheets on a scale of 1,000 yards to an inch. Though Roy himself described the survey as ' a magnificent military sketch rather than a very accurate map,' the work was evidently done with great care. Contours were, of course, not at that date in use, the hills being drawn in with skilful brush work which has the effect of making them stand out as if in relief. With its striking colouring the map, which is preserved in the map room of the British Museum, is a thing of considerable beauty.

Some doubt has been suggested as to the roads shown on Roy's map, and though these doubts do not appear to be supported by Sir David Dundas' account of the work, it may well be that many of the subsidiary routes marked as roads were, in fact, little more than tracks. However this may be, it would seem a fair assumption, in many cases supported by other evidence, that the routes shown by Roy indicate routes then in use by contemporary traffic, of which droving traffic formed at least a part.

> Arrowsmith, *Memoir relative to the Construction of the Map of Scotland*, 1807
>
> *The Early Maps of Scotland*, Royal Scottish Geographical Society and *Early Scottish Maps and Travel* (Moir), Royal Scottish Geographical Society

APPENDIX E

(*page 89*)

THE BRIDGE OF AWE

CURIOUSLY little information is available as to the date of the building of the old bridge of Awe, the three-arched stone bridge which stands a short way upstream from the modern bridge on the main road to Oban. In an article which appeared in Vol. X of the Proceedings of the New York State Historical Association written by the Secretary of the Association, the writer ascribes the building to Captain William Pitman, a friend of Major Duncan Campbell of Inverawe who was killed at Ticonderoga in 1758 and gives the date of the building of the bridge as 1756. In the Rev. John Smith's *General View of the Agriculture of the County of Argyll* published in 1798, however, the Author, after referring to the work of the late Captain Archibald Campbell of Glen Lyon in improving the roads of the County, adds the following passage :

' The same public-spirited gentleman was the means of throwing bridges over the two largest rivers in the county, Aw and Urchay, by obtaining liberal subscriptions from the Duke of Argyll, Lord Breadalbine, and other heritors. Both, under his management, were executed for £1,000, a sum which was long thought to be much less than was requisite for the first of them ; which shows that public money is capable of doing much more than is generally done with it. Indeed, these works would have been executed for still less money, if an unfortunate accident had not given the contractor a just claim for more than the sum agreed upon. The water of Aw, which discharges at one outlet all the collected streams of an extent of country near 50 miles in length and from 6 to 10 in breadth, is remarkably large and rapid, and subject to sudden rises. After the work was begun in a very dry season, it was carried on with all possible expedition, but just as the arches were locked, and before there was time for removing the timbers, a sudden flood swept timber and stone before it, and obliged the undertaker to recommence his labours. The second attempt succeeded ; and this useful bridge has since withstood every trial.'

APPENDIX F

(page 141)

FALKIRK TRYST IN 1849

'Having carried our readers to the Highlands we must, at the risk of being somewhat episodical, request that on their return south they will accompany us to Falkirk Moor on the second Monday or Tuesday in either September or October. They will there witness a scene to which certainly Great Britain, perhaps even the whole world, does not afford a parallel. We doubt whether we do not much under-rate the whole number of sheep collected at 100,000. Mr Paterson, Mr Sellers, Mr Kennedy and Mr Cameron of Corachoilie will each have several thousands on the ground. We have heard that this last patriarch has 50,000 head of cattle and sheep on his several farms. . . . No stranger accustomed to the bustle and the crowd, the handling and the haggling of an English fair, would suspect that transactions of a magnitude to which Barnet, St Faith's, and Wey Hill afford no parallel was on the eve of taking place. On a portion of the moor adjoining the sheep ground . . . a wooden pent-house about five feet square announces itself by exterior placard to be the ' Royal Bank of Scotland ' ; the British Linen Company, The Comercial Bank and every other banking company north of the Tweed appear there by similar wooden representatives. The purchasers come to the fair provided with Letters of Credit and stepping into the tabernacle to which they are accredited bring out in large notes the amount required. These are handed to the vendor in an adjoining booth and are probably in a very few minutes at his credit with the issuer or one of his rivals. . . . There are three trysts held every year—the first in August, the second in September and the last and largest in October. The cattle stand in a field in the parish of Larbert at a distance of nearly three miles from Falkirk, at a place called Stenhousemuir. The field on which they assemble contains above 200 acres, well-fenced and in every way adapted for the purpose. The scene, seen from horse-back, from a cart, or some erection, is particularly imposing. All is animation, bustle, business and activity ; servants running about shouting to the cattle, keeping them together in their particular lots and ever and anon cudgels are at work upon the horns and rumps of the restless animals that attempt to wander in search of grass or water.

The cattle dealers of all descriptions chiefly on horse-back, are scouring the field in search of the lots they require. The Scottish drovers are for the most part mounted on small, shaggy, spirited ponies that are obviously quite at home among the cattle ; and they carry their riders through the throngest groups with astonishing alacrity. The English dealers have, in general, large, stout horses, and they pace the ground with more caution, surveying every lot carefully as they go along. When they discover the cattle they want, they enquire the price. A good deal of riggling takes place, and when the parties come to an agreement, the purchaser claps a penny of arles into the hand of the stockholder, observing at the same time ' It's a bargain.' Tar dishes are then got, and the purchaser's mark being put upon the cattle, they are driven from the field. Besides numbers of shows, from 60 to 70 tents are erected along the field for selling spirits and provisions. The owners of these portable taverns pay 2s 6d for the ground they occupy on the first Tryst, and 4s 6d for each of the other two. . . . In one of these tents a few gentlemen attend from the Falkirk Bank to accommodate the dealers with the money they require. Many kindle fires at the end of their tents, over which cooking is briskly carried on. Broth is made in considerable quantities, and meets a ready sale. As most of the purchasers are paid in these tents, they are constantly filled and surrounded with a mixed multitude of cattle dealers, fishers, drovers, auctioneers, pedlars, jugglers, gamblers, itinerant fruit merchants, ballad singers and beggars. What an indescribable clamour prevails in most of these party-coloured abodes !

Far in the afternoon, when frequent calls have elevated the spirits and stimulated the colloquial powers of the visitors, a person hears the uncouth Cumberland jargon and the prevailing Gaelic, along with the innumerable provincial dialects, in their genuine purity, mingled in one astounding roar. All seem inclined to speak ; and raising their voices to command attention, the whole of the orators are obliged to bellow as loudly as they can possibly roar. When the cattle dealers are in the way of their business, their conversation is full of animation, and their technical phrases are generally appropriate and highly amusing.'

Gisborne, *Essays on Agriculture*, 1854, 15 et seq.

APPENDIX G
(*page 209*)

THE EFFECT OF TURNPIKES ON DROVING

THE serious view taken by the drovers of the establishment of tolls which they considered unwarranted encroachments on their ancient rights, may be judged from the proceedings of two meetings which took place in the year 1827. On 3rd September of that year a meeting of the Freeholders, Justices of the Peace and Commissioners of Supply of the County of Sutherland was held at Dornoch. This meeting ' having taken into consideration the present condition of the ancient drove-road leading from the most Northern parts of Scotland to the central Counties of England, and the great importance of preserving the same free from interruption,' came to the following resolutions :

1. That the servitude of driving Cattle and Sheep along the said drove road, has existed from beyond the memory of man, and still does exist without interruption, except in one or two instances of little importance.
2. That the Meeting, however, have seen with regret, that several attempts have been made of late years, to interrupt the right of passing this road, in different parts of Scotland, either by the imposition of heavy tolls, or by entirely shutting up the road itself, under the authority of local Acts of Parliament, which it is conceived it was not the intention of the Legislature should be applicable to this ancient and peculiar right of way, while the same remains free and uninterrupted throughout England.
3. That the preservation of this right of way is of the utmost importance to all the breeding district of the country.
4. That this Meeting therefore will use its best endeavours to preserve the said drove road, and those connected with it, from interruption during such a period of the year as shall be required for driving stock to market, whether the same shall be best effected by an application to Parliament or otherwise.

. . . . . .

(Copy Resolutions found among *Sutherland Estate Papers*)

On 11th September ' a numerous and respectable Meeting of the Breeders of Cattle and Sheep, in the Highlands and Lowlands of Scotland, and the Dealers and Feeders of Stock, who are in the practice of attending Falkirk Market ' was held at the Red Lion Inn, Falkirk, ' called in consequence of the great and increasing damage sustained by themselves personally, and by the public, by reason of the encroachments, which have, of late years, been made on the ancient drove-

242

ways, leading from the different districts of Scotland, to the Falkirk Trysts, and from thence southward to the English Borders.' The following resolutions were unanimously adopted :

1st.   That beyond all memory of man, the present Landholders and Farmers of Scotland, and their ancestors, have possessed a right of passage, for the stock bred in the pastoral district, to go to market, and to the feeder and consumer of such stock.

2nd.   That this right of passage existed, for the most part, through sequestered parts of the country, where the stock had sufficient width of passage, and not meeting with the horses, carts, carriages, &c. which obstruct the common highways, the animals reached their destination in good health.

3rd.   That, in the progress of improvement within the last forty years, almost every county in Scotland has obtained its private Act of Parliament, authorising parties interested in each particular district, to make turnpike roads suited to the convenience of that district, to confine all thoroughfares to these turnpikes, and to levy tolls for their maintenance.

4th.   That in virtue of these powers, the ancient drove way was first begun to be encroached upon about twenty years ago, but, in so few instances, that for many years no serious injury was done ; and people submitted willingly to an inconvenience which they considered of little importance, compared to the public advantage derived from the turnpikes.

5th.   That, of late years, however, measures have been used, in various places, along the ancient drove-way, to confine the cattle and sheep in their passage entirely to turnpike roads ; and the consequences which have already arisen from the exposure, during so long a journey, of animals, of their wild habits, to the concussion of horses, dogs, mail coaches, and carriages of all descriptions, are so serious, that, after impeding, by their numbers, the progress of all other travellers, who use the Turnpikes, they arrive at their destination in a diseased and foundered state, to the great injury of the owner, who is compelled to pay extravagantly for receiving damage and to the public who consume this diseased stock.

6th.   That these effects have already followed from the partial measures which have been used in various places to prevent the stock from passing along its ancient drove-way, and confining them to Turnpikes. But if the measures of the Turnpike makers be completed, and the droves confined to Turnpikes during their whole passage, then, assuredly, it will be impossible for the breeders of cattle and sheep to bring them to market, worth to the purchaser the expense of their travelling, and the valuable supply of animal food now received by the consumer ; the profit derived by the farmer and feeder, and the rents paid to the landlord from the above species of stock, must, in a great measure, cease.

7th.   That this Meeting feel satisfied that it is only necessary to point out to a British public the injustice and impolicy of the measures complained of, to induce a complete revisal of the various Turnpike Acts threatening so great an evil ; and an equitable arrangement calculated to enable the owners of cattle and sheep to bring them to market in a sound and healthy state ; they paying a fair remuneration, and no more, for whatever facilities shall be afforded them along their journey.

.   .   .   .

(Sutherland Estate Papers)

It is evident, however, that the troubles of the drovers from this source persisted, for in 1833 drovers from the North of Scotland, complaining of the effect of customs dues and tolls, particularly in Perthshire and Stirlingshire, on the traffic in cattle and sheep, urged the construction of a general drove road as recommended by Telford on which no tolls would be payable. Six years later a movement was on foot for the establishment of trysts at Spean Bridge in September and October. The reasons urged were the tolls on the roads, the heavy customs dues at the market, the exorbitant charges made by farmers for grazing in the neighbourhood of the existing Trysts and the damage caused to the stock by the long drive to Falkirk. It was then estimated that 50,000 sheep were driven from the Highlands and Western Isles for the September and October markets at Falkirk, 20,000 going by the western road through Lochaber and Rannoch and 30,000 by the eastern road through Badenoch and East Perthshire.

(Inverness Courier, 17th April 1833 and 17th July 1839)

BIBLIOGRAPHY

* Of the sources listed in the Bibliography those which have proved most valuable are marked with an asterisk

MANUSCRIPT SOURCES

RECORD OFFICE, H.M. REGISTER HOUSE, EDINBURGH

Bell, Thomas. *Manuscript letters (contained in Reid's Calendar of papers found at Dumfries)*.

* *Breadalbane Papers.*

Papers in connection with Process of Division of Commonty

(*a*) of Sheriffmuir, (*Durie Decreets*, 2 Dec. 1772, and *Register of Decreets*, Vol. 586).

(*b*) of Falkirk (*Durie Decreets*, 19 Dec. 1807, and *Register of Decreets*, Vol. 835).

(*c*) of Gretna (*Mackenzie Decreets*, 9 Aug. 1700, and *Register of Decreets*, Vol. 612).

(*d*) of Reddingsrigg and Whitesiderigg (*Mackenzie Decreets*, 11 Mar. 1773, and *Register of Decreets*, Vol. 638).

Forfeited Estates Papers. Perth. Portfolio 21G., 21 Jan. 1771.

Records of Custom Dues collected at Kelso in 1683.

Sinclair of Mey (Caithness). *Manuscript letters.*

NATIONAL LIBRARY OF SCOTLAND, EDINBURGH

Balfour, Sir James of Denmylne. *The Chief Passages from the River Tay to the River Dee through the Mountains.* (Spalding Club Collection.) MS 33.2.27.

PUBLIC RECORD OFFICE, LONDON

Victualling Board Records (Admiralty).

Victualling Board Records (War Office).

BRITISH MUSEUM

Young, Arthur. *The Elements and Practice of Agriculture.* 44 Vols. (B.M. 34821 to 34864).

ROYAL BANK OF SCOTLAND

Minute Books.

BRITISH LINEN BANK

Minute Books.

CLERK OF THE PEACE, STIRLING

Justices of the Peace for the County of Stirling. *Minute Book of Quarter Sessions*, 6 Dec. 1819–

DUNROBIN CASTLE

Sutherland Estate Papers.

245

BONSER, KENNETH J., LEEDS
  MS (unpublished) on *Scottish Drovers and Drove Routes in Yorkshire in the Mid-eighteenth Century.*

STEWART, JOHN, FALKIRK
  MS (unpublished) *Falkirk Tryst.*

OFFICIAL PUBLICATIONS

Acts of the Lords of Council in Civil Causes, 1496–1501, Vol. 2, 1918.
* *Acts of the Parliament of Scotland* (Record Edition). 12 Vols., 1814–75
Border Papers 1560–1603. 2 Vols., 1894–6.
Exchequer Rolls of Scotland, 1264–1600. 23 Vols., 1878–1908.
Historical MSS Commission. *Mar & Kellie Papers,* 1904.
* Marwick, Sir J. D. *List of Fairs and Markets held in Scotland,* 1890.
Napier, Crofters' Commission. *Report on the Highlands.* 5 Vols., 1884.
Nautical Survey. New edition, 4 Dec. 1912. (Lochalsh and Kyle Rhea.)
* *Register of the Privy Council of Scotland,* 1st, 2nd and 3rd Series, 1545–1689. 1877–1933.
Report of Select Committee on Cultivation, etc. of Waste Lands, 1795.
Report of Select Committee on Finance (Vol. 13 of House of Commons Committees), June 1798.
* *Report of Select Committee on Promissory Notes in Scotland and Ireland,* 1826.
Report of Commissioners on Public Roads in Scotland, 1859.
* *Reports of Commissioners for Highland Roads and Bridges.* 3 Vols., 1803–60.
Report of Committee on Hill Sheep Farming in Scotland, 1943.
Report by George Brown on most important lines of Highland Roads, 1803, in 1st Report of Commissioners for Highland Roads and Bridges, Appendix C, pp. 23–9 *supra.*
Rotulae Scotiae. 2 Vols. (Record Commission), 1814–19.
Rymer, *Foedera.* (Record Commission), 1816–69.
State Papers. Domestic. Charles II, 1663–64.
Statutes of the Realm.
Survey and Reports of the Coasts and Central Highlands of Scotland in Autumn of 1802. Thomas Telford, 1803. (See Vol. I of *Reports of Commissioners for Highland Roads and Bridges, supra.*)

BOOKS

Acworth, William M. *Railways of Scotland,* 1890.
Aikin, Arthur. *Journal of a Tour through North Wales in 1787,* 1797.
* Alexander, William. *Notes and Sketches of Northern Rural Life in the 18th Century,* 1877.
Anderson, George and Peter. *Guide to the Highlands,* 1834, 1842 etc.
Anderson, James. *Account of the present state of the Hebrides,* 1745, 1785.
Anderson, John. *State of Society and Knowledge in the Highlands . . . at the period of the Rebellion, 1745,* 1827.
Arrowsmith, Aaron. *Memoir relative to Map of Scotland published . . . in year 1807.* Bound with 3rd Report of Commissioners for Highland Roads and Bridges.

BIBLIOGRAPHY

Bannatyne Club. 56. *Liber Sancte Marie de Melros*, 1837. 89. *Chartulary of Newbattle Abbey*, 1849. 100. *Black Book of Taymouth*, 1855.

Barron, James. *The Northern Highlands in the 19th Century.* 3 Vols., 1903-7.

Belsches, Robert. *General View of the Agriculture of the County of Stirling*, 1796.

Boswell, James. *Journal of a Tour to the Hebrides with Samuel Johnson.* Edited by F. A. Pottle, 1936 (Isham edn.).

Brand, John. *Brief Description of Orkney and Shetland*, 1701 (reprint 1883).

Brewer, E. Cobham. *The Historic Note-book*, 1891.

Brigg, John Jeremy. *The King's Highway in Craven : being notes on the history of the Yorkshire portion of the Keighley and Kendal turnpike Road*, 1927.

Brown, Peter Hume. *Early Travellers in Scotland*, 1891. *Scotland before 1700 from contemporary Documents*, 1893. *History of Scotland.* 3 Vols., 1899-1904. *Scotland in the time of Queen Mary*, 1904. *Legislative Union of Scotland and England*, 1914.

Buchanan, Rev. John Lane. *Travels in the Western Hebrides from 1782 to 1790*, 1793.

* Burt, Edward. *Letters from a Gentleman in the North of Scotland*, 5th ed., by R. Jamieson. 2 Vols., 1822.

Cadell, Henry Moubray. *Story of the Forth*, 1913.

Campbell, Alexander. *A Journey from Edinburgh through parts of North Britain.* 2 Vols., 1st ed., 1802.

Campbell, John. *Full description of the Highlands of Scotland*, 1752.

Chalmers, G. *Caledonia.* 8 Vols., 1887-1902.

Chambers, Robert. *Domestic annals of Scotland.* 3 Vols., 1858-1861.

Chambers, William. *History of Peeblesshire.* 3 Vols., 1864.

Cinncinnatus Caledonius (John Gordon Barbour). *Lights and Shadows of Scottish Character and Scenery*, 2nd Series, 1825.

* Corrie, J. M. *The Droving Days in the southwest district of Scotland*, 1915.

Croal, George. *Living Memories of an Octogenarian*, 1894.

Culley, George. *Observations on Live Stock*, 1807.

Davidson, John, and Gray, Alexander. *The Scottish Staple at Veere*, 1909.

Defoe, Daniel. *A Tour thro' the whole Island of Great Britain in 1724 . . .*, 6th ed. 4 Vols., 1762.

De Quincey, Thomas. *Autobiographical sketches*, Vol. 14 of *Works* (edition of 1863).

Dixon, John H. *Gairloch in North-west Ross-shire ; its Records, Traditions, Inhabitants and Natural History*, 1886.

Don, William Gerard. *Archaeological Notes on Early Scotland relating more particularly to the Stracathro District of Strathmore in Angus* (Brechin 1896).

Donaldson, James. *General View of the Agriculture of Elgin or Moray*, 1794 ; *General View of the Agriculture of Kincardine or the Mearns*, 1795.

Donaldson, John E. *Caithness in the 18th Century*, 1938.

Donaldson, M. E. M. *Further Wanderings in Argyll*, 1926.

Fletcher, Joseph Smith. *The Making of Modern Yorkshire (1750-1914)*, 1918.

Forbes, Rev. Robert, Bishop. *Journal* (Rev. J. B. Craven's edition), 1886.

Forfeited Estates Papers, 1715-45. Scottish History Society, 1st Series, Vol. 57, 1909.

* Fraser, George Milne. *The Old Deeside Road*, 1921.

Fraser-Mackintosh, Charles. *Letters of two Centuries from 1616 to 1815.*

Gartmore MS. *An Inquiry into the Causes . . . of Rebellion . . . in the Highlands*

247

of Scotland, 1747 ; printed as appendix in Jamieson's 5th edition of Burt's *Letters from a Gentleman in the North of Scotland*, Vol. 2, at p. 159, 1822.

Gilbey, Sir Walter. *Farm Stock 100 years ago*, 1910.

Gillespie, R. *Round about Falkirk*, 1879.

Gilpin, Rev. William. *Observations on several parts of the Counties of Cambridge-shire, Norfolk, etc.*, 1809.

Gisborne, Thomas. *Essays on Agriculture*, 2nd ed., 1854.

Graham, Henry Gray. *Social Life in Scotland in the 18th Century*, 1901.

Graham, Rev. Patrick. *General View of the Agriculture of Stirlingshire*, 1812.

Graham, R. B. Cunninghame. *A Hatchment*, 1913.

Grant, Mrs Anne, of Laggan. *Letters from the Mountains*, *1773–1807*, 6th ed., 2 Vols., 1845.

Grant, Mrs Elizabeth, of Rothiemurchus. *Memoirs of a Highland Lady*, 1807, 1898.

Grant, I. F. *Economic History of Scotland*, 1934 ; *Social and Economic Development of Scotland before 1603*, 1930.

Hall, Rev. James. *Travels in Scotland*, 1807.

* Hamilton, Henry. *The Industrial Revolution in Scotland*, 1932.

Hardie, R. P. *The Roads of Medieval Lauderdale*, 1942.

Henderson, John. *General View of the Agriculture of Sutherland*, 1812.

Heron, Robert. *Journey through the Western Counties of Scotland in Autumn of 1792*. 2 Vols., 1799.

Highlands of Scotland in 1750. Edited by A. Lang, 1898.

Hodgson, John C. *History of Northumberland*, 1820–58.

Hogg, James. *A Tour in the Highlands in 1803*, 1888.

Hughes, P. Gwyn. *Wales and the Drovers*, 1943.

Hurtley, Thomas. *A concise account of some Natural Curiosities in the environs of Malham in Craven, Yorkshire*, 1834 (1st ed. 1786).

Innes, Cosmo. *Sketches of Early Scottish History*, 1861.

Institute of Historical Research. *Bulletin*, Vol. 3.

Iona Club, Vol. 1. Transactions of 1835 (*Collectania de Rebus Albanicis*). Edited by Donald Gregory and W. F. Skene, 1839.

Islay, The Book of. Edited by G. Gregory Smith, 1895.

Islay, The Stent Book of, 1718–1843. Edited by Mrs Lucy Ramsay of Kildalton, 1890.

Johnson, Samuel. *Journey to the Western Islands*, 1775.

Johnson, Walter. *Byways in British Archaeology*, 1912.

* Johnston, Rev. Bryce. *General View of the Agriculture of the County of Dumfries*, 1794.

Johnstoun, Alexander, of Kirkland. *Description of the Parish of Morvenside in Stirlingshire*, 1723 in Macfarlane's Geog. Collections, Vol. 1, p. 317 (Scot. Hist. Soc., 1st Series, 51, 1906).

* Keith, George Skene. *General View of the Agriculture of Aberdeenshire*, 1811.

Keith, Theodora. *Commercial Relations between England and Scotland 1603–1707*, 1910.

Keltie, J. S. *The Scottish Highlands*. 2 Vols., 1883.

Knox, John. *Tour through the Highlands of Scotland and the Hebride Isles in 1786*, 1787.

Larkin. *A Tour in the Highlands in 1818*, 1819.

Leslie, Rev. Wm. *General View of the Agriculture of Nairn and Moray*, 1811.

Lloyd, J. *Historical Memoranda of Breconshire*, 1903–4.

Logan, James. *The Scottish Gael.* 2 Vols., 1831.

* McCombie, William. *Cattle and Cattle Breeders,* 1867.

Macculloch, John. *Highlands and Western Isles.* . . . 4 Vols., 1824.

McCulloch, John Ramsay. *Dictionary . . . of Commerce,* 1856.

MacDonald, Rev. Angus and Archibald. *The Clan Donald,* 1896–1904.

* MacDonald, James. *General View of the Agriculture of the Hebrides,* 1811.

McDowall, William. *History of the Burgh of Dumfries,* 1867.

MacFarlane's Geographical Collections. 3 Vols. Scot. Hist. Soc., 1st Series, 51–3, 1906–8.

MacGill, W. *Old Ross-shire and Scotland.* 2 Vols., 1909–11.

McIan, R. R., and Logan, James. *Highlanders at Home,* 1848.

MacIver, Evander. *Reminiscences.* Edited by Rev. George Henderson, 1905.

MacKenzie, Alexander. *History of the Munros,* 1898.

Mackenzie, Rev. William, and J. Nicholson. *History of Galloway.* 2 Vols., 1841 (published anon).

Mackenzie, W. *Old Skye Tales,* 1934.

Mackenzie, W. Mackay. *The Scottish Burghs,* 1949.

Macky, J. *Journey through Scotland,* 1723.

MacLeod, Rev. Norman. *Reminiscences of a Highland Parish,* 1871.

Macpherson, David. *Annals of Commerce.* 4 Vols., London 1805.

Marshall, Rev. Wm. *Historic Scenes in Perthshire,* 1880.

Marshall, Wm. *General View of the Agriculture of the Central Highlands,* 1794 ; *Rural economy of Norfolk,* 2nd ed., 2 Vols., 1795.

Martens, Georg Friedrich Von. *Recueil de Traités,* 1st Series, 2nd ed., tome 2.

Martin, Martin. *Description of the Western Isles of Scotland, circa* 1695, 1703, 1st ed. Edited by D. J. Macleod, 1934.

Mathieson, W. Law. *The Awakening of Scotland, 1747–97,* 1910.

Maxwell, Sir Herbert. *Memories of the Months,* 5th Series, 1909.

Millar, A. H. *History of Rob Roy,* 1883.

* Mitchell, Sir Arthur. *List of travels and tours in Scotland, 1296–1900* (Suppl.), 1902.

* Mitchell, Sir Arthur, and Cash, C. G. *Topography of Scotland.* 2 Vols., 1917 (Scot. Hist. Soc., 2nd Series, 14 and 15).

* Mitchell, Joseph. *Reminiscences of my life in the Highlands.* 2 Vols., 1883, 1884.

Munro, Neil. *History of the Royal Bank of Scotland, 1727–1927,* 1928.

Murray, David. *The York Buildings Company,* 1883.

Naismith, John. *Observations on the different breeds of sheep and the state of Sheep Farming in the Southern Counties of Scotland,* 1795.

New Spalding Club. *Historical Papers, 1699–1750.* 2 Vols., 1895, 1896.

* *New Statistical Account of Scotland.* 15 Vols., 1845.

Newte, Thomas. *Tour of England and Scotland in 1785,* 1791.

Nimmo, Wm. *History of Stirlingshire,* 1st ed., 1777.

Pease, Howard. *The Lord-Wardens of the Marches,* 1913.

Peebles. *Charters and Documents relating to Peebles, 1165–1710,* 1872. Scottish Burgh Records Society.

Pennant, Thomas. *A Tour in Scotland, 1769* ; and *A Tour in Scotland and Voyage to the Hebrides, 1772.* 3 Vols., 1790.

Pococke, Richard. *Tours in Scotland, 1747, 1750, 1760,* Scot. Hist. Soc., 1st Series, Vol. 1, 1887.

Porteous, Alexander. *History of Crieff,* 1912.

Postlethwayt, Malachy. *Britain's Commercial Interest Explained and Improved.* 2 Vols., 1757.

Ramsay, John. *Scotland and Scotsmen in the 18th Century.* Edited by Alexander Allardyce, 1888. 2 Vols.

Retail Meat Trade, Vol. 1, Gresham Publishing Co., 1929.

Ridpath, George. *The Border-History of England and Scotland,* 1776.

Robertson, Sir C. Grant. *England under the Hanoverians,* 1911 and 1939.

Robertson, George. *Rural recollections,* 1829.

* Robertson, James. *General View of the Agriculture of Inverness,* 1813.

Robson, James. *General View of the Agriculture of Argyll and West Inverness-shire,* 1794.

Roger, Rev. James. *General View of the Agriculture of Angus,* 1794.

Rogers, Rev. Chas. *Social Life in Scotland from early to recent times.* 3 Vols., 1884-6.

Royal Scottish Geographical Society. *The Early Maps of Scotland,* 1936.

Salmond, J. B. *Wade in Scotland,* 1938.

Savary Des Bruslons, Jacques. *Universal Dictionary of Trade and Commerce.* Translated by Malachy Postlethwayt. 2 Vols., 1751-5.

Scotland Described. . . . 3rd ed., Edinburgh 1806.

Scott, Sir Walter. *The Highland Clans with a particular account of Rob Roy and the Macgregors,* 1856 ; *The Two Drovers.*

* Sinclair, Sir John. *Statistical Account of Scotland.* 21 Vols., 1791-9 ; *Analysis of Statistical Account.* 2 parts, 1825, 1826 ; *General View of the Agriculture of the Northern Counties, including counties of Cromarty, Ross, Sutherland and Caithness, and islands of Orkney and Shetland,* 1795.

Singer, Rev. William. *Agricultural Survey of Dumfries,* 1812.

Smiles, Samuel. *Life of George Moore,* 1878 ; *Life of Telford,* 1867.

Smith, Adam. *Wealth of Nations,* 1887.

Smith, Alexander. *A Summer in Skye,* 1866.

Smith, James. *The Exact Dealer's Companion,* Edinburgh, 1727.

Smith, Rev. John. *General View of the Agriculture of the County of Argyll,* 1798

Smith, Samuel. *General View of the Agriculture of Galloway,* 1813.

Somerville, Rev. Thomas. *My own Life and Times, 1741-1814.* 1861.

Souter, David. *General View of the Agriculture of Banff,* 1812.

Spalding Club. *Collections for a history of the Shires of Aberdeen and Banff,* 1843.

Steuart, John. *Letter Book, 1715-52* (Scot. Hist. Soc., 2nd Series, Vol. 9, 1915).

Stevenson, Robert Louis. *St. Ives.*

Taylor, John (The Water-Poet). *Works,* 1630.

Third Spalding Club. *The Book of Glenbuchat,* 1942.

Thornton, Col. T. *Sporting Tour through Northern parts of England and . . . Highlands of Scotland,* 1804.

Topham, Edward. *Letters from Edinburgh,* 1776.

Tough, Douglas L. W. *The last years of a Frontier,* 1928.

Trevelyan, G. M. *English Social History,* 1944.

Tytler, Patrick Fraser. *History of Scotland,* 2nd ed., 1841-50.

Ure, Rev. David. *General View of the Agriculture of Dumbarton,* 1794.

BIBLIOGRAPHY

* Walker, Rev. John. *Economical History of the Hebrides and Highlands.* 2 Vols., 1808.
* Webster, James. *General View of the Agriculture of Galloway,* 1794.
Wight, Andrew. *Husbandry.* 6 Vols. 1778.
Wilson, James. *Annals of Hawick, 1214–1814,* 1850.
Wordsworth, Dorothy. *Journals, 1798–1828.* Edited by W. Knight, 1924.
* Youatt, W. *Cattle, their breeds, management and diseases,* 1834. (Library of Useful Knowledge.)

ARTICLES, PAMPHLETS, ETC.

Adam, M. I. *The Causes of the Highland Emigrations of 1783–1803.* Scot. Hist. Rev., Vol. 17, pp. 73–89, 1920 ; *The Highland Emigration of 1770.* Scot. Hist. Rev., Vol. 16, pp. 280–93, 1919.
Campbell, Duncan. *Highland Shielings in the Olden Times.* Transactions of Inverness Scientific Society, Vol. 5, pp. 62–90, 1896–9.
Celtic Magazine. Vol. VIII, p. 586.
Curle, James. *The Leg from a Roman Bronze Statue found at Milsington.* The History of the Berwickshire Naturalists' Club, xxix, p. 195.
Dumfries and Galloway Courier. *Notes and Queries,* 1913.
Farmers' Magazine, The, Edinburgh, 1804.
Fraser, G. M. *Highways and Bridges in Aberdeenshire in 1739.* Third Spalding Club Miscellany, Vol. 1, pp. 233–4, 1935 ; *An Old Drove Road over the Culblean.* Article in Aberdeen Free Press, 7th June 1921.
* Fussell and Goodman. *18th Century Traffic in Live Stock.* Economic History (Supplement to Economic Journal), Vol. 3, No. 11.
Highland Society *Transactions,* 1803, Vol. 2, pp. 169 and 204 ; 1816, Vol. 4, pp. 1–65 ; Vol. II, New Series, pp. 4–16.
Highland and Agricultural Society *Transactions,* Vol. 8, 4th Series, p. 147, 1876.
Inglis. *The Roads which led to Edinburgh.* Proceedings of Society of Antiquaries of Scotland, Vol. 50 (Vol. 2, 4th Series), pp. 18–49, 1915–16.
Jenkins, R. T. *A Drover's Account Book.* Caernarvonshire Hist. Soc. Trans., 1945.
Johnman, Rev. W. A. P. *Highways and Byeways.* Transactions of Hawick Archaeological Society, 1917.
Lloyd, J. *The Black Cattle Droves.* Historical Memoranda of Breconshire 1903.
MacAdam, Ivison. *Notes on the Ancient Iron Industry of Scotland.* Proceedings of Society of Antiquaries of Scotland, Vol. 9, New Series, pp. 89–131, 1886–7.
McGrouther, T. *The Cattle Trade with England.* Falkirk Arch. and Nat. Hist. Soc. Proceedings, Vol. 3, p. 45, 1938–9.
McIntire. *The Fords of the Solway.* Trans. Cumberland and Westmorland Ant. and Arch. Soc., Vol. 39, New Series, pp. 152–70, 1939,
MacIntosh, Wm. of Borlum. *Essay on Enclosing,* 1729. *A short scheme . . . by means of the Military Road made by General Wade . . . to stop depredation and theft so destructive to the Northern Counties of Scotland.* Edinburgh, 1742.
Mackenzie, Sir Kenneth S. *General Wade and his Roads.* Inverness Scientific

Society Transactions, Vol. 5, pp. 145–77 ; *Military Roads in the Highlands.* Inverness Scientific Society Transactions, Vol. 5, pp. 364–84.

McKerral, Andrew. *The Tacksman and his Holding in the south-west Highlands.* Scot. Hist. Rev., Vol. XXVI, pp. 10–25, 1947.

* Miller, Rev. Thos. *Origin of the Falkirk Trysts.* Proceedings of Falkirk Arch. and Nat. Hist. Soc., 1936.

Moir, D. G. *Early Scottish Maps.* Royal Scot. Geog. Soc.

Murray, Sir Patrick. *Memorial respecting the Road from Yetts of Muckhart through Glendevon and Gleneagles into Strathearn,* 1814. (In Patent Office Library, London.)

Reid, R. C. *Some Letters of Thomas Bell, Drover, 1746,* in Trans. Dumfriesshire and Galloway Nat. Hist. and Ant. Soc., Vol. XXII, 3rd Series,

Robertson, Rev. Archibald Aeneas. *Old Tracks, Cross-country Routes and ' Coffin Roads ' in the North West Highlands,* 1943.

Ross, Alexander. *Old Highland Roads.* Proceedings of Gaelic Society of Inverness, Vol. 14, pp. 172–93, 1887–8.

Simpson, W. Douglas. *Early Castles of Mar.* Proceedings of Society of Antiquaries of Scotland, Vol. 63 (Vol. 3, 6th Series), pp. 102–38, 1928–9.

* Skeel, Caroline. *The Cattle Trade between England and Wales from the 15th to the 19th centuries.* Royal Hist. Soc. Trans., Vol. 9, 4th Series, 1926.

Souvenir of the Highland Show, Dumfries, 1910.

* *Stirling Journal and Advertiser* (files in Stirling Public Library).

Thompson, William. *Cattle Droving between Scotland and England.* British Archaeological Assoc, Vol. 87, New Series, pp. 172–83, 1932.

LEGAL REPORTS, ETC.

Campbell v. *Campbell,* 1777. 5 Brown's Supplement to Morison's Dictionary of Decisions, p. 599.

* *McGregor* v. *Lord Breadalbane,* 1846. Court of Session Cases (9 Dunlop's Reports), p. 210.

McKenzie v. *Bankes,* 1868. Court of Session Cases (6 MacPherson's Reports), p. 936.

* Signet Library *Collection of Old Session Papers.*

Scottish Rights of Way Society v *Macpherson,* 1887. Court of Session Cases (14 Rettie's Reports), p. 875.

Torrie v. *Duke of Athol,* 1848. Court of Session Cases (12 Dunlop's Reports), p. 328.

Winans and Chisholm v. *Lord Tweedmouth,* 1888. Court of Session Cases (15 Rettie's Reports), p. 540.

MAPS

Armstrong, Mostyn J. *Map of Peeblesshire,* 1773.

Edgar, Wm. *Map of the River Forth,* 1745.

Elphinstone, John. *Map of North Britain,* 1745.

* Roy, William, General. *Survey of Scotland, 1747–55.* MS (British Museum).

Taylor, George, and Skinner, Andrew. *Survey of the Roads of Scotland,* 1839.

Thomson, William.　*Atlas of Scotland*, 1832.
　　　　　　　　　　Map of Selkirkshire, 1824.
　　　　　　　　　　Map of Peeblesshire, 1821.
Ordnance Survey of Scotland, 6 in. to 1 mile.　1st edition 1863.

The Maps printed with the Reports of the Commissioners for Highland Roads and Bridges and in the Volumes of the New Statistical Account of Scotland have also been used.

INDEX

18

PRINTED IN GREAT BRITAIN AT
THE PRESS OF THE PUBLISHERS